AR(

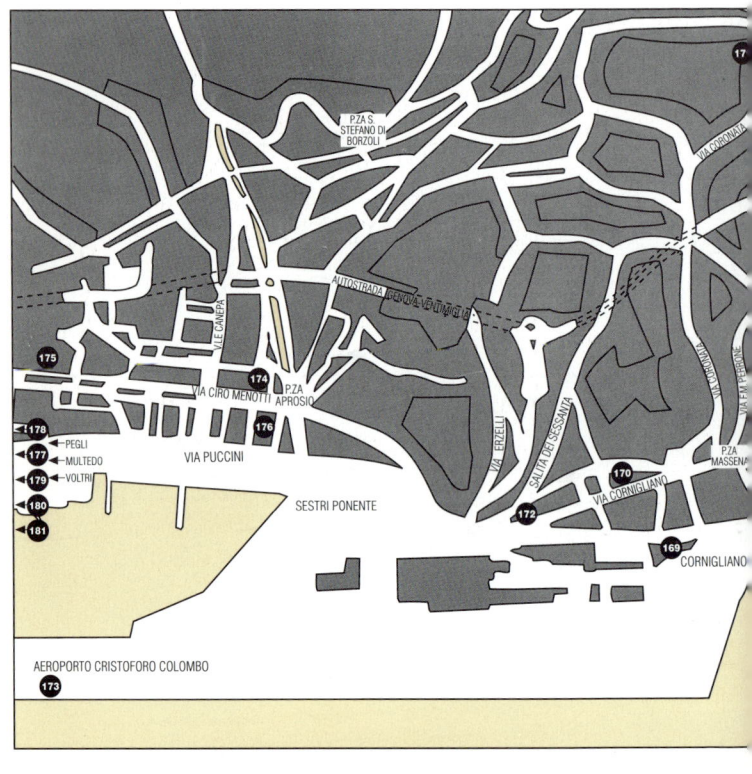

*The numbers on the maps refer to the individual entries;
the larger ones indicate the start of a section.*

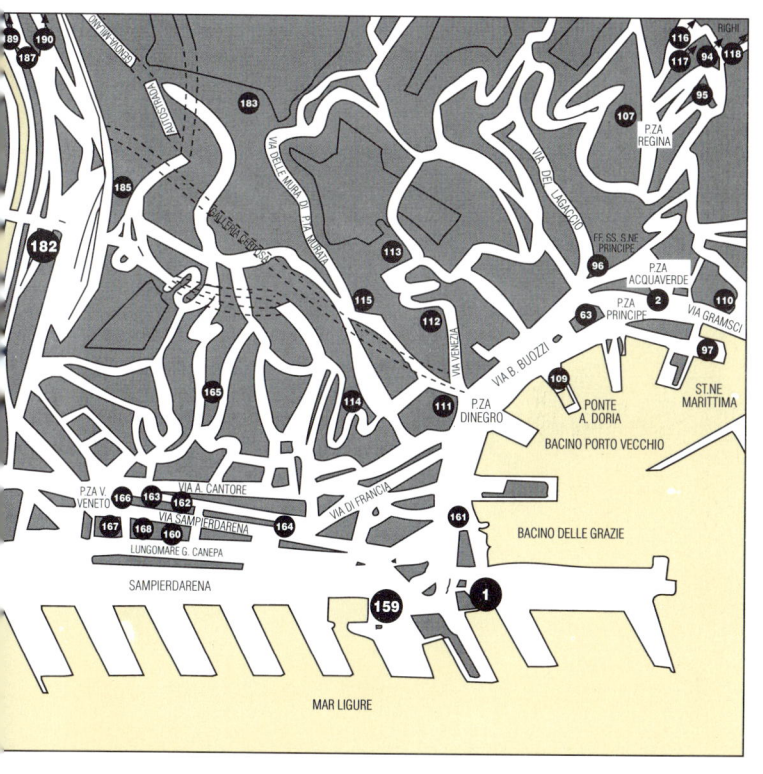

The numbers on the maps refer to the individual entries; the larger ones indicate the start of a section.

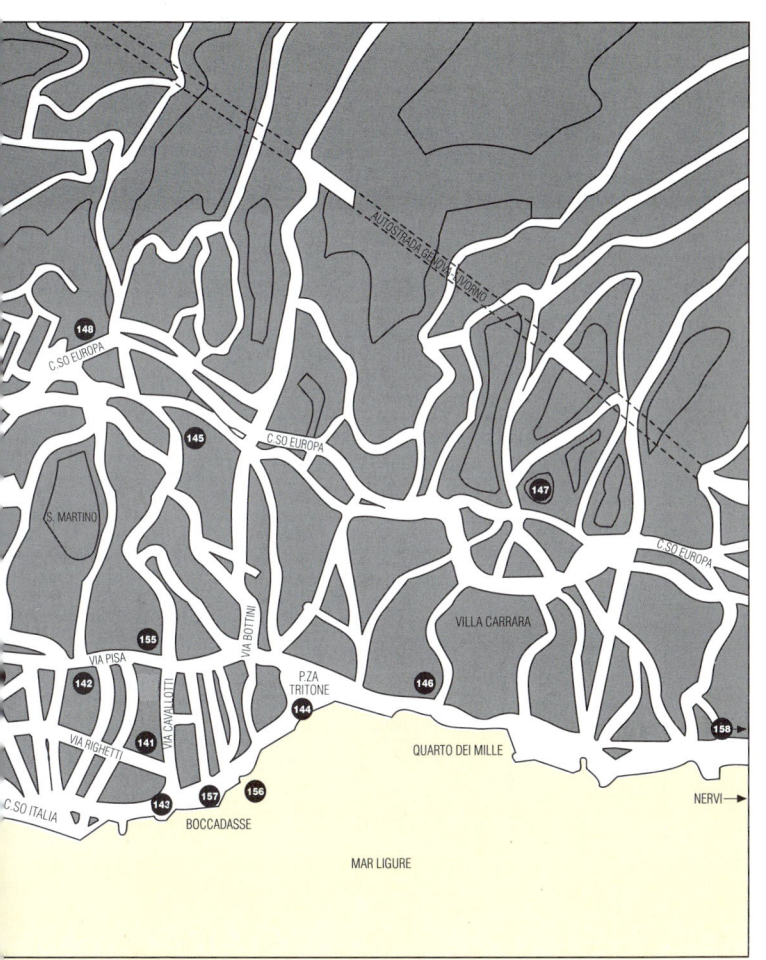

The numbers on the maps refer to the individual entries; the larger ones indicate the start of a section.

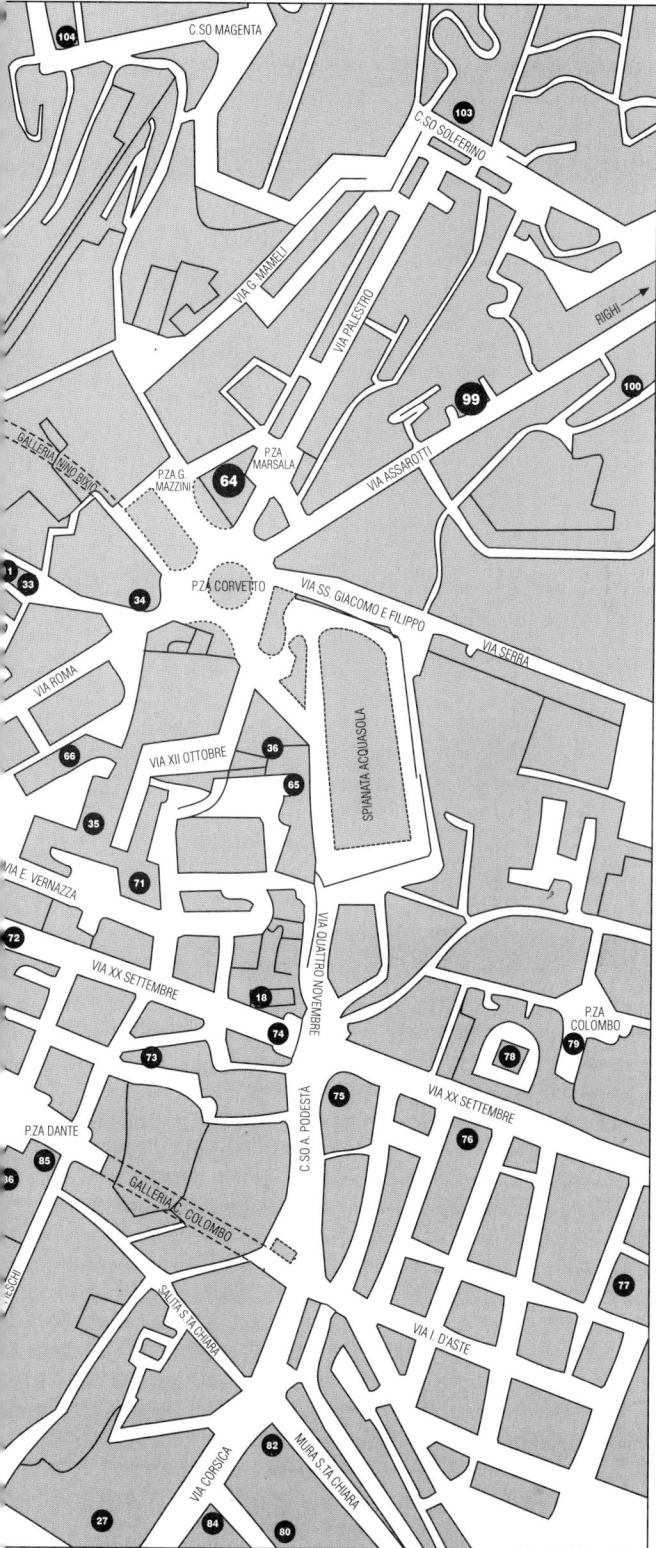

ARCHITECTURAL GUIDES
GENOA

PROJECT AND PHOTOGRAPHS
BY LORENZO CAPELLINI

EDITORIAL CO-ORDINATION
BY ENNIO POLEGGI

UMBERTO ALLEMANDI & C.

CONTENTS

13 ENNIO POLEGGI
Introduction

17 ENNIO POLEGGI
I. The medieval walled city

42 NICOLÒ DE MARI
II. The city of the old walls: modern buildings

96 ENNIO POLEGGI
III. The city of the old walls:
contemporary and present-day buildings

136 EMMINA DE NEGRI
IV. The city of the new walls

160 PAOLO CEVINI
V. Val Bisagno

182 CARLO BERTELLI
VI. Albaro and the eastern suburbs

207 PAOLO CEVINI
VII. Sampierdarena and the western suburbs

235 GIORGIO PIGAFETTA
VIII. Val Polcevera

249 Bibliography

251 Index of places

254 Index of names

AUTHORS OF THE ENTRIES

Carlo Bertelli	C. B.
Saveria Cardona	S. C.
Luisella Cefeo	L. C.
Nicolò De Mari	N. D. M.
Emmina De Negri	E. D. N.
Laura Diaceri	L. D.
Ilaria Forno	I. F.
Riccardo Forte	R. F.
Maria Paola Gerbaz	M. P. G.
Francesca Ghigliotto	F. G.
Maurizio Maggiali	M. M.
Anna Maria Nicoletti	A. M. N.
Ennio Poleggi	E. P.
Roberta Porsenna	R. P.
Giulio Sommariva	G. S.

Luisa Videsott assisted with the project; Clara Altavista and Riccardo Forte collaborated on the new edition. The maps of Genoa were drawn by Caterina Gori and the photographs were printed by Patrizio Parolini. The photographs of No. 2 (church of San Giovanni di Prè), No. 52 (church of San Siro) and No. 171 (oratory of the Assunta) are by the Soprintendenza per i Beni Architettonici e Ambientali della Liguria; those of No. 173 (Christopher Columbus airport), No. 143 (new lido at Albaro) and No. 181 (Voltri port) are by the Studio Fotografico Merlo (Genoa). Translated by Idem, a division of Addware Europe Ltd., Glasgow.

INTRODUCTION
ENNIO POLEGGI

A guidebook is no more than a sterile list if it does not actually guide the visitor in the right direction, indicating with precision what he has hastily to grasp; it is harder to find a finely balanced guidebook which does not succumb to myth and a celebratory manner, but this is something we will see later. In accordance with the publisher's aims, which are intriguing for those working in architecture faculties, we left aside all theoretical fads and concentrated on the useful: for the city and its visitors, for the challenge of communicating with our readers and for group spirit. Another choice we deemed useful for those waiting to get their bearings and visit a special series of works was the topographical succession which moves from the historic centre to the suburbs and from East to West, also reflecting historic expansion.

The most important aspects of the urban landscape in Genoa and of its architecture are to be found on a pi-shaped axis, formed by the coastline and two valleys (Bisagno and Polcevera) which rise towards the Appennines. From the Ripa at the heart of the city in the port to the city limits one travels through the memories and marks of the first medieval walls, the Mura Vecchie and Mura Nuove (Old and New Walls) and through the city laid out in the natural amphitheatre of its setting (about 900 hectares) to the 19th-century expansion of the suburbs - so closely bound to the customs of the walled town - which were later incorporated into the city itself.

The thematic character of this guidebook required us to slot each of the buildings described into one of the eight sections, aligning considerably different itineraries in the same area like in a Chinese box. These seemed obvious precautions to take in a volume made up of individual descriptions which are fragmentary in their concision of dates and comments but - and we declare it right away in these "instructions for use" - Genoa is a difficult city from the traditional point of view of architecture; indeed, it derives from its special nature an unfavourable criticism which is hard to reverse as is the incredible lack of luck it has had with tourists over the past century.

These would seem to be the same reasons that prevent any building in the world from being encapsulated in a single photograph: it is not just a matter of the traditional limits of a medium which has become an art-form because of this very fact, but also of the accretion of all the impediments of a stratified urban organism together with that "fifth façade" which only Genoese houses have, formed of terraces and attics dotted between slate roofs and perhaps linked with passageways to higher roads winding along the steep hillsides. In this way, the single buildings become urban architecture before the spectator's eyes.

From the air, Genoa seems to be a tidily laid out city but to explain the deceptive order of the central areas, which for different reasons date from remote rather than recent times, it is not enough to make a distinction between the government of the old regime and the town-planning schemes of the last 150 years.

Genoa has remained a rising city, as Giorgio Caproni sang; the detached blocks which lie dotted along the bottoms of the valleys or along the curved hillside avenues, curtain after curtain, from the mid 19th-century middle-class residences to the cheap housing of this century show this to be astonishingly true as did the old "bird's eye view" prints of the past. A surface of windows and roofs laid out across valleys which filled in the post-war period and occasional "breakthroughs" high up where some still green ridges reveal the existence of a comb-like series of crests dropping to the Tyrrhenian sea. In this guide, any desire simply to describe risks becoming bogged down in the knotty question of terms used in building, architecture and urban landscape: in Genoa more than in any other city, the contiguity between these tends to blur and indeed to disappear altogether in the last category, so strong is the cohesion between one building and the next and between buildings and public spaces, to the point that they coincide with entire chunks of urban construction.

In the early days of the ancient regime, the principal factor in defining construction habits was certainly the physical characteristics of the "site", together with the quick exhaustion of building land in a setting dominated by the aristocratic clans. In short, without going back too far and ignoring the categories, it is not easy to describe Genoa's pre-industrial architecture when one thinks of the long survival of the city's walls and how, although not lacking, isolated buildings are in the main attached to their neighbours or to raised passages, in styles and period divisions unknown to the traditional connoisseur of architecture.

Despite the unification of original buildings into larger complexes, the visitor will still be able to recognise medieval buildings, especially the little 15th-century palaces which are unfailingly decorated with flowery entrances, and also the greater number of two to three hundred quality palaces erected between the mid 16th century and mid 17th century, even though these often incorporated old walls marked from their earlier use.

Given the narrow, uninterrupted lacing of streets, a visit can only be fruitful if one walks along looking upwards where hanging arches, string courses and openings clearly indicate with their changing styles the many stories which characterize the high points of the city's history and, in substance, the living habits of its citizens. Large-scale demographic movements, together with the loss of the legends and oral tradition which were a feature of this early industrial city, aggravate today's lack of recognition of a setting transformed by heavy-handed redevelopment and neglect.

Less patience (but also less imagination) is required for examining contemporary architecture in a city as naturally panoramic as Genoa; starting with the "viewing points" or age-old belvederes left us by history which provide valuable opportunities to take in the most important buildings and architecture which interest us, whilst enabling us also to appreciate the ways in which the patrons of the last century wished to set them into the landscape.

As well as the stately platform of the Porta del Molo, from which the eye gazes over the historic double horizon of sea and land, the most suitable belvederes for a first overview are those built on the upper Circonvallazione (ring road). However, one can also climb higher, along roads weaving their way parallel to the coast, as far as the 12 km long parapet on the Mura Nuove (New walls), or, if one has seen everything in the 900 ha of the walled city, go to the districts along the coast and lateral valleys and start again in the same way.

One will note with astonishment that it is always with building development on hillsides that architects and ways of life contrast, producing complex results which can reach heights of great originality. To summarise, it is here that the secret of a form of habitation lies which - thanks to Liguria's position as a frontier throughout history - has seen various influences, fleeting passages and the great mass of culture of the siglo des Genoeses between the mid 16th and mid 17th century which placed Genoa in the history of European architecture. Put simply, we would like the visitor as he wanders around to stop at the point where he can best understand how - in its conquest of air, light and a "view" - the city has often freed itself from the fleeting infatuation with a style to integrate it instead into its own idiom and adapt it to the inevitable verticality of the place. It might be the period of the black and white bands originating in Tuscany and decorating 13th-century churches and great private entrance ways and copied in the houses of merchants and aristocrats. Of inestimable importance too was the period which began with the opening of Strada Nuova, when the skill of the great Italian architects transformed itself into the incredible conquest of an architecture diagonally crossing all exterior and interior changes in level in a free or built-up area, to the extent that Pevsner affirmed that the first signs of Baroque "space" appeared here. This is a paradoxical statement if we remember that the land made the symmetrical grids of Rome or Turin an impossibility here; there is indeed a search for long perspectives and trompe-l'œils but these are all internal and appear in stairs, nymphaea, salons and naves and so up to vaults and domes to blend in with the frescos which are here an integral part of the architecture.

The list of examples lengthens, in part thanks to the engineering and typological innovations of the 19th-century, to include the brief, ringing season of Coppedè at the start of the 20th century but especially, given the widespread use and effectiveness of the results, the new Hennebique system. The revolution brought about by reinforced concrete in a city like Genoa must have produced an impact similar to that of the arrival of the Antelami masters at the end of the early medieval period; the speed of planning and production of the concrete met the requirements of the programmes for a newly revitalized port faced with competition from the recently opened Suez canal and Alpine passes, just as new carpentry techniques had been vital in building in the past.

Even today, Genoa is going through profound changes amongst controversial uncertainties and brave decisions, including the bold adoption of avant-garde techniques and forms, abandoning the sense of prudence which has always accompanied the individual who knows he might find himself alone and unexpectedly in a storm.

We leave to the reader the fortune of discovering the points which draw the attention of the individual and public in general to a city which is notoriously little-known and misunderstood in its most "cultural" aspects, and excluded from the circuit of Italian cities of art (which is to say excluded from virtually any flow of tourists or international promotion). There has been no lack in recent years of important contributions, some by the authors of this guide, which have tried to change a situation which had become intolerable for a city which had ceased to live its period in the architectural sense, after having been a great player in Mediterranean and European history of shipping, business and banking in the West.

I.
THE MEDIEVAL WALLED CITY
ENNIO POLEGGI

THE HISTORIC CITY TODAY

The surprising conservation and densely stratified nature of the walls and ground, which a Council ruling ("Organic study", 1984) enclosed within a perimeter roughly coinciding with the walled area of the 14th century, merit a brief but direct examination and an illustration of the most general problems thrown up by the present day's conjunction of studies and town-planning choices.

THE STREET PLAN

Until the late Middle Ages, the walled area expanded in three successive boundaries which, in the 14th century, coincided with the "thousand paces" of Roman times (roughly 1,480 m) measured from the old market of San Giorgio; between the construction of the 9th-century walls around the old hill of Castello and that of the 12th-century walls, the early street plan did not undergo radical changes, simply being extended towards the interior without changing character.

Even today, if one starts from the water's edge, it is possible to follow the whole system, noting that the structure bases itself upon a rigid comb plan, hinging on the coastal axis running behind the houses of the Ripa and from which just four major branches lead upwards (Via San Bernardo, Via Canneto il Lungo, Via Luccoli and Via della Maddalena).

The town filling the gaps between these four roads is also medieval but formed more slowly, with narrower access streets which led towards the heart of areas dominated by the most powerful families and to the marginal quarters inhabited by poor craftsmen and the general populace. Apart from the change of direction - caused by the creation of the 19th-century centre inland of the coast - the street plan has remained unchanged even though larger buildings are visible today than would have been the case in the past: these are the modern and even contemporary structures which have absorbed the medieval plots without changing the original framework, especially in the most profitable and representative areas. The division of the land is also visible through the boundary changes caused by the wide avenues created by demolishing old houses to allow later monumental buildings to have more air and views.

Only uphill of the original settlement, next to the 14th-century walls have 16th and 19th-century constructions occasionally closed off or interrupted any expansion with imposing boulevards and squares which now encompass - like a picture frame - the precious heritage of a substantially medieval city which still needs to be made the most of.

MAIN FEATURES

The structural map suggested by the streets acquires greater interest if those ancient buildings and places are remembered which have characterized the identity and landscape of the various urban areas for their importance in the life of the city and their artistic worth.

Starting from the sea, like in an old "bird's eye view", we first of all find the old parish and family churches near which the family house was then erected. Some were transformed between the 16th and 17th century, such as the first cathedral of San Siro, San Luca (of the Spinola family), San Pietro in Banchi, Santa Maria delle Vigne, Santa Maria Maddalena and San Giorgio, which used to house the standard of the City Council. Others still preserve a medieval aspect, although altered by 19th-century restorations, such as the cathedral of San Lorenzo, San Matteo (of the Doria family), San Donato, Santa Maria di Castello, Sant'Agostino and Santa Maria del Carmine. The most charming in tourists' eyes is the Commendam of San Giovanni di Prè by the sea which, with the rooms of the hospice and monastery of the Knights of St John of Jerusalem, strongly evokes the memory of the Crusades and great pilgrimages which used to gather here before embarking.

Together with the Palazzo del Mare, which rises at the centre of the Palazzata della Ripa, and the remaining towers, the temples of the early parishes and powerful noble families are undoubtedly the most recognisable part of the "genius loci". However, a visitor used to the stereotypical Italian city will be surprised at the lack of a "Piazza" which Genoa has never had, except in some way with the arcades of the Ripa and the small indoor markets of Banchi, Soziglia and San Giorgio. This is an unusual aspect of the town and one which goes some way to explain the original narrowness of the cathedral square, which historians attribute to the fragmentary structure of Genoese society, which had always been arranged around private squares run like independent citadels.

Less recognisable are the few remaining sections of medieval walls, although the monumental two-towered gateways of Santa Fede and Sant'Andrea do survive to the west and east of the perimeter begun in 1155. Only the Archi, Pila and Molo gates survive, too, of the later internal and seaward walls of the 16th and 17th centuries, whereas the whole bastioned perimeter can be seen in almost its entirety along the ridges of the mountains surrounding the historic centre.

However confused the hasty visitor may be in seeking out the monuments which form the historic landscape of Geona one by one, he has only to climb to the Castello de Albertis (1892), to the L. Montaldo belvedere (close to the Castelletto) or to San Silvestro (the original castrum, today home to the Architecture Faculty), to rediscover all of their glory in the richness of effects which towers, steeples and monumental palaces trace against the backdrop of the Ligurian Sea. Genoa is a naturally panoramic city, provided with many viewpoints which the 19th-century hillside roads have exploited to the full, despite the recent arrival of some tall, atypical buildings.

PALACES AND HOUSES

The main feature of the town plan, occupying an area of about 150 hectares, comprises an impressive collection of monumental residential buildings, over 200 of which rise in the centre. Of these, over 40 are medieval, the rest being from the modern era with rare exceptions from the last century. Almost all are completely visible except for a few of the medieval palaces in which, however, the height can be discerned. These surprising aristocrats' homes await a suitable study and a new function to remove them from the ignorance of an idealistic historiography and from neglect.

This explains Genoa's present-day lack of appeal as a city of art for tourists, although these very features were enthusiastically described by travellers of all ages, from Petrarch to Rubens, the great Flemish painter, who produced a series of prints of the main palaces in Genoa (1652).

Most of these palaces, especially those of the modern era, are built in the large triangle formed by Via San Luca, Via Luccoli and Via Garibaldi. Indeed it is from this last street (originally called Strada Nuova, 1550-75) and from its first 10-12 palaces, owned by the main bankers and ship-builders of the Spanish crown, that renewal in the crowded medieval city began, reaffirming the city's ancient title of "proud".

This is not to say that the medieval palaces surviving from the Middle Ages are of any lesser interest. Despite numerous accretions, they still boast stately pointed archways and richly sculpted doorways, bearing witness to the existence of a varied and long-lived process of search for form and typology which is not always easy to follow in other Italian cities because of the scarcity of surviving examples. In conclusion, it must be added that there is no lack of more modest houses in the odd gaps and more marginal parts of the historic centre which are equally interesting, such as the ranks of houses which can be attributed to the poorer classes of the 12th-13th centuries, or entire quarters of rental housing built as speculative ventures by the aristocracy in the 18th century.

All this makes Genoa into an exceptional place for research for those disciplines which in recent years have applied themselves to urban planning, from the history of town-planning to "post-classical" archaeology which here finds abundant opportunity to study material from the medieval and modern world. The unusual richness of the State Archives and the City Council's Historic Archives, which house an enormous amount of papers from public sources, especially notarial documents, has contributed to this trend.

ITINERARY
SINGLE ROUTE: FROM SAN GIOVANNI DI PRÈ TO SANT'AGOSTINO

If we exclude the Lanterna and the church of Santo Stefano as being too far apart and distant and so best reached by public transport, the itinerary which guides the visitor around the architecture of medieval Genoa can be followed in chronological order and without topographical interruptions from west to east.

From the railway station of Porta Principe or the maritime one of Ponte dei Mille and Ponte A. Doria, the church and hospice of San Giovanni di Prè are easily reached. After following the full length of Via Prè, an old suburb in the west, go through the Porta di Santa Fede - turning left here for Piazza della Nunziata one can reach the Carmine and follow Via del Campo to Piazza Fossatello then right into Via A. Gramsci which leads to the start of the great Palazzata of the Ripa.

Once its centre has been reached at Palazzo San Giorgio, go straight uphill along the major Banchi axis of Via Orefici - from which a road to the left leads to Santa Maria delle Vigne - and Via Luccoli where one may see the Macello Nuovo (new slaughterhouse, at nos. 16 and 18) before returning to the Campetto and left to Piazza San Matteo, "curia" of the Doria family.

The Cathedral is just a little higher, to the south and on the right after the Archbishop's palace. From the southern edge of Piazza San Lorenzo, walk along Via Chiabrera to Via Canneto il Lungo which, followed uphill (to the left), leads to Palazzo Maruffo (no. 23). Soon, one comes to the church of San Donato at the crossroads with Salita Pollaioli.

From here, turn right along Via San Bernardo, the old platealonga of the medieval merchants, to climb (along Vico Giustiniani) to Piazza Embriaci and the great complex of Santa Maria di Castello. After the visit, turn right, passing in front of the Embriaci Tower and, follow Via Santa Maria di Castello to pass Piazza Santa Croce and arrive at Piazza Sarzano - an ancient "Corso" or avenue and the Genoese's viewpoint over the sea - where one can find the Museo di Sant'Agostino (no. 21) and the Architecture Faculty, where this guide was planned and produced.

1
The Lanterna Lighthouse
LARGO LANTERNA
BUS 8, 30, 34

This symbol of the city rises 85 metres from its base and 117 metres above the sea. Comprising two slender square columns crowned by three levels of well-proportioned embrasures, the Lanterna has always functioned as a lighthouse and navigational aid for sailors; a function it maintains to this day with a light beam visible 33 miles away. Located at the extreme west of the town on a natural promontory, the site already had a guard tower in 1128. In 1507, Louis XII built the Briglia citadel upon it and during the reconquest, the upper part of the Lanterna was damaged and remained out of use until 1543 when the Council Fathers had it restored by some Antelami masters under Martino da Rosio. During the construction of the Mura Nuove (completed in 1633), the tower became an integral part of the perimeter, constituting the main point of coastal defence for the San Benigno promontory. The Lanterna has undergone numerous restorations. In 1785, the architect, Gregorio Petondi, had the City Council's arms painted on the north side, and this was later overpainted with the Kingdom of Sardinia's arms. [E. P.]

2
Church and Hospice of San Giovanni di Prè
SALITA DI SAN GIOVANNI; PIAZZA DELLA COMMENDA
BUS 1, 2, 3, 7, 8, 32

The San Giovanni di Prè complex (first mentioned in 1180) was built within the area owned by Santo Sepolcro by the Antelami masters who had been working in Genoa since the 11th century. It is also possible that masons from beyond the Alps belonging to the same order of Knights of St John of Jerusalem were employed on the site. The Hospice, with quarters for the knight monks and pilgrims travelling to the Holy Land, was directly linked to the church to which access was gained via an internal doorway.

The church is on two levels; the ground-plan of the lower church reveals a nave and two aisles with cross-vaults, whereas the upper one has a far broader area with the upper central nave corresponding to the lower nave and aisles. Reconstruction work was carried out in 1508 on the Commenda's lower porch and upper gallery, raising its height with a second gallery. In 1731, with the upper church beginning to hold services for the public, it became necessary to open a new entrance on the opposite side at the centre of the apse (Salita San Giovanni di Prè). This caused the closing off of the first bay inside and the construction of a pseudoapse. The highly elongated cross-vaults, which are rectangular with square ribs, the robust colonnade and the transept piers are a powerful, rare example of a strongly stylized and well-preserved medieval structure.

[R. P.]

3
Porta di Santa Fede (dei Vacca) and Porta di Sant'Andrea (Soprana)

PIAZZA DELLA DARSENA; VICO DRITTO DI PONTICELLO
BUS 15, 17, 20, 32, 35, 36, 41, 41, 42

The Porta dei Vacca, once called Porta di Santa Fede from the name of a little church erected just outside the walls and today under restoration in its 17th-century version, was built at the same time as the Sant'Andrea gate. The latter at the opposite entrance in the walls built between 1155 and 1161 also boasts two towers. In the 18th century, the north tower was incorporated into Palazzo Serra; the southern one has been freed from additions built over it in the 1960s. Porta Soprana, or Sant'Andrea, was built over an earlier, 9th-century entrance next to the monastery of Sant'Andrea which was demolished at the start of this century to make way for Via Dante. It reveals a single, large pointed arch with archivolts, flanked by two imposing horseshoe-shaped towers with the rounded part pointing outwards. Of some interest is the text on the foundation stone set into the southern intrados of the archway in which the personified gateway addresses the visitor who enters.

With its original function coming to an end following the construction of the defensive boundary of the 14th century (1320-47), Porta Soprana was transformed into dwellings; at the end of the last century, the north tower was restored by Alfredo D'Andrade along clear Romantic lines; restoration of the southern tower was undertaken by Orlando Grosso (1938).   [R. P.]

4
Church of Nostra Signora del Carmine
VIA BRIGNOLE DE FERRARI
BUS 39, 40

The Nostra Signora del Carmine complex was begun in 1262 in the ancient suburb alongside the 12th-century walls which was first developed by the Benedictines of San Siro and then by the Carmelites in the area of Vallechiara, Sant'Agnese and Guastato where agriculture flourished alongside trade and crafts. The work lasted until the beginning of the 14th century when the northern cloister was added to church and convent. The church was enlarged in the 15th century with the addition of two bays towards the façade; the work was perhaps undertaken at the same time as the reconstruction of the bell tower in 1417. Other changes followed, with part of the wall of the right-hand aisle being knocked down to add the present chapels to be found on that side. Today, the church is divided into a nave and two aisles, with the nave being much higher and illuminated by single-light windows; it is cross-vaulted with strongly-defined ribs. Despite much rebuilding and recent restoration, the interior preserves the suggestion of the Gothic architecture, highlighted by the arches with archivolts, vaulting ribs, demi-shafts on corbels and the two clustered piers. [R. P.]

5
Palazzata della Ripa
FROM PIAZZA DELLA DARSENA TO PIAZZA CAVOUR
BUS 1, 2, 3, 7, 8, 12, 15

This great architectural complex is virtually unique in Europe in its preservation of original features and monumentality. It was decreed in 1133/34 by the Council Consuls to make use of the central coastal area, and required private householders to build an arcade about 900 m long in exchange for permission to build their homes above.

From the Porta di Santa Fede in the west (now Piazza della Darsena) to Piazza del Molo to the east (Piazza Cavour), the Ripa is also an eloquent testimonial of the great urban transformations which Genoa / understood as an organic unit comprising town and port / has undergone in its double role as a major means of communication (harbour, frontier, market) and important place of residence. On the eve of the dramatic changes brought about by the actual reorganisation of the historic port, the Ripa appears changed only at the ends. The first arcaded length at the western entrance has been hidden by the Sardinian *carrettiera* [road] (1835/40) which did not touch the palaces above (Ripa scura); the opposite length (Ripa di Coltelleria) was demolished and partly reconstructed as rental accomodation after 1870 to make room for Via Vittorio Emanuele II (now Via F. Turati), an access point for the future coastal ring road. The expansion of the town and the tumultuous industrial developments produced by a transit port (1875/82) did not erase its original monumentality even though they removed the Ripa from being a central part of the city's life.

Indeed, the first part we see when approaching from the west is also the only section to have been "restored" in the late-Romantic taste of the end of the last century, with medieval doors and windows being reinvented and the 16th-17th-century mezzanines which hid the arches of the arcades demolished (these survive in the section between Vico del Serriglio and Vico dell'Olivo).

The Ripa overall provides a magnificent horizon of buildings in which are plainly visible its architectural origins and to which we still have to attribute a place in the building practices which are peculiar to Genoa, influenced by the countless limitations of the site, by the society which created it and by later requirements of the port. If we must pick out a few exceptional palaces, it is worth noting the palazzi Negrotto-Durazzo, Cybo-Cellario, Remondini and Pallavicino placed next to each other in Via del Campo, and palazzi Grimaldi-Fabiani, Serra Gerace, Pinelli, Passano (with the Morchi tower) and Gentile between Via al Ponte Calvi and Via al Ponte Reale, brutally interrupted by a demolition of buildings which had just survived the Second World War; and finally, the palazzi Cattaneo, Durazzo and De Marini-Croce Bermond placed around Piazza di Banchi and Piazza De Marini, as well as behind the historic Palazzo di San Giorgio.   [E. P.]

6
Palazzo San Giorgio
VIA DELLA MERCANZIA 2 (VIA FRATE OLIVERIO)
BUS 1, 2, 3, 7, 8, 12, 15

The original nucleus of the palace was built in 1260 by friar Oliverio for the Captain of the *popolo*, Guglielmo Boccanegra, between the port and the public arcades of Sottoripa in what was then effectively the very heart of the city. Originally intended as a seat of government dominating the sea, its role changed with the fall of Boccanegra and it became the headquarters of the customs. At the start of the 15th century, the palace was assigned to the Banco di San Giorgio, a government body controlling the state's consolidated debt and instrument of effective executive power over all of the workings of the medieval Commune and later of the oligarchical Republic. The form of the original building changed in 1570 with a drastic restructuring which completely altered its look and incorporated the older structure in a new enlargement towards the sea. It took on a compact look with typically Genoese Renaissance decorations, including the façade, originally produced by Antonio Semino but rebuilt a few years later by Lazzaro Tavarone (1606-8). At the start of the 19th century, with the fall of Genoa to the French and the abolition of the Banco di San Giorgio, the building fell into neglect. In 1878, with a partial demolition averted, restoration work began under the direction of A. D'Andrade. In 1912, L. Pogliaghi finished this work and repainted the decorations of the façade facing the sea. The grand staircase leading to the "sala delle Compere di San Giorgio" is a coeval work by A. Crotta. [R. P.]

7
Church of Santa Maria delle Vigne
PIAZZA DELLE VIGNE
BUS 1, 2, 3, 7, 8, 12, 15, ~~15~~, 35, 41, ~~41~~, 42

Santa Maria delle Vigne, probably built around the 10th century between the cathedral of San Siro and the Soziglia stream as the headquarters for the most powerful canonical collegiate church after San Lorenzo, became a parish church in 1147 during the expansion that was later encompassed in the walls of 1155. Because of its central position, the church underwent numerous transformations; still surviving from its Romanesque origins is the bell tower, probably built in the 12th century, from which an archivolt provides a passage from the church to the cloister which preserves a strongly archaic character in its stocky columns and cubic capitals. The present aspect of the church maintains the basilica plan of the original but reveals the effects of repeated 16th-century renovations; by 1588, these had reached the choir (Gaspare della Corte). This was a long period of transformation which Daniele Casella (1640-42), assisted by Giovanni Battista Bianco, son of Bartolomeo, accelerated, replacing the eight columns of the nave with another four, taller coupled columns to raise the arches of the nave and remove the imitation women's gallery. Finally, as well as interventions on the vaults in the aisles, the lantern was also replaced by a dome. In essence, this was a Baroque transformation which succeeded in removing every vestige of the Romanesque building. From the middle of the 18th century, decoration began within the church with the painting of frescos in the nave, and work continued until the early years of the 20th century. The façade also remained unfinished until 1842, when Ippolito Cremona designed the present front. [R. P.]

8
Macello Nuovo (New Slaughterhouse)
VIA LUCCOLI 16/18
BUS 18, 19, 20, 30, 35, 39, 40, 42

Located in the busiest shopping area of the city around the Soziglia market, the Macello Nuovo has two main fronts giving on to the present-day Vico dei Macelli di Soziglia and on to Via Luccoli. Built between 1291 and 1292 by the Commune, it was amongst the most significant public projects of the time, in part because of its financing, derived from the sale and rent of the housing above. The architectural model is that adopted throughout the Middle Ages in Genoa: houses placed next to each other and set above a colonnade with a strict hierarchy for each floor, here taking the appearance of a single palace. On the east side of the ground floor were the entrance and space for two dwellings whereas on the west were the shops for butchering (?) and selling meat. Of some interest is the rich, perhaps imported, figurative decoration on the capitals of the colonnade in Via Luccoli. This survived the closing-off of the arches and introduction of two new stairs in the 16th century.

The building of this public project is evidence of the prestigious results obtained in Genoa by the intense residential research in little more than a century, starting with the planned construction of the houses and colonnades of Ripa Maris (1133). [E. P.]

9
Church of San Matteo
PIAZZA SAN MATTEO
BUS 15, 18, 19, 20, 30, 35, 39, 40, 41, 41, 42

This, the Doria's family church, was founded in 1125 by Martino Doria, rebuilt in 1278 and refurbished on the basis of designs by G. A. Montorsoli and later G. B. Castello il Bergamasco at the behest of Andrea Doria. Between 1308 and 1310, at the behest of the prior, Andrea da Goano, a *magister Marcus Venetus* built the square cloister with its pointed arches and coupled columns; this is reached from the piazza. Only the façade has survived virtually unchanged of the original 13th-century church. This is simple and severe with its facing of alternating black stone and white marble bands in which a continuous text which recounts all of the Doria family's victories marks the earliest example of dynastic celebration. In the entrance lunette, there is an old mosaic with St Matthew and, at the base of the right-hand window once decorated with trilobate arches, there lies a Roman sarcophagus, a battle trophy from Curzola, which was placed here in 1323 when the Doria's bodily remains were no longer laid to rest in the Abbey of San Fruttuoso di Capodimonte. Within, the Gothic plan is almost hidden by the 16th-century alterations; Montorsoli, indeed, was responsible for the restructuring of the presbytery, the construction of the crypt with the tomb of Andrea Doria and the marble decoration of the apse and dome (1547-49). Ten years later, Castello took Montorsoli's place and restructured the whole building (1557-59), eliminating the columns, moving the pulpits and frescoing the ceiling of the nave, with the assistance of Luca Cambiaso. [R. P.]

10
Palazzo Lamba and Palazzo Andrea Doria (ex Lazzaro Doria)
PIAZZA SAN MATTEO 15/17
BUS 15, 18, 19, 20, 30, 35, 39, 40, 41, 41, 42

The piazza is closed off on the uphill side by the church and Palazzo Branca Doria, in which the cloister is located, whilst looking round in an anticlockwise direction, we see the palace of the Capitano del Popolo, Domenicaccio, another Doria palace (Quartara), the most eminent palace of Lamba Doria and that of Andrea Doria. The palace donated by the Commune to Lamba Doria (on the right), the victorious admiral at Curzola in 1298, belongs to a model which is typical of other noble residences of similar date. As in the case of the Macello Nuovo, it was divided vertically into two single-family residences. After war damage inflicted in 1945, Mario Labò's restoration reopened the great colonnade on the ground floor; remnants of the original building include the side mullioned windows with four lights, whereas the openings in the façade show a clear Mannerist style. The next-door palazzo (no. 17) was donated in 1528 by the Senate to Andrea "Liberator of the Nation", although originally built by Lazzaro Doria in 1468. Even though what we see today is the result of a comprehensive restoration undertaken in the 1930s by Orlando Grosso in a flowery Gothic style, with highly decorated windows and often polylobate embellishments laid over the traditional kaleidoscopic black and white facing, it still reveals the shift in taste and lifestyle which occurred at the end of the 15th century, together with the widespread presence of Lombard craftsmen whose work is here represented by the fine marble porch. [E. P.]

11
Palazzo Spinola dei Marmi
PIAZZA DELLE FONTANE MAROSE 6
BUS 18, 19, 20, 30, 35, 39, 40, 42

Palazzo Spinola, which since 1832 has looked out on to a raised piazza flanking the continuation of the present-day Via Luccoli, was built between 1445 and 1459 for Giacomo Spinola on two parcels of land owned by the family on which an old tower had previously stood. As well as revealing traditional late medieval features, the façade has five niches with marble statues of illustrious members of the family in conformity with an unusual tradition in celebrating family dynasties. These are attributed to the Lombard, Bissoni, who, together with Leonardo Riccomanni, was the first to bring the new Tuscan culture to Genoa. The kaleidoscopic façade was transformed by the introduction of 16th-century windows (see sides), by the reintroduction of the mullioned four-light windows (1903, arch. Aurelio Crotta under supervision of A. D'Andrade) and by the numerous lowerings of the street level which required the introduction of bas-relief panels to re-balance the general proportions (c. 1870).
In recent years, the building has undergone great and widespread reconstruction which has restored the 15th-century "hall" on the piano nobile. Despite wide-ranging internal changes, one can still perceive the original solution adopted for the hillside site as can be seen from the terrace at the rear. [E. P.]

12
Cathedral of San Lorenzo
PIAZZA SAN LORENZO
BUS 12, 15, 1̵5̵, 17, 19, 30, 4̵1̵

The present complex, bounded to the east by the archbishop's residence and to the north by the Canons' cloister and baptistry, was built alongside the Porta di Serravalle within the 9th-century walls after the original site outside the walls to the west of the XII Apostles (now San Siro, 4th century) was left, as is revealed by the oldest remains. Of the original church, begun in 1099 and consecrated whilst still unfinished by pope Gelasio II in 1118, the great proto-Romanesque, Lombard, north door (of San Giovanni, c. 1160) and its contemporary to the south, the Porta di San Gottardo, which is more in Nicolo Pisano's style still remain. After the 1222 earthquake, the site was reopened *ex novo* by Franco-Norman craftsmen, as is shown in the plan with its two towers and the design of the lower façade. After an interruption in the middle of the century and fires in 1296, the wooden roof and the lower order of the nave (1307-12) were rebuilt, reusing such capitals and columns as had survived; the apse was also rebuilt. In the 15th century, various chapels were opened in the left-hand side, together with the larger one dedicated to St John the Baptist, Genoa's principal patron saint (begun 1451, G. Gaggini), and work continued on the façade. Of the two bell-towers, the left-hand one remained unfinished but was topped by a loggia built by G. di Gandria (1445-47), whereas the other was finished in 1522. In the middle of the 16th century, a renovation programme was started, with the Perugia architect, Galeazzo Alessi, building a dome over the transept on an octagonal drum supported by four large piers.

He also roofed the nave, aisle and presbytery (1556) with barrel vaults. The decoration was Mannerist in style and included statues by G. A. Montorsoli and G. G. della Porta set in the transept and presbytery (1541-53) as well as later frescoes by L. Tavarone in the choir (1624). The façade, damascened by the taste for reusing Roman elements, spans at least three centuries: the lower order is dominated by three great, multicoloured, splayed doorways of French style, whilst the black and white decorative bands embrace other, later openings and the 15th-century rose window. The severe setting of the piazza, which was originally higher and narrower, derives from the stairs with Carlo Rubatto's lions which were built as part of the continuation of Via San Lorenzo to the port (c. 1840), an indispensable through-route and main entrance to the new heart of the city at Piazza San Domenico (now Piazza R. de Ferrari). After passing the Gothic innernarthex which dates from the same period as the façade, we find the interior is characterized by a bare, medieval solemnity despite the gold and coloured splendour of the broad apse which is scarcely attenuated by the dark stalls of the choir. The whole complex was restored following a programme drawn up by a commission (1894-1900) comprising Alfredo D'Andrade, Camillo Boito, Luigi A. Cervetto and M. Aurelio Crotta who later became director of the project. The 18th-century altars in the right-hand aisle were removed but the 15th-century chapels on the left were preserved. The aim was to restore the cathedral to its medieval character. [E. P.]

13
Palazzo dei Maruffi and Tower
VIA DI CANNETO IL LUNGO 23
BUS 15, 17, 30, 32, 36, 41, 41

The sole surviving example of a relatively unchanged noble medieval residence (single-family palazzo with flanking tower), the building boasts a grand entrance with an archaic single archway and equally archaic ashlar facing on the tower which is well-preserved despite the lack of crenellations on the crown. Other examples along the Ripa di Castello or in the 13th-century centre have been re-absorbed into 16th-17th-century palaces within which the form of the tower can sometimes be discerned. The Embriaci tower is one of these latter; it is harder to make out the remaining examples of degli Alberici (Piazza San Giorgio), Dentuti (Via Sottoripa) and Piccamiglio (Via del Campo). The alternative style of tower is of the sort we see at the Macello Nuovo (Via Luccoli 16-18) and attached to the Palazzo Lamba Doria (Piazza San Matteo) - the latter only from the outside; these belong to a more "civic" type. Both comprised a commercial area (raised colonnade) and a residential area on the upper storeys, with separate functions for each floor as in every medieval city palace; in Genoa there were always three or four storeys. The upper part would rise above the black Promontorio stone base. Usually, this was in brick while the black and white decoration on the walls, which is of clear Pisan influence, was only permitted to powerful families. Large openings divided into several lights with small columns and capitals bearing floral decoration would be opened in the façade; the slate roof might have had a crenellated parapet. [E.P.]

14
Church of San Donato
PIAZZA SAN DONATO
BUS 15, 17, 30, 32, 36, 41, 41

First evidence of the church dates from the 11th century but it was twice enlarged in the following century; still visible are the exterior octagonal covering of the dome (*tiburio*) and crossing tower dating from the first half of the 12th century. The reconstruction of the nave and aisles towards the entrance, which maintained and reused part of the external walls and original monolithic columns by the apse can probably be dated to the second half of the century. The plan we find today - nave and two aisles roofed in wood and three apses - is the result of this work. Despite the restructuring of the 18th century and Michele Canzio's Neoclassical refurbishment of the nave, the Romanesque San Donato has survived thanks in part to D'Andrade's restoration (1888) and another in 1925 which reconstituted arbitrarily sited original elements into a strongly expressive whole. The porch on the façade is an interpretation by D'Andrade of the San Gottardo portal in the cathedral. The acute splays of the portals, the piers, the octagonal sectioned arches, capitals and reused Roman architrave date from the medieval enlargement. The nave and aisles, restored after the last war, are dominated by the reused Roman columns and capitals which in number are second only to Santa Maria di Castello, and characterized by the two-light mullioned windows of the unusual pseudo women's gallery. The refurbishment of the octagonal crossing tower, which rises in three levels from a pendentive dome of Byzantine derivation, dates from the 19th-century restoration. [R. P.]

15
Church and Convent of Santa Maria di Castello
SALITA SANTA MARIA DI CASTELLO 15
BUS 12, 15, 18, 17, 32, 35, 41, 41

Situated on the hill which saw the earliest siting of the city, it is one of the earliest churches dedicated to Mary (658 AD?) and was mentioned in 1049 as having a parsonage. The Romanesque church dates from the first quarter of the 12th century. The nave and aisles with transept and three apses were built under the patronage of Embriaci and de Castro by the Antelami masters who were to provide impetus for the whole of Genoa's architectural history.

It is the most impressive example of local Romanesque architecture, boasting the highest number of reused Roman columns and capitals in the city (3rd century AD), and was restored by Maurizio Dufour in 1859/60.

The original ceilings in the aisles were replaced at the beginning of the 13th century with rib vaulting and that in the nave was renewed in 1445 after Eugenio IV made the church over to a Dominican order (1441) as a result of its previous poor administration under the Canons. A year later, they began building the convent (1452/1513) and gave the church its present aspect: the opening of side chapels and a first elongation of a choir and half-dome (1448/49). The apse was enlarged again and a dome later built (1589).

The original plan, divided into three by pilasters and crowned by hanging arches owes its present aspect to the restorations of 1925 and 1948. The only decorative feature in the entrance is a Roman cornice of the 3rd century AD with leaves facing griffins.

The Dominican convent which replaced the Canonical collegiate church is articulated around two cloisters on three very simple orders along the south side of the church (1445-70), around the kitchen garden and the cloister of the infirmary (1513). After the recent restorations (1961-65), it is possible to understand once more the strong theological, mystical and political message conveyed by the refounding order in an extensive fresco cycle executed around the middle of the 15th century. The convent houses an exceptional collection of antiphonies and incunabula, as well as ex-votos and panel paintings which are preserved in a museum. These not only bear witness to the convent's troubled early history but also to the richness of the Lombard and Piedmontese schools of painting, drawn there towards the end of the 15th century by the Dominican order and the patronage of the greatest families and members of the city's government. [E. P.]

16
Church of Sant'Agostino
PIAZZA R. NEGRI; PIAZZA SARZANO 21
BUS 15, 17, 30, 32, 35, 41, 41, 42

Founded by the Augustinians in 1260 with the name of Santa Tecla, it is one of the rare Gothic churches to have survived the destruction of ecclesiastical buildings of that period, even though it went through a century-long period of restoration.
It was constructed with humble materials, with marble and cut stone used for a little decoration in the façade, the tall columns and cube-shaped capitals. The 14th and 15th centuries saw renewed building activity with the demolition of the side trusses and raising of perimeter walls, with some single-light windows being blocked off and oculuses opened under the new vaults. The choir was also enlarged. In the 17th century, further major work was undertaken in Baroque style.
The present-day façade in black and white bands with a pointed arch portal and lunette by G. B. Merano (17th century) is divided into three by pilasters and motifs which extend right up to the dentilled pitches of the roof, with blind arcading and romboid panels. The bell tower has two and four-light mullioned openings on four levels and is decorated with square tiles and crowned by cusps and four side pinnacles which, unusually, are faced with polychrome majolica from Albissola.
After the suppression of 1798, the neglect of the whole complex, including a triangular and a square cloister, was such as to cause the historian, Federigo

Alizeri (1859) to propose it being turned into a sculpture museum. From the end of the century to the 1930s, the complex was the object of a number of studies and careful restoration projects which saw the participation of A. D'Andrade, Antonio Barabino and O. Grosso who sited a museum of Casacce in the church (1939).

Only after the realization of the project to set up a museum of sculpture and architecture (1977-82, F. Albini, F. Helg, A. Piva), which necessitated the destruction of the second cloister, did the site acquire a new identity which is now integrated with the church, used as an auditorium. [M. M.]

17
Embriaci Tower
SALITA ALLA TORRE EMBRIACI
BUS 12, 15, ~~15~~, 17, 32, 35, 41, ~~41~~

This is the most well-known and venerable of the private towers and rises alongside Palazzo Brignole Sale (16th century, previously called Embriaci) between the lower piazza of the same name and the upper one - now called Piazza di Santa Maria in Passione - thus revealing the military might of the cliques in the decades during the formation of the Commune. It is roughly 41 metres high, and is entirely built of rusticated ashlar with thin openings in the walls to admit light. Below the cornice at the top, there are three orders of projecting blind arcading crowned by square crenellations which characterize the whole structure, although these were only added after a restoration in 1923. As is well-known, the towers were used for attack and defence but we note that their close proximity actually defused their danger, so we have to conclude that their use was also in large part symbolic. Despite this, an order dated 1160 instructed Lanfranco Bacemo that his tower *de mari* should not exceed 80 feet (about 24 m), although the Embriaci were subsequently relieved of this obligation as a result of their daring deeds in the Holy Land. In 1228, the Embriaci built another tower of brick with wolf's mouth openings just within the Porta di Sant'Andrea (Salita Prione 35) which was to all extents and purposes a fortress. This was immediately sold to the Fieschi family. In the 13th century, the private towers numbered at least 66, but this had dropped to less than half that figure by the end of the 15th century. [E. P.]

18
Church of Santo Stefano
PIAZZA SANTO STEFANO
BUS 15, 17, 18, 19, 20, 30, 36, 39, 40, 41, 41, 42

The church was built by Bishop Teodolfo II (960), on a site where there was perhaps already a Longobard church dedicated to St Michael, as a Benedictine abbey to colonize the eastern edge of the city from Porta Soprana to Val Bisagno and the coast to the east. In the 13th century, it was still an important stabilizing power in the control of the area extending beyond the Oltregiogo. The present building is unusual in having a single nave and an extremely high presbytery; it was built towards the end of the 12th century (consecrated 1217). In the 14th century, Lombard workmen added a new dome covering (*tiburio*) and terracotta belfry; the tower beneath is a medieval, or even Byzantine military construction. The monastery and surrounding area were included within the city only after the 1320-47 walls were built. Thus, after these were altered in 1536, Santo Stefano came to find itself close to the eastern gate of the city where the new Via Giulia would terminate in the mid 17th century. With the progressive development of the central urban area, and especially with the opening of Via XX Settembre (1898-1910) which revealed the remains of an impressive pre-Roman necropolis from Santo Stefano to Sant'Andrea, the church was raised higher than the ground around to such an extent that when the octagonal, exterior dome covering, semi-circular apse and the brick dome were restored by D'Andrade, he had to add a colonnade beneath in neo-Gothic style (1912-16). During the most recent restoration under Carlo Ceschi (1946-55), a crypt was revealed. [M. M.]

II.
THE CITY OF THE OLD WALLS: MODERN BUILDINGS
NICOLÒ DE MARI

The interventions of the modern era within the walls, built from 1536 onwards on the outline of the fourteenth-century walls (1320-50), bear witness to the many stances gradually taken by the various economic, cultural and entrepreneurial policies towards the urban fabric of the "finished" city of 1200.

The city centre was abandoned in the 19th century in the face of changed social and demographic conditions which encouraged expansion beyond the fortified city and the growth of ever greater urbanisation of the hills behind. Before this, however, between the 16th and 18th centuries the largest city centre of its type in Europe underwent a series of urbanistic and architectural changes of varying scale and importance which aimed to renew the extraordinarily dense medieval city, the result of successive accumulations and the reflection of a mercantile society which looked to the harbour area as its sole economic resource.

THE 16TH CENTURY

The city of "hotels" - spontaneous noble associations aimed at economic and political control and heirs of the ancient "factions" - imposed a style of building in the 15th century led by Lombard "Antelami" masters who had been operating for some time in the city, characterized by the closing of the commercial façade on the road and the introduction of hall, courtyard and stairs at the rear. However, it was only in the 16th century that the Genoese architectural culture adopted more mature designs and more aware entrepreneurial programmes. The new political stability deriving from the arrival of Andrea Doria in 1528, the betrayal to France under François I and the alliance with Spain under Charles V, the successful conversion of the traditional maritime and mercantile economy to a capitalist, financial one based upon asientos and exchange and the rapid growth of a new rich "nobility" constitute the principal starting points for a renewal which took form as a result of Andrea Doria's cultural aspirations: from 1529, he invited artists from the school of Raphael to work at Fassolo, and these were soon followed by architects such as Galeazzo Alessi and Giovanni Battista Castello, who brought with them the latest trends from Rome. Above all, however, the period was to be marked by an extraordinary fruitfulness in urban and construction projects, both public and private.

The crowded medieval fabric of the town was altered to make way for more elaborate buildings. The reworking of the Campetto-Soziglia axis, the creation of aristocratic squares of the Doria-Invrea in Via del Campo and the De Franchi between San Siro and the Maddalena, and the opening of Via Imperiale between Campetto and San Lorenzo and Via Doria to San Matteo are just some of the examples of a widespread phenomenon which touched upon the whole of the 13th-century city. The new streets and squares were fronted by new houses built upon the rubble of demolition on a grand scale to allow for an easier execution of the new spatial discoveries of the previous century, which find their definitive expression in the buildings of Strada Nuova.

However, it was above all the large public projects, like Strada Nuova itself, which bear witness to the changed cultural conditions and desire for self-glorification of the dominant families in a city which had only recently strengthened its fortified boundary walls.

Strada Nuova (1550-83) which was at once a carefully thought-out speculation, a plan to enlarge and tidy up the surrounding area and an opportunity for the new aristocracy to exhibit its new power and cosmopolitan culture; the Banchi complex (1575-95) which was a skilfully self-financing operation and at the same time the celebration of an economic system at its peak; the enlargement and refurbishment of the medieval Palazzo Ducale (starting in 1590) made possible by large private contributions and the symbol of a renewed political faith, are the three examples which best exemplify the material culture of the city in the "century of the Genoese".

THE 17TH CENTURY

With the 16th-century fervour for renewal, as exemplified by Rubens' prints (1652), coming to an end, the 17th century saw a relative immobility in building; a sign of a feared political and economic instability which were confirmed by the prudent construction of the new city walls (decreed in 1626) and of the Molo Nuovo (decided in 1636). This lack of movement left unrealised a number of projects which sought to resolve the pressing and difficult problems of through routes and access links in the newly-congested and "finished" city; these were left to the following century. Although there was considerable activity on a small scale (often adding embellishments to earlier buildings), few important construction projects were started. Only the dreadful results of the French bombing of 1684 were to restore a necessary and unexpected vigour on both fronts.

In this setting, of particular importance were the spread of new religious foundations on the one hand and, on the other, the construction of the monumental Balbi road, "end of a move to expansion" (Poleggi), which, between the end of the 16th century (1587) and the first 20 years of the 17th century (1622), saw the failure of additional residential buildings near to, and on the model of, Strada Nuova. Traced under the supervision of the Council Fathers between 1601 and 1613 with evident spatial references to the 16th-century "districts" and attention to the traffic problems unrelated to the division into lots of the 16th century, the new road (started 1616) was actually the last opportunity for the spatial experiments begun in the 15th century. It was at the same time a masterly test for Bartolomeo Bianco, last and perhaps most famous exponent of that secular Lombard presence which in the 17th century seemed to return and impose its experience as masters and directors of works.

The image of the city in the 17th century, however, cannot fail to take into account the new religious foundations as well. These began towards the turn of the preceding century with building sites opened by the Theatines (1583), the Somaschi (1586) and the Jesuits (1589). They were to spread considerably in the 17th century on the wave of a renewed religious fervour and rediscovered desire to show a presence.

The main players were the reformed congregations, alongside sporadic "curial" or noble projects, with complexes slotted into the wide spaces created between the old and new city walls. However, they also appeared within the older walls and in the midst of the crowded medieval fabric, where they often restored ancient ecclesiastical buildings and adapted pre-existing constructions to use as convents.

THE 18TH CENTURY

The Age of Enlightenment, restrained by political timidity, was to confirm trends formulated by the urban culture of the preceding century, although some infrastructural works which had shown themselves to be indispensable were undertaken. Amongst these, the opening of Strada Nuovissima (1778-86; today called Via Cairoli) was fundamental; it provided a link between Strada Nuova and Via Balbi and thus a new through - route within the ancient walls.

Although, as mentioned above, the bombs of 1684 were to provide renewed stimulus to a building sector which had been idle to all extents and purposes since the end of the 16th century, this was to take concrete form (alongside purely speculative ventures) for the most part in the completion of town-planning schemes which had already been defined (Strada Nuova, Via Balbo), or in more or less superficial reworkings of decorative displays. Against this setting, the first timid projects for the building of theatres gain some importance. Appearing very late (and now lost again), these reveal the first indications of an international culture which found their greatest exponent in the figure of Emanuele Andrea Tagliafichi.

ITINERARIES
FIRST ROUTE: FROM PIAZZA CARICAMENTO TO PIAZZA DI CARIGNANO

Walk along Via San Giorgio to arrive at the charming piazza of the same name with the two Baroque churches of San Giorgio and San Torpete. After a brief detour to Piazza Cattaneo to see Palazzo Cattaneo designed by Bartolomeo Bianco (1623), take Via dei Giustiniani to the nearby piazza with some interesting 17th-century palaces at nos. 6 and 7. Then follow the parallel Via San Bernardo, home to a number of important 15th-century (nos. 8-10-12-14-16) and 16th-century buildings (nos.29-31 and no. 26 in Piazza San Bernardo). Arriving at Piazza Ferretto, turn left along Salita Pollaiuoli to reach Piazza Matteotti with the 18th-century façade of Palazzo Ducale and the 17th-century one of the Gesù of the right. Returning to Piazza Ferretto and going behind the church of San Donato, climb up Stradone Sant'Agostino, opened in 1687 with interesting examples of working-class housing to reach Piazza Sarzano (church of San Salvatore, 17th century) and, crossing the bridge of Via Ravasco (1728), the Piazza di Carignano dominated by the Basilica dell'Alessi (begun 1552). With a slight detour along Via Santa Maria and Via Lata, one comes to the Noviziato dei Gesuiti di Sant'Ignazio (1673-c. 1725).

SECOND ROUTE: FROM PIAZZA BANCHI TO ACQUASOLA

Following Via al Ponte Reale, one reaches the monumental Banchi complex. After a look at Via San Luca and a quick detour to Piazza De Marini to see the 16th-century courtyard of Palazzo Croce Bermondi (no. 1), take Via Orefici to reach the important hub of Piazza Soziglia and Piazza Campetto with Palazzo Casareto-De Mari (no. 2) and Palazzo Imperiale (no. 8), before climbing Via Scurreria which lies opposite the entrance to the latter. Cross Piazza Invrea (with the interesting painted façade of no. 4), to arrive at the 18th-century Piazza Scuole Pie with the church of the same name. Return to Piazza Campetto and proceed to Piazza delle Vigne with its 12th-century church and Palazzo di Domenico Grillo (1545-60) and then follow Via Luccoli, observing the façade of the 16th-century Palazzo Franzone in Piazza Lucoli. Cross Piazza Fontane Marose to reach Salita Santa Caterina and Palazzo Spinola (no. 3) and Piazza E. Lanfranco with Palazzo Doria which can be dated to 1541-43 and which is now the prefecture. The last part of the route crosses Piazza Corvetto behind the old walls of Acquasola to arrive at the Annunziata di Portoria (entry from Via IV Novembre).

THIRD ROUTE: FROM PIAZZA FONTANE MAROSE TO PIAZZA ACQUAVERDE

The last route follows the axis comprising Via Garibaldi (Strada Nuova), Via Cairoli (Strada Nuovissima) and, through Piazza della Nunziata, Via Balbi (Strada dei Balbi), with the following detours: from Via Garibaldi to the Maddalena church (lane behind the chancel of the Maddalena); from Via Cairoli to the churches of San Siro (Via San Siro) and San Luca (Via San Luca); from Via Bensa, connecting to Piazza della Nunziata, to Via Lomellina and the Filippini complex and as far as Piazza Fossatello, a sizeable area divided into lots in 1539, and a precursor of Strada Nuova, where one may admire Palazzo Pallavicino-Rayper, dated 1503 (no. 2).

19
Porta del Molo
PIAZZETTA PORTA DEL MOLO
BUS 90

The construction of the "Muragliette", as this part of the 16th-century walls was called, took place at the same time as the project for the Porta del Molo by G. Alessi realized by Antonio Roderio between 1551 and 1553. This date, engraved in the marble plaque on the outside of the arch, provides a certain date for the completion of the work. The project began in 1550 when Alessi was instructed to provide a military complex which would be linked to the new walls being constructed and guarantee both the city's defence and the regulation of traffic for the purposes of extracting duty. It would also supply a convenient route between the Molo and the city and be an important element in the urban landscape. With his design for the Porta del Molo, Alessi set the city's seaward entrance in a fine exedra with niches, pilasters and half-columns on Mannerist drums, the whole enclosed within two pincer arms. On the city side, the opening appears like a trilithic portico with three arches divided by Doric pilasters; the inside, divided into five bays covered with a single barrel vault with the road perpendicular to the main symmetrical axis, underwent many alterations in the 19th century, including a radical one by General Della Porta (1869). [M. M.]

20
Churches of San Giorgio and San Torpete
PIAZZA SAN GIORGIO
BUS 12, 15

The two Baroque churches of San Giorgio and San Torpete transform the small square they face (once the site of a market) into a highly refined setting which is almost unique in the medieval town. The old church of San Giorgio dates back to 964 and used to stand in the southern part of the area now occupied by the present building. It was rebuilt in a completely new style by the Theatines from 1697 onwards.

The architect is unknown; it may be Giacomo Lagomaggiore, the state architect, who in 1693 signed the plan attached to the request to the Council Fathers, explaining the variations to the façade proposed and which reflects the unusual curvilinear solution actually built. Alternatively, it might have been Gio Batta Sanguineti, called Spinzo, who in 1697 received payment from the Theatines for some drawings and a model. The hypothesis of the Lombard architect, Giovanni Antonio Viscardi, has also been advanced. He worked for the Theatines towards the end of the century and was responsible for the sanctuary of Santa Maria Ausiliatrice at Freystadt (1700-8) which has close similarities to this church in Genoa.

The ground-plan, with an octagonal hall and deep, radial side chapels surmounted by a dome on a high drum with windows, reveals the influence of the northern Po Valley and invites comparison with other churches in the city, especially with Santa Maria della Sanità, perhaps designed by Giovanni

Ponzello (1614). The bell tower was adapted using an existing medieval tower and incorporated into the adjacent building in Via dei Giustiniani (no. 2), which was transformed into a convent after 1687 and documented in 19th-century plans which have been recently discovered.

The old church of San Torpete dated from the 12th century and was rebuilt after 1730 using a design by Gio Antonio Ricca Jr., called il Gobbo. The small family church of the Cattaneo household faces the piazza with a classicizing façade with pilasters and niches. The interior features an elliptical space divided into three small apses and covered by a dome on a drum. It also has a presbytery set along identical geometrical lines. The precious character of the whole is established by the rich decoration which helps create a continuous, enveloping environment. [L.D.]

21
Palazzetto Criminale (State Archives)
VIA T. REGGIO 14
BUS 12, 15, ~~15~~, 17, 19, 30, ~~41~~

In its present role as a public building (the State Archives), it does not immediately reveal the importance it had in the development of a Genoese style of architecture. It marked the first attempt to build a new type of building in the guise of a court house, with the prominent use of the familiar Genoese covered stairway. Decreed in 1581 to provide a modern structure (until then the only real jail had been the Malapaga for debtors on the Molo), it was located where the 13th-century Palazzo del Podestà used to stand, between Palazzo Ducale and the Arcivescovado. It also stood on one side of the Cathedral Canons' cloister with adjoining land and houses which gave rise to long-standing court cases before the owners could be evicted.

For this reason, it was built in two phases (1581-92 and 1593-98) using the old Serravalle tower (which can still be made out on the west side). It housed the civil and penal courts, jails (public and secret), the examining board and chapel. It also included a belvedere terrace for the doge who could reach it from the adjoining palace which was reconstructed during the same period. With the transfer of the jail (1818) designed by G. Cantoni and C. Barabino, it became the offices of the prestigious and exceptional Archives of the Republic, of the Banco di San Giorgio and of the Notaries (from 1155). [E. P.]

22
Archbishop's Palace
PIAZZA G. MATTEOTTI 4
BUS 12, 15, 1̶8̶, 17, 19, 30, 4̶1̶

The palace, dating back to the first half of the 16th century, is in part a reconstruction of an older building. In 1133, Innocent II removed the bishop's see of Genoa from Milan's jurisdiction, raising it to the rank of Metropolitan for which Siro II, the city's first archbishop, had a new palace built between the end of the 15th century and the start of the 16th.

In 1530, the warehouse and powder factory beneath caught fire, gutting the palace. The archbishop, Innocenzo Cibo, had it rebuilt, entrusting the task to Domenico Marchesi da Caranca, called il Caranchetto. In 1577, the archbishop, Cipriano Pallavicino, began enlarging the eastern side of the palace, a task continued by his successor with the construction of a hall, loggia and stairway. Today, the lack of unity in the project resulting from successive juxtapositions is still quite clear.

In the last century, following the demolition of the wings of Palazzo Ducale, the entrance to the building was moved from the north façade, where it used to be, to its present location on the square. The palace was damaged during the Second World War with the loss of some of the frescos in the salone by Luca Cambiaso. The cobbled courtyard follows the design of the roof of the Museo del Tesoro di San Lorenzo, designed by Franco Albini; its presence being revealed in the palace basements. [I. F.]

23
Palazzo Ducale
PIAZZA G. MATTEOTTI
BUS 12, 15, ~~15~~, 17, 19, 30, 35, 41, ~~41~~, 42

Today, we see the palace with the monumental Neoclassical façade by Simone Cantoni, decorated with imposing coupled columns and trophies on the upper storey which bear witness to the influence of early French Neoclassicism, and the two regular avant-corps designed with academic correctness by Ignazio Gardella in the 1860s. It is on a C plan and covers an area of 6,000 square metres, enclosing a volume of 200,000 cubic metres. Work began on the palace in 1291 following a decision taken by the Capitani del Popolo to provide a headquarters for the Commune. The palazzo degli Abati, of which we can see a loggia with three arches and two storeys of openings on Via T. Reggio opposite the Archbishop's palace, enclosed an adjacent, older, rusticated "casa dei Fieschi" with a tower of seven floors (la Grimaldina, which was made taller in 1538 with the addition of a belfry) to create a single structure.

The present Palazzo Ducale was designed by Andrea Ceresola, called il Vannone, a state architect, who began building work in 1587. Work lasted for a considerable period covering the whole area and reusing elements from the earlier building. Below the western courtyard, recent restoration has uncovered the great hall called "del munizioniere", with cross-vaulting set on eight pillars with enormous capitals taken from earlier 14th-century constructions. Within, the splendid, empty, immense spaces created by Vannone are laid out on the ground floor (actually scenically set above Piazza Matteotti). The great hall, covered by an outsized vault held up by an avant-garde technological invention which transferred the weight to metal chains set into the walls, is separated only by a double curtain of columns from two courtyards: that to the west presents an elegant corner solution with entablature and an architraved cornice above the columns in a sophisticated Mannerist style. The austere staircase starts from the centre of the hall and is in keeping with the cerimonial nature of a class of government which was already looking to Spain. A first, shallow flight divides into two symmetrical stairs: the one on the left leads to the loggia of the western courtyard and separates the part of the palace with the Doge's apartments and the chapel. Here, in the middle of the 17th century, Carlone glorified the salient moments in Genoa's history around the Virgin Mary as Queen of Genoa, in his paintings. The two large reception rooms of the Maggior and Minor Council lie above the hall following the 16th-century plans, but they were refurbished in the 18th century. A fire in 1777 provided Simone Cantoni with the opportunity to make radical changes: the two rooms were doubled in height and redecorated in line with 18th-century notions of ceremony, using rich marble and stucco effects. The brick and stone roof held in balance without chains is completely original. However, by 1861 it was already necessary for I. Gardella to intervene to resolve problems of movement. He replaced the large masonry arches of the great room with trusses in steel and cast iron (Polençau) which have emerged in recent restoration. [E. D. N.]

24
Church of SS. Ambrogio e Andrea Il Gesù
PIAZZA G. MATTEOTTI
BUS 12, 15, 15, 17, 19, 30, 35, 41, 41, 42

Built for the College planned by the Jesuits for the site of Sant'Ambrogio - an area of great strategic importance given its proximity to the centre of political power (Palazzo Ducale) and one-time site of an early-medieval construction of the same name given from 1582 to the Society of Jesus - the present church represents one of the most important examples of late 16th century Genoese religious architecture. Traditionally attributed to Tibaldi and, more recently, to G. B. Lantana, the project is now unanimously attributed to the Jesuit artist and architect, Giuseppe Valeriani, partly on the basis of indications contained in the *Historia Domus Professae Genuensis* manuscript by Father Giulio Negrone. The construction was financed by Father Marcello Pallavicino and began on 1 August 1589. The main structure was completed between 1592 (building of the transept) and 1603 (completion of the roof), which year the church was reserved for the sole use of the new Casa Professa after the Jesuits withdrew from the scene. In 1599, with the completion of the first phase of the work on the rest of the complex, work began upon the façade and continued until 1637, although involving only the lower part of the structure. The present upper storey, although coherent with the original design as reproduced by Rubens (1652), actually dates from 1891-92. The plan of the building, slightly modified as a result of work undertaken in 1636 in the presbytery by Orazio Grassi (chapels of San Francesco Saverio and of the Sacro Cuore), is unusual given the Jesuit context, despite strong similarities with the order's church in Naples which was also designed by Valeriano (Gesù Nuovo). It provides an interesting link between the central scheme of five domes deriving from Bramante (San Pietro) - in which we can perhaps suggest a debt to the nearby basilica by Alessi in Carignano (1552) - and the longitudinal design with lateral chapels which are more in keeping with Counter-Reformation trends. The decoration in the interior is extremely rich, with frescos dating from the 1630s produced in line with a precise didactic and iconographic programme set out by the Society.

Rapid mention must also be made of the Casa Professa of which the church used to be an integral part. It was a building of little architectural interest occupying a long patch of ground behind the present structure and put up unevenly in a number of phases over a period of about 80 years (1595-1678). The initial project was perhaps altered by Orazio Grassi, essentially because of the difficulties encountered in acquiring the site. It was demolished at the beginning of the 20th century as part of the overall plan which saw the creation of Piazza R. De Ferrari. [N. D. M.]

25
Ponte di Carignano
VIA E. RAVASCO
BUS 32, 35

The Ponte di Carignano (1718-24) was constructed as a natural link between the Carignano and Castello hills which are divided by the valley of the Rio Torbido, at the same time as the façade of Santa Maria Assunta in Carignano was completed. This was designed to be the perspective backdrop of a road which had already been planned by Stefano Sauli in the latter half of the 16th century, probably following a suggestion from G. Alessi. Only at the start of the 18th century did Domenico Sauli entrust the French military engineer, Gerard de Langlade, with the task. De Langlade had become the main military architect of the Republic and director of the first school of military architecture which opened in 1713 and trained such architects, engineers and topographers as Matteo Vinzoni and Gaetano Tallone. Two solutions were presented: the first foresaw a straight bridge but was rejected because of the expense that would be incurred in expropriating residents beneath; the second, successful, plan allowed for four powerful, high arches set along a broken line amongst the houses of the district of Via Madre di Dio, now destroyed by a town planning scheme of the 1970s. [M. M.]

26
Church of Santa Maria Assunta in Carignano
PIAZZA CARIGNANO
BUS 32, 35

Building began in 1552 under the patronage of the Sauli family and with a design by Galeazzo Alessi, who followed the whole project even after moving to Milan and Perugia, as is revealed by the correspondence with the Sauli and the directors of works, Bernardino Cantone, Domenico and Giovanni Ponzello, Bernardo Spazio and Angelo Doggio. The last letter, dated 1569, informs us that the lower part of the structure was complete. The dome was begun in 1568 and completed in 1603. The ground plan is in the form of a Greek cross, with a central dome and four corner spaces with smaller domes, and has no precedent in the local culture, nor any analogies with contemporary Counter-Reformation churches. It is, instead, conceived along Roman and Sangalloesque designs of perfect geometry. Decoration is kept to a minimum in the Corinthian capitals, and in the caissons of the vaults with an extremely refined interweaving of lines of the apse vault. The statues on the pillars of the dome were added by Puget, who in 1668 followed the example of the redecoration of St Peter's in Rome. The division of the interior into four identical zones around the dome is echoed in the exterior with a similar spatial and volumetric symmetry. The dome is grandiose, with a drum boasting mighty serliana arcading and terraces which follow the central ones along the top of the roofs, allowing the town to be seen from the top of the hill upon which the Basilica rises; an external feature of the city which can be admired from the sea and from afar. [E. D. N.]

27
Church and Novitiate of Sant'Ignazio (State Archives)
PIAZZA SAN LEONARDO 2
BUS 35

The Jesuits' Novitiate, constructed between 1676 and 1683, and its church (1723-24) face the small square, an important hub of communications in centuries past in Carignano. Backing on to the hilltop, it comprises a 16th-century villa which reveals a picturesque disposition of structures and a varied use of loggias set within a geometrically defined plan. Acquired by the Jesuits in 1660, it was used as the first nucleus of the Novitiate to which further buildings were later added. Completely bare of decoration, these are purely functional structures and the contrast between the large, severe spaces of the Jesuit building and the cheerful polychromy of the villa residence could not be greater. Used in the 19th century as a barracks, it was seriously damaged by bombs in the last war and was subsequently abandoned. In 1985, with its new intended use as State Archives, salvage and restoration began on this important project, linked to the concept of re-use, by Angelo Sibilla.

To date, the church has been restored (on a centralized longitudinal plan with a large domical vault on diagonal pilasters, it is full of light thanks to the large windows in the wings), as has the villa, which was decorated with frescos, by Andrea Semino and helpers. The church is to serve as a multipurpose space, whereas the villa will be used for administrative staff and documentation on Columbus. The book stacks (with 15 kms of shelving) are nearing completion and new structures are being built. [E. D. N.]

28
Loggia dei Mercanti
PIAZZA BANCHI
BUS 1, 2, 3, 7, 8, 12, 15

The construction of the Loggia, designed by A. Ceresola, called il Vannone, and G. Ponzello between 1589 and 1595, brought to a close the City Council Fathers' 20-year programme of restructuring and improving Piazza di Banchi, the old commercial and city centre. Considered to be one of the wonders of the city, it was built by the same architects assisted by the same artists (Daniele Casella and Taddeo Carlone) who were working on the church of San Pietro. An analogous form of self-financing was also employed by including a number of shops in the structure.

The loggia encloses a single hall with perimeter arches on coupled columns which are closed on two sides. It has a tent vault and the roof is supported without internal supports thanks to an extraordinary piece of carpentry comprising a trellis of beams which hold up the roof and from which were hung the wooden centering of the vault beneath. In 1839, the building was given to the Chamber of Commerce and restored on the basis of a project by G. B. Resasco, with the arches being closed with windows and a door being opened on to Piazza Senarega. From 1855, it housed Italy's first Commodities Exchange. In 1942, a bombing raid caused the loss of the roof and the restored loggia was only opened in 1950. By then, it had lost its original commercial role and was taken over by the City Council for cultural events. [I. F.]

29
Church of San Pietro in Banchi
PIAZZA BANCHI
BUS 1, 2, 3, 7, 8, 12, 15, 32

Built in the latter half of the 16th century at the behest of the Republican Senate as a token of thanks for the end of an outbreak of plague, it stands on a site where there already used to be a church dedicated to San Pietro della Porta, of which there is mention in the 10th century. The work was entrusted to the State Architect, Bernardino Cantone, who produced an initial design in 1572, but it was actually completed before 1585 by Andrea Ceresola, called il Vannone, assisted by Giovanni Ponzello.

The old church of San Pietro, the main building on the square, was built above a number of shops. The unusual arrangement which enabled the project to be self-financing through the sale of the shops on the ground floor, imposed serious constraints on the architects but it was reproposed for the new church. Built on such an unusual raised base, the present church recalls a reduced version of Alessi's design for Santa Maria Assunta in Carignano with its forming a perspective backdrop for the square. A broad terrace with balustrade in marble along the perimeter of the construction underlines the division between the sacred and the commercial areas and provides space for socializing.

The interior is strongly centripetal and is harmoniously proportioned and displays a unified decoration with architectural and sculptural works by Daniele Casella and Taddeo Carlone, frescoes by Andrea Ansaldo and Paolo Gerolamo Piola, and stucco work by Marcello Sparzo. [I. F.]

30
Palazzo Imperiale
CAMPETTO 8
BUS 1, 2, 3, 7, 8, 12, 15, 15, 18, 19, 20, 30, 41, 41, 42

The palace was built by Vincenzo Imperiale using a project by G. B. Castello to replace some existing medieval structures. The work was undertaken between 1555 and 1560, which date is engraved above the entrance. Towards the end of the 16th century, the palace was already enlarged at the behest of Gio Vincenzo Imperiale. The project was by Andrea Ansaldo and it considerably altered the original proportions of the building. In the 17th century, the palace was raised by a floor.

The façade, with its two *piani nobili* and mezzanine, recalls Castello's Roman training, as is also true of the palaces of Tobia Pallavicino (1558) and Nicolosio Lomellino (1563), both in Strada Nuova. The decoration on the upper part reveals many analogies with the motifs on the palace of Nicolosio Lomellino and it is possible to see in them cosmogonal meanings which reflect the patron's interests. The decoration must have been conceived for close viewing from beneath: going down Via Scurreria which was opened up opposite the entrance to the palace in 1584, it is not possible to grasp the unified meaning of the composition. The interior was probably conditioned by the existing structures as is suggested by the hall which is placed asymmetrically to the entrance and the stairs which climb on the right-hand side of the courtyard. In this case, too, just as with the palace of Tobia Pallavicino (1558), Castello succeeds in creating dramatic effects and unique perspectives. [L. D.]

31
Church of SS. Nome di Maria e Angeli Custodi Scuole Pie

PIAZZA DELLE SCUOLE PIE
BUS 12, 15, ~~15~~, 17, 19, 30, ~~41~~

The church is best known under the name it takes from the fathers of the Scuole Pie, or Scolopi, who built the "new" church between 1708 and 1713, after restructuring part of a neighbouring block from 1627. Salaried by Domenico Sauli, the director of the project was Gio Giacomo Ricca, a secondary figure in a family of established architects and master builders from the area (Gio Antonio, Antonio Maria, Gio Antonio Jr.). He may also have been the author of a design which originated from the family's workshop. Set as a charming backdrop to the square which takes its name from the church, the façade reveals the double function of the building, with two floors reserved as a residence for the fathers (built later) set above an architectural structure comprising two orders with tympanums which frame the richly-decorated doorway and unusual curtained window. The interior of the church, built using the outer walls of a pre-existing and irregular structure, presents a single space, a presbytery with a flat end wall and side chapels which are modest because of the conditions imposed by the site. It represents an explicit reuse of the forms imported from Lombardy and used by the Scolopi at Savona (San Filippo Neri, 1648-51, demolished) and in the initial project for San Biagio di Oneglia (1704), and subsequently spread throughout the region. The interior features a rich display of tribunes screened with wooden grates, served by stairs set behind the diagonal piers in the central hall. The decoration of the mid 18th century is especially rich. [N. D. M.]

32
Palazzo Fieschi Ravaschieri, De Ferrari
VIA SAN LORENZO 17
BUS 12, 15, ~~15~~, 17, 19, 30, ~~41~~, 41

The palace was rebuilt for Sinibaldo Fieschi on the family's ancient site near the cathedral. Through Manfredo Ravaschieri, he had received a project from Scamozzi who was in Genoa in 1611. The master builder was Bartolomeo Massone and work was completed in 1618.

The surface of the façade is exceptional for its alternating black and white stripes which recall medieval houses and which we see here in a 17th-century revival. In line with Mannerist taste, however, are the ambiguous half-man, half-beast masks which are similar to those of Palazzo Tursi.

With the opening of Via San Lorenzo in 1839, the palace, which used to face the small cathedral square (about half the present size), had to be partially sacrificed: the façade was moved back a few metres and rebuilt preserving proportions and ornaments. The interior rooms are decorated with frescos by S. Galeotti and Domenico Piola.

The decoration in those rooms giving on Via San Lorenzo was redone after the road was opened; in the Sala dell'Aurora, for example, in the same way as for the façade, Giuseppe Isola reused the damaged fresco to restore to the composition the unity it had earlier had. [E. D. N.]

33
Palazzo Spinola Pessagno
SALITA SANTA CATERINA 3
BUS 18, 19, 20, 30, 35, 36, 41, 42

Tomaso Spinola's palace was built between 1558 and 1561, but the decoration was only finished after 1574, when the building was purchased by Luca Negrone. The architect was perhaps G. B. Castello; this is suggested by similarities in layout and decoration on the front with Palazzo Imperiale at Campetto (1555). The façade, with two *piani nobili* and two mezzanine floors, reworks in vertical format the layout borrowed from Palazzo Branconio dell'Aquila in Rome (Raphael, 1525), and is characterized by the crescendo of decorative motifs as one moves upwards. According to recent studies, the painted and sculpted elements in this façade are not just part of the structure but have an important semantic value since they throw light on otherwise undocumented aspects of local culture. The same is true of the façades of Palazzo Imperiale and Palazzo Podestà in Strada Nuova (1563). The vigorous articulation of the perspective, of which the entrance with herms is an important part, contrasts with the interior where the only reminder of Castello is provided by the three-mullioned window which screens the single flight of stairs on the ground floor. This solution was also used for two symmetrical flights in the contemporary palace of Tobia Pallavicino in Strada Nuova (1558). Overall, the bare interior almost constitutes a regression when compared to the palaces being built in Strada Nuova. Only the richly-frescoed rooms of the *piani nobili* are of any note. [L. D.]

34
Palazzo Doria Spinola (Prefecture)
LARGO E. LANFRANCO 1
BUS 18, 19, 20, 30, 35, 36, 41, 42

Built for Antonio Doria between 1541 and 1543 close to the Porta dell'Acquasola, in 1624 it became the property of the Spinola di San Pietro family, and in 1876 was ceded to the City Council; it now belongs to the Province and houses the offices of the Prefecture. The raising of a floor between 1793 and 1797 and the mutilations caused by the opening of Via Roma (1877) and the new town layout (demolition of Galleria Spinola, cutting off of the right-hand corner, creation of a high base and destruction of the garden), have profoundly altered the original design which can be seen in drawings by Rubens. The compact, block-like volume of the building is characterized by an hall which opens out on a courtyard with two levels of loggia. The courtyard-garden sequence must have been less clear, with the latter being barely perceptible along a corridor. The project has been attributed to a collaboration between B. Cantone, who was definitely employed on the site, and G. B. Castello, called il Bergamasco, whose presence is not documented but is strongly suggested by a stylistic analysis of the decoration (star-shaped crosses in the vaults in the entrance porch, panels with masks and telamons in the courtyard) which bears witness to an "up-to-date, elegant" figurative culture. Of great interest is the 16th-century fresco cycle, although little remains of the painting on the façade (L. and P. Calvi). Within, however, there are works by Giovanni and Luca Cambiaso and others by A. and F. Calvi, as well as a gallery of views of the city on the first floor. [G. S.]

35
Church of Santa Marta
PIAZZA SANTA MARTA 2
BUS 18, 19, 20, 30, 35, 36, 41, 42

Of the vast convent which began to appear from the 12th century at the edge of the city, little remains after tempestuous events and the destruction of the Portoria district. Apart from the church itself, the capitular room and the nuns' refectory survive, both now absorbed into modern buildings. The first church, dedicated to San Germano, is documented in 1234 and was used by a community of Humiliati. The old, single-nave, church was transformed in 1535 and took on its present aspect. Suppressed in 1797, the complex was given over to the Congregazione degli Operai Evangelici in 1826. The church's modest sloping façade with small blind arches crowning the whole (resulting from a restoration in 1961) appears within a narrow courtyard, in clear contrast to the rich interior. The ground plan comprises a nave and two aisles divided by piers; the two aisles are lower and cross-vaulted with rectilinear ends; the nave has a lowered vault and ends in a deep apse which is dramatically dominated by a sculpture of the saint "in glory" by F. Parodi. The monastic role of the church is highlighted by the presence of the upper choir which extends down the nave. Of great importance are the cycles of frescos executed during the 17th and 18th centuries by the greatest exponents of the Genoese school (G. B. Carlone, V. Castello, D. and P. G. Piola, L. De Ferrari, D. Parodi). [G. S.]

36
Church of SS. Annunziata di Portoria (Santa Caterina)

VIALE IV NOVEMBRE 5R
BUS 15, 17, 18, 19, 20, 30, 36, 39, 40, 41, 41

The complex of the Annunziata di Portoria - better known as Santa Caterina - was required by the Protectors of the Hospital of Pammatone to enlarge a structure which in 1471 Sixtus IV had decreed should fulfill all of the city's hospital needs (of this building, only the central courtyard, absorbed into the 19th-century courthouse, survives today). Construction began in 1488 on a building which was to be architecturally autonomous and used by the Congregation of the Observants, the only link with the hospital being an airy passage leading to the women's infirmary. Large alterations were made as the site was developed, as a result of the Acquasola walls being built in 1537. With part of the lost space being reclaimed, the presbytery area was rebuilt in 1556 thanks to Battista Grimaldi.

Considerable work was also undertaken in the 18th century: after 1737, the votive chapel of Santa Caterina Fieschi was erected by enlarging the existing entrance tribune on one side; the façade, as a consequence of this, was modified, and only the classicizing double doorway (1521) survives of the original design; finally, 1772 saw the creation of the large staircase which now links the chapel of the saint with the narrow entrance square - a monumental solution for the functional relationship between hospital and convent. Also dating from the 18th century is the transformation into pilasters of the existing black and white drum columns of the nave. [N. D. M.]

37
Strada Nuova
VIA GARIBALDI
BUS 18, 19, 20, 30, 32, 35, 36, 41, 4̶1̶, 42

The creation of Strada Nuova was decisive for the image of the city in the 16th century, and one of the most important urban projects in Europe. An event which had major political, social and economic repercussions, it was named Via Maggiore in 1558, or Aurea, and in 1882 was given its present name of Via Garibaldi. It first saw the light of day in the middle of the 16th century under Doge Luca Spinola with the specific aim of obtaining the money needed for urgent restoration to the Cathedral of San Lorenzo but it also embodied the desire for show expressed by a social class at the height of economic prestige deriving from intense financial dealings with the greatest powers in Europe and strengthened by the return of Andrea Doria at the helm of the Republic in 1528. Another important objective was to improve the area uphill of the church of the Maddalena and to move the existing brothel to the Castelletto. Conceived as a residential quarter rather than a road (Labò) and only transformed into a major route with the completion in 1786 of Strada Nuovissima (Via Cairoli), the *Via aurea dei genovesi* was managed with a precise building programme controlled by the Magistrato dei Padri of the City Council. For the most part, it was completed between 1558 and 1588 with the construction ⁄ in the parcels of land sold at auction in 1551, 1558⁄59 and 1561 ⁄ of eight of the palaces allowed for in the original project (four downhill and four uphill, starting from today's Piazza Fontane Marose). To these were added other buildings which did not appear in this project and which broke the mirror-like symmetry of the rigorously geometric blocks. These were the residence uphill of Nicolò Grimaldi and downhill that of Baldassare Lomellino. The grandiose complex, which was soon to appear in a book by Rubens (1652), although it was only actually completed in the 18th century, has recently thrown up some unresolved problems of attribution: although the literature categorically excludes the traditional claim that Alessi was responsible for the whole route (Vasari), and suggests in his place Bernardo Cantone da Cabio from Como and the key figure of the Magistrato dei Padri of the City Council, it is also true that the cultural and figurative elements in the overall plan seem today to suggest a strong figure such as the master from Perugia working alongside Cantone and once in the employ of Alessi in the Carignano site (1552), as were other architects working in Strada Nuova. Extending about 250 m behind the hill of Montalbano and with a slope of 1°, Strada Nuova is an extraordinary example of the "hillside building" which already figured prominently in Genoa. In this case - especially in the uphill palaces - it provides a series of solutions which are not only decisive for later developments in Genoese architecture, but which place this road amongst the very first examples of the new Baroque style. [N. D. M.]

38
Palazzo Pallavicino-Cambiaso
(Banca Popolare di Brescia)
VIA GARIBALDI 1
BUS 18, 19, 20, 30, 32, 35, 36, 41, 41, 42

Agostino Pallavicino's palace, built between 1558 and 1560, was one of the first on Strada Nuova and rises at the most representative point of the road, opening the way with its two fronts (the eastern one being altered as a result of the opening in 1864 of Via Interiano). The rather narrow site upon which it was raised was acquired in the second public auction (1558) and was indicated in the "model" as being the fourth site on the upper side. The palace is attributed to Alessi with the certain participation on the site of Bernardino Cantone. Even if we ignore the age-old question about the presence or absence of Alessi in the Strada Nuova project, it cannot be denied that some motifs on the façade, such as the frieze and, above all, the windows on the ground and first floor recall Alessi's Palazzo Marino in Milan, which was also begun in 1558. However, the Genoese palace is more sober and restrained and bare of the decoration which adorns the Milanese palace; it depends more on chromatic than plastic effects. The ground plan, with its succession of hall-stairs-courtyard on the ground floor, and the salon on the upper floors is innovative for the role of the stairs which are placed asymmetrically between hall and courtyard, thus accentuating the feeling of a sudden breakthrough of the latter. The motif of the three arches screening the start of the flight can be found in the contemporary palaces of Tobia Pallavicino in Strada Nuova and of Tomaso Spinola in Salita Santa Caterina, both of which can be attributed to Castello.   [L. D.]

39

*Palazzo Spinola Gambaro
(Banco di Chiavari e della Riviera Ligure)*
VIA GARIBALDI 2
BUS 18, 19, 20, 30, 32, 35, 36, 41, 41, 42

Built for Pantaleo Spinola between 1558 and 1569 by Bernardo Spazio and completed by Giovanni Pietro Orsolino, it clearly owes a debt to Alessi with its almost cubic volume, sloping roof and the façade set with five axes of windows and divided into three with a central element which is set slightly back from the side elements. The imposing, rough structure has only the massive doorway remaining of its original decoration, with Doric columns crowned by an arched tympanum and statues of Prudence and Vigilance.

The original plan was marked by a rigid symmetry. The hall and room on the ground floor corresponded to the loggia and salon on the 'piano nobile', with service rooms associated with the residential function of the palace relegated to the mezzanine floors. The interior decoration is by the Carlone brothers and Domenico Piola, who also executed the fresco, the "Allegory of Peace", in the vault of the central salon. It did not undergo any alterations until the latter half of the 17th century when it was provided with an octagonal courtyard closed on one side with a double-storey nymphaeum surmounted by a balustrade at the same height as the *piano nobile*. Owned by the Gambaro family in 1844, the palace was purchased by the Banco di Chiavari e della Riviera Ligure in 1923 to be used as its central office. Its new use required the covering of the courtyard which on the ground floor has been transformed into a banking hall. [I. F.]

69

40
Palazzo Lercari Parodi
via Garibaldi 3
bus 18, 19, 20, 30, 32, 35, 36, 41, 41, 42

The construction is one of the last on Strada Nuova and was started by Franco Lercari after 1571. It was almost certainly terminated by 1578, when Ottavio Semino executed the frescos on the second floor. An unusual feature of the palace is the position of the main part of the building on two floors housing the main residential quarters, which is set back from the road and set behind a screen (originally open and laid out as a loggia). This is linked to the palace by a series of service rooms. The architect remains unknown although the building recalls Alessi's Villa Grimaldi-Sauli in its use of a deep courtyard with a loggia placed in front of the palace, a plan which anticipates the *cours d'honneur* of the Parisian *hôtels particuliers*. The façade is on three levels and presents a rusticated band in high relief recalling a Tuscan order and an architectural division with Ionic and Corinthian columns and pilasters on the upper levels. The sides giving on to the courtyard are bare of all formal qualities. Within, to the left of the hall and at the end of the courtyard, there is a stairway with two flights, which takes up the Genoese model of a light staircase, and leads to an antechamber on the first floor, once linked to a hanging garden behind, which no longer exists. The decoration, given by Lercari to Luca Cambiaso, Ottavio Semino and the Calvi brothers takes its style from a local late Mannerism, and has been in part damaged by 19th-century work. Today, the palace is used as a private residence but also houses some offices. [G. S.]

41
Palazzo Pallavicino Carrega
(Chamber of Commerce)
VIA GARIBALDI 4
BUS 18, 19, 20, 30, 32, 35, 36, 41, 41, 42

Modified during the course of the 18th century after it was acquired by the Carrega family, the second palace on the downhill side of Strada Nuova was built for Tobia Pallavicino between 1558 and 1561 to a design by G. B. Castello, called il Bergamasco. Despite the 18th-century work, the original building, built on a lot sold in the 1558 auction, can still be easily made out. The 16th-century front has two floors and further mezzanines and was changed with the addition of floors in 1710-14, but the original aspect can be seen in Rubens' book (1652). There are clear Roman echoes, with reminiscences of Raphael in the treatment of surfaces and Antonio da Sangallo the Younger in the windows of the basement floor. Overall, the façade is very different in its originality to others by the same architect, such as that of Palazzo Podestà (1563), also in Strada Nuova, and Palazzo Imperiale (1555) in Campetto. The interior plan, with a hall, stairs, salon and garden on the ground floor, loggia and room on the upper floors, is simple but characterized by notable organic unity. The staircase is a fundamental element in the composition; it boasts two symmetrical flights, one blind, providing a dramatic setting which once again confirms Castello as a precursor of compositional themes which would be fully developed in the Baroque period. Between 1727 and 1740, the palace was enlarged, occupying the area of the old garden, and the *galleria dorata* built, one of the outstanding examples of Rococo art not just in Genoa but in the whole of Europe. [L. D.]

42
Palazzo Spinola
(Deutsche Bank)
VIA GARIBALDI 5
BUS 18, 19, 20, 30, 32, 35, 36, 41, 4̶1̶, 42

Built between 1558 and 1564 by Angelo Giovanni Spinola and designed by Giovanni Ponzello, further work was undertaken on the site after 1572 by Giulio Spinola. The palace, which stands out for its austere monumentality, was conditioned by the steep slope behind. In the original project, the tripartite plan shows the clear influence of Alessi, with two shallow wings to the rear enclosing the courtyard and the interior based upon a single axis of symmetry. In the use of the space, particular attention was paid to the large room on the piano nobile which appears on the façade corresponding to three axes of windows and is exceptionally high. Around 1580, the courtyard was doubled in depth and the wings extended towards the hanging garden dug into the hillside, with the link between piano nobile and garden behind being formed by broad terraces located over the wings.

The creation of Piazza Portello destroyed the original bond between the palace and the natural environment and required a new front which was built in 1928. The palace preserves an important, unified pictorial cycle with frescos by Bernardo Castello, Andrea Semino and Lazzaro Tavarone. The only palace in Strada Nuova to be owned until the 20th century by the same family as the original patron, in 1926 it was sold to the Banca d'America e d'Italia. At present, it is the Deutsche Bank's headquarters and also houses a private club on the piano nobile. [I. F.]

43
Palazzo Doria Spinola
VIA GARIBALDI 6
BUS 18, 19, 20, 30, 32, 35, 36, 41, 41, 42

Building was begun by brothers G. B. and Andrea Spinola, high-ranking members of the mercantile aristocracy which had backed the creation of Strada Nuova in 1563. The director of the project was Bernardino Cantone but G. B. Castello was also present, as is evidenced by some drawings of architectural details. The ground plan repeats the standard hall-courtyard (today partly closed off)-garden pattern, which only varies in the inclusion of a wall between two loggias. This partly hides the essentially private garden from view (and contrasts with the public, "ceremonial" area of the hall-courtyard), and reinforces the tunnel view which leads from the entrance doorway through the colonnade to a nymphaeum set into a wall at the end of the garden. On the piano nobile, the spatial rhythms are inverted and the palace opens out with a loggia at the rear but is closed off towards the large central salon. In the course of 18th-century work following the French bombardments of 1684, an extra floor was added to the building and a new front built, designed by A. M. Ricca. The solemn essentiality of the original façade, of which the windows are preserved, was replaced by a stucco Baroque front in superimposed orders.

The immensely rich collection of paintings owned by the Doria has been dispersed, but the palace preserves an interesting cycle of frescos (A. Semino and L. Cambiaso). The piano nobile is now occupied by council offices but the upper floors have maintained their character of private residence. [G. S.]

44
Palazzo Lomellini Podestà
VIA GARIBALDI 7
BUS 18, 19, 20, 30, 32, 35, 36, 41, 4̶1̶, 42

This is the fourth palace on the uphill side of Strada Nuova and was built on land acquired in the first auction in 1551 by Luca Grimaldi and later sold to Leonardo Gentile and then to Nicolosio Lomellino. Construction began in 1563 and introduced some important innovations such as the stucco decoration on the façade and the elliptical hall, which formed the hub of the ground plan and was a precursor of forms which were to become typical of the following century. Its architect was Giovanni Battista Castello, called il Bergamasco, who must have played a dominant role despite the certain presence on the site of Bernardo Cantone. The façade, which has one level of windows on the side looking to the east, is entirely decorated with motifs to which recent studies have attributed precise cosmogonical significance. Today, the unity of the whole appears slightly altered as the doorway has been replaced (18th century) and the parapets on the ground-floor windows removed. The U-shaped ground plan should be noted which, in common with other palaces on the uphill side of the road, introduces an animated relationship with the land behind. The interior features the elliptical hall, a focal point to which all the viewpoints of the design converge and from which they spread out; the shorter axis of the ellipse corresponds to the penetrative axis which "breaks" through the palace via a progression of hall, courtyard, nymphaeum and garden - an internal itinerary which links the road to the Montalbano hill behind. [L. D.]

45
Palazzo Cattaneo Adorno
VIA GARIBALDI 8-10
BUS 18, 19, 20, 30, 32, 35, 36, 41, 4̶1̶, 42

The last palace to be built in the first stretch of Strada Nuova was that of Giacomo and Lazzaro Spinola, begun in 1584 and completed in 1588. The site, the fourth on the downhill side, had already been acquired in the 1551 auction by the Vivaldi family who sold it in 1568 to Stefano Lomellini. The unknown architect is probably one of those local or skilled Lombard masters destined to remain anonymous and still working in 16th-century Genoa. The unusual presence of two patrons led to the creation of a "condominium" type of residence with a fairly simple interior based on a symmetrical distribution of rooms along a central axis lying at right-angles to the façade. The façade itself clearly shows the two distinct houses in the two identical, Mannerist-inspired doorways which confer a monumentality on the whole.

Considerable space is given over to the decoration which repeats the motifs of Palazzo Podestà opposite (1563). In the following centuries, the palace was spared any large-scale intervention from an architectural point of view and it has survived virtually intact. It is worth noting the building standing at the end of the garden which, although it appears in Rubens' prints (1652) - which even out the decidedly triangular form - has never been noted despite being of some interest for the presence of a frescoed spiral staircase. [N. D. M.]

46
Palazzo Grimaldi Doria-Tursi (Town Hall)
VIA GARIBALDI 9
BUS 18, 19, 20, 30, 32, 35, 36, 41, 41, 42

In 1564, Nicolò Grimaldi bought from Luca Grimaldi a vast tract of land upon which was to rise the most important of the Strada Nuova palaces. To this area, he added other lots obtained from the fathers of San Francesco in 1568. This led to the modification of the original project which had been prepared in 1564 by Giovanni and Domenico Ponzello. The considerable size of the area and, above all, the steep slope of the terrain, provided the opportunity for trying and testing solutions which would be particularly valuable for the architecture of the following century.

In size and complexity, the façade exceeds any other erected in Genoa in the 16th century. Built on top of the imposing base which continues beyond the body of the palace to include and screen off the gardens, it was completed in 1596 with the addition of two side loggias which the new proprietor, Gio Andrea Doria, had built. Its unusual extension along the flanks of the palace highlights the depth of the building and within which the whole interior is characterized by the succession of hall-courtyard-staircase.

The axis which pierces through the building is especially accentuated from the courtyard which is traditional in its superimposition of the two Doric and Ionic orders, but completely innovative in its rectangular plan. It is no longer the centre of the composition as in 15th-century palaces but a route. This dynamic concept is further stressed by the staircase which connects hall and court-

yard on different levels, as well as by the monumental stairs which close the luminous, broad, open space. After a first flight, the latter divides into two divergent stairs leading at a right-angle to the upper loggia, adopting a model which is reminiscent of Spanish imperial stairs. The vertical distribution is not just a simple solution to a practical problem but a fundamental element in the architectural composition, rich in innovative values and stagy effects.
In this sense, a precedent is provided by the stairs with two symmetrical, divergent flights constructed by Castello in the nearby palace of Tobia Pallavicino (1558), whilst a later example may be found in the Jesuit college of Via Balbi (now the University) designed in the first half of the 17th century by Bartolomeo Bianco. As far as the interior layout is concerned, the formal rooms - partly decorated in the mid 19th century - were concentrated at the front of the palace with the salon placed behind the three central windows in the façade whereas independent apartments looked out on to the gardens. [L. D.]

47
Palazzo Brignole (Bianco)
VIA GARIBALDI 11
BUS 18, 19, 20, 30, 32, 35, 36, 41, 41, 42

The palaces rises in place of the house built in the first half of the 16th century by Girolamo Grimaldi for his second son, Luca. The 16th-century building was a cube with a courtyard of limited size and a main front dominated by corner loggias and an entrance on Salita San Francesco. After 1580, the palace was transformed by the heirs of Luca Grimaldi with the addition in the garden of an external wing comprising superimposed loggias to bring it into line with the splendour of the other residences in Strada Nuova. Following its acquisition by Maria Durazzo Brignole, owner of Palazzo Rosso, the palace was restructured in 1711 with a project by Giacomo Viano. It was at this time that it was given its new name of Palazzo Bianco to contrast with the other. Viano's plan was limited by the boundary and volume of the existing palace. A new entrance and main façade were created giving on to Strada Nuova, and the resulting problem of the interior was resolved using an adapted version of the solution used in the hall of Palazzo Tursi with the aim of linking the various parts of the building while maintaining the same level as the original ground floor. In 1889, it was part of the Galliera bequest to the City Council to be used as a museum and in 1951, after serious war damage was repaired, the Galleria di Palazzo Bianco reopened. The new layout, undertaken by Caterina Marcenaro with a project by Franco Albini, became the model for contemporary museums in its use of spaces and exhibitive rigour. [I. F.]

48
Palazzo Brignole (Rosso)
VIA GARIBALDI 18
BUS 18, 19, 20, 30, 32, 35, 36, 41, ~~41~~, 42

The palace closes the long array of palaces in Strada Nuova to the west and was built between 1671 and 1677 for Ridolfo and Gio Francesco Brignole Sale. It derives its name from the dark red of the plaster used in the rustication, cornices, tympana and masks of the façade. Nowadays, it is attributed to P. A. Corradi. Commissioned to design a building destined to be used by two brothers of equal rank, he resolved the problem by creating a double piano nobile, as Il Bianco had already done (no. 59).

A main block runs around the high courtyard and opens out on the seaward side into airy loggias facing the garden. The building is conditioned by the presence of smaller structures laid out at right angles and linked via suspended passageways. The dynamic flow of the spaces is complemented by the rich cycle of frescos (1682-92) which give the illusion that the vaults are actually open to the luminous sky and filled with figures (G. De Ferrari, D. and P. G. Piola, A. Carlone) or break down the walls in a perspective whirl of ramps and courtyards (N. Viviano). Donated to the City Council in 1874 by the last descendant of the Brignole with the condition that no changes be made, it was beautifully restored and refurbished by F. Albini after suffering damage from bombs, in collaboration with C. Marcenaro, Director of the Ripartizione Belle Arti. It now houses the Galleria Civica which includes collections of minor arts as well as the Brignole-Sale collection of pictures. [G. S.]

49
Palazzo Grimaldi della Meridiana
SALITA SAN FRANCESCO 4
BUS 18, 19, 20, 30, 32, 35, 36, 41, 41, 42

Built by Gerolamo Grimaldi for his eldest son, Gio Battista, between 1541 and 1545, its main façade gave on to Salita San Francesco with two side wings giving on to two gardens uphill and downhill. It introduced a new freedom in the internal distribution of rooms, with a succession of open and green spaces in a continuous play of perspective with the various elements of the building. The 16th-century structure, with its double role as decentralised city palace and almost suburban family home, constitutes one of the first and most significant examples of the renewal of Genoese architecture. In the first half of the 17th century, using a plan by Giacomo Lagomaggiore, structural changes involving the roofing over of the entrance courtyard were made with the aim of creating as many rooms as possible.
At the end of the 18th century, following the opening of Strada Nuovissima (Via Cairoli), the palace was restructured by Giacomo Brusco to the extent of transforming the southern, lateral façade into the main one. It was at this point that the sundial which has since then been a typical feature of the building was painted on the façade. At the start of the 20th century, Evans Mackenzie commissioned some internal restructuring work from Gino Coppedè who changed the original layout and use of space. The decoration is by G. B. Castello, whilst Luca Cambiaso frescoed the vault of the salon and one room on the ground floor. It now houses council offices and a nursery school. [I. F.]

50
Palazzo Spinola (National Gallery)
PIAZZA INF. AND SUP. DI PELLICCERIA 1
BUS 18, 19, 20, 30, 35, 36, 41, 4̸1, 42

With elegant juxtaposed fronts, the palace faces two minor roads at the centre of a densely-built area, the centre in medieval times of various crafts, the *Pellipariæ*, whence the name of the street. It was constructed at the end of the 16th century by Francesco Grimaldi, absorbing some already existing houses (traces in the irregular trapezium of the plan and in some walls). The original building - a main structure with asymmetrical wings connected by a two-storey screen with a loggia on the top floor and the entrance opposite where it is now - is documented in the prints published by Rubens (1652) and recalls the form used for Palazzo Lercari-Parodi in Strada Nuova (1571-78). After passing through the hands of the Pallavicino and Doria families, in 1732 it became the property of the Spinola household who, in 1958, donated it to the Italian state. The present *facies* may be dated overall to the first half of the 18th century when major modifications were made, such as the raising of the loggia (already closed by 1650) with the addition of a mezzanine and a second "Gallery", the substitution of the painted perspective views (traces visible on the courtyard walls) with a Rococo stuccoed decoration and the renewal of the internal decoration, especially on the second floor (S. Galeotti, L. De Ferrari) for the important paintings. The two *piani nobili*, which maintain the look of an aristocratic home, now house the Galleria Nazionale di Palazzo Spinola in accordance with the wishes of the donors. The upper floors house the recently arranged Galleria Nazionale della Liguria. [G. S.]

51
Church of Santa Maria Maddalena
PIAZZA DELLA MADDALENA
BUS 18, 19, 20, 30, 35, 36, 41, 41, 42

The little church of the Maddalena is mentioned by 1182, but it was radically altered from the end of the 16th century by the Somaschi fathers who were ordered to fill a gap left empty when the Theatines moved to the more convenient quarters of San Siro (1575). An early project by G. Ponzello backed by Franco Lercari, patron of 1581, remained on paper and the church was eventually redesigned completely by A. Ceresola, 'il Vannone,' who reversed its orientation, rendering communication easier with the nearby Strada Nuova (Via Garibaldi). Work began in 1586 with the new backing of G. B. Spinola and terminated in 1589 with the construction of the façade portico (now made visible again thanks to restoration in 1911). The church's interior, however, took on its present form only after 1635 when, following a project presented by the Somaschi and with work being interrupted between 1646 and 1660, the single nave with deep side chapels was divided into three, separated by screens of coupled columns, a late use of a form already adopted in the restructuring of San Siro (1586). The construction of the dome and transept also date from the 17th century, whereas the interior frescos are mainly 18th century. The adjacent college finished in 1622 was probably designed by Ceresola and has suffered considerable alteration. It now houses the rich archive and library of the Somaschi fathers. [N.D.M.]

52
Church of San Siro
VIA SAN SIRO
BUS 18, 19, 20, 30, 35, 36, 41, 41, 42

The church of San Siro, built in the *borgo* [district] around the 4th century and dedicated to the 12 Apostles was left outside the 9th-century medieval walls, and had to share its early role as cathedral with San Lorenzo, before ceding this to the latter altogether. Assigned in 1006 to the Order of Benedictines which rebuilt it in Romanesque style, the church went through a long period of decay until the arrival in 1575 of the Theatines who just three years earlier had installed themselves in the Maddalena (1572). The building of today is the result of a complex reconstruction imposed by the partial collapse of the structure in 1580. The programme of reconstruction, which began in 1583, foresaw the replacement of the old monastery with a vast monastic complex; this latter was greatly damaged by the opening of Strada Nuovissima (Via Cairoli) in 1786. Actual work began in 1586 and came to an end in 1613, except for the dome which was finished in 1619. There is some doubt as to whether the architect was the Theatine, Andrea Riccio, or Andrea Ceresola, 'il Vannone', to whom the project has been traditionally attributed. Reproduced by Rubens (1652) but perhaps never built, the original design for the façade was replaced by the Neoclassical surface we see today, a 19th-century construction by Barabino (1821). The interior of the church is characterized by the coupled columns which frequently appear in civil architecture of the period and were employed several times in Genoese and Ligurian Counter-Reformation churches (Maddalena, Vigne). Of note, too, is the 17th-century decoration. [N. D. M.]

53
Church of San Luca
VIA SAN LUCA
BUS 18, 19, 20, 30, 35, 36, 41, 41, 42

Assigned in 1589 by Sixtus V to the Spinola and Grimaldi families as their family church, the origins of the small church of San Luca date back to the end of the 12th century. Built between 1188 and 1189 by Oberto Spinola on land belonging to his brother-in-law, Oberto Grimaldi, it was later raised to collegiate status by Innocent VIII, a nobel Genoese of the Cybo family, who on 10 May 1485 decreed it was to be perpetually under the patronage of the two families. The present building is the result of a radical transformation begun in 1626 which required the almost total destruction of the existing structure; some traces of this remain in the apse. The design was traditionally attributed to the Lombard Carlo Muttone, whom local records show to have been the architect of SS. Croce e Camillo (1667), but he was perhaps only responsible for the façade. On the basis of documents, the project has recently been attributed to B. Bianco. Set picturesquely between Piazza di San Luca and the palaces of the Grimaldi and Spinola families, the façade features a slightly projecting central area with classicizing elements enclosed within paired pilasters, and is especially noteworthy for the rich stuccoed decoration. The interior is also richly decorated and has a single nave based upon models found in the plains of the Po with very shallow side chapels and a juxtaposition between the broad central dome and deep apse. [N.D.M.]

54
Via Cairoli
BUS 18, 19, 20, 30, 35, 39, 40, 41

The opening of Strada Nuovissima ⁄ now called Via Cairoli ⁄ dates back to 1778 in response to an overriding need to connect Via Balbi and Via Garibaldi. It cut through the heart of the city, interrupting roads that climbed towards Castelletto and required the demolition of part or all of many buildings. This, in turn, meant that some of these were combined or that old routes were blocked to provide a regular front on the road. This led to owners' attempts to get the most advantageous route possible and to the architect, Gregorio Petondi, choosing to trace out a curved road. Some of the most interesting palaces include that of Gian Tomaso Balbi (no. 18 on the corner with the Zecca), restructured during this period by Petondi. The palace already had an imposing façade on Strada Lomellina below, and this was connected to the new façade with complex open, symmetrical stairs in harmony with the concept of continuous space. The three palaces which adjoin each other at nos. 8, 10 and 12 were designed by G. B. Cervetto for the Cambiaso family soon after 1786 and resulted in old routes being closed to achieve a regular alignment on the new road. Delicate stucco decoration and the greater importance accorded the central palace reveal the Neoclassical care taken even for rented palaces. Other problems arose at the meeting point with Strada Nuova: the gardens which were located at the end were destroyed; from the site emerged Palazzo Grimaldi (della Meridiana), with its long southern side which was renewed in Giacomo Brusco's refined, 18th⁄century classicising façade. [E. D. N.]

55
Palazzo Lomellini Patrone
(Regional military headquarters)
LARGO ZECCA 1
BUS 18, 19, 20, 30, 35, 39, 40, 41

Built by Giacomo Lomellini between 1617 and 1619, it has one entire side adjoining another building and reveals the restrictions of restructuring within the old city centre. The south-western corner was cut off to allow Via P. E. Bensa to be widened.

As in many other Genoese palaces, the façade must have had a frescoed decoration of architectural features, but the only remaining echo of this surviving is the imitation rustication in the base. The interior plainly shows the restrictions imposed by the site with a small courtyard thrust towards the boundary wall; in 1922, two columns were added and the whole courtyard roofed over with cross-vaulting, thereby losing all sense of light. The same Giacomo Lomellino, the Republic's doge in 1625, had the palace frescoed by Domenico Fiasella in about 1625-30. The decoration filled the whole palace with a cycle of paintings illustrating Ansaldo Cebà's poem, *La Reina Esther*, with precise references to the defence of liberty and the virtues of the man in government and thus to the political situation in Genoa. [E. D. N.]

56
Church and Oratory of San Filippo Neri
VIA LOMELLINI 10
BUS 18, 19, 20, 30, 35, 39, 40, 41

Fronting the 17th-century Via Lomellini, the Filippini's building represents one of the greatest examples of Genoese Baroque religious architecture, despite its lack of uniformity. The project was launched thanks to a large bequest from Camillo Pallavicino (1642) and building began about ten years after the provisional locating of the Congregation at the Pallavicino family church of San Pancrazio (1646). After the site was acquired, a modestly-sized church was constructed in 1657 but this was replaced after 1674 by a larger structure, perhaps initially with the intervention of P. A. Corradi (Labò). Work continued until 1721, and the new church could also make use of the area Palazzo Adorno used to stand on. The date of the adjacent oratory is less certain. Elliptical in form and set out along different axes, tradition has attributed it to G. B. Montaldo. At all events, construction began before 1753, as this was when the rich decoration was started. Even less is known of the monastery which was constructed in an irregular form between the two main buildings and even over the church, and features a unique - for Genoa - sensibility deriving from Borromini and Guarini. This also appears in the slight concavity of the upper part of the church's façade, which was never completed but decorated with a later doorway (1762). The interior of the church features a remarkable "serliana" solution to the four side chapels: these are intercommunicating via passages cut behind the piers. [N. D. M.]

57
Church of SS. Annunziata del Vastato
PIAZZA DELLA NUNZIATA
BUS 18, 19, 20, 30, 35, 39, 40, 41

Facing the piazza of the same name with the monumental 19th-century pronaos - part of an uncompleted project (G. B. Resasco, 1841) - the church was built in 1520 by the Minorites of St Francis on the site of an earlier Romanesque building erected by the Humiliati in 1228 (Santa Marta). Initially dedicated to San Francesco del Guastato, the building was rededicated to SS. Annunziata when the church was given in 1537 to the Order of the Franciscan Observants. Under the patronage of the Lomellini family from 1591 onwards, considerable modifications were brought to the plan and volumes of the church. In the closing years of the 16th century, the presbytery was doubled in depth and the dome raised over the crossing between nave and transept. The early years of the next century saw the rustication of the façade as well as the addition of an entrance bay and the transformation of the smaller aisles into side chapels. This last operation brought the original basilica plan with nave, four aisles and transept into line with the latest Ligurian late-Mannerist trends. By the middle of the 17th century, the marble facing of the architectural elements had been completed (1616-25), as had the important illusionistic fresco decorations in the nave, transept and dome (1625-38), whereas the period between 1620 and 1650 saw considerable enlargements in the adjacent convent, today used to house two secondary schools (Liceo Classico and Convitto C. Colombo). [N.D.M.]

58
Palazzo Balbi-Cattaneo Adorno
VIA BALBI 1
BUS 18, 19, 20, 30, 35, 39, 40, 41

Built for Gio Agostino Balbi from 1618 from a project by Bartolomeo Bianco (design signed 7th February), it was the first palace to be built in Strada dei Balbi. It is unusually broad and this aspect is further emphasised by the four corner wings which terminate in loggias built along the side gardens. A high base follows the slope and isolates the severe façade, devoid of all decoration, from the road.
The interior featured the use of divergent stairs which used to connect the road-level hall with the higher courtyard, highlighting rather than minimizing the change in level. These stairs figured in the above-mentioned design, in Rubens' posthumous book (1652) and in a splendid drawing by Fragonard. They were rebuilt by Andrea Tagliafichi in 1774-78 who modified both hall and courtyard, linking them with a single flight as wide as the room and decorated with two statues placed against the first columns. The imposing severity of the hall contrasts with the famous, brilliantly-conceived internal staircase, built without supporting columns and of the greatest technical skill, in the most refined taste of the 18th century. One of the most important private collections of paintings is displayed in the splendid salons. [E. D. N.]

59
Palazzo Balbi-Senarega
via Balbi 4
bus 18, 19, 20, 30, 35, 41

Designed by Bartolomeo Bianco, this palace was constructed between 1616 and 1620 for Giacomo and Pantaleo Balbi on a site adjacent to the family's *domus magna*. The commission required the creation of two apartments of equal architectural prestige for the two brothers and was resolved with the solution of a double *piano nobile*. The simple, severe façade is divided in three vertically by a slight projection of the wings and by the variation in setting of the windows (closer together at the centre). Horizontally, these are defined by simple string courses separating each floor. The engravings published by Rubens in the second edition (1652) document the original look of the building which reveals an innovative spatial conception in the articulation of the spaces between portico and courtyard with the doubling of the colonnade, and in the opening of the upper loggias on the seaward side. In 1645, a restructuring programme was started by F. M. Balbi, almost certainly following a design by Pier Antonio Corradi. Bianco's Baroque use of space was emphasised by the demolition of the southern wall and the creation of a perspective view which drew the eye along a long garden bounded by colonnaded porticos to a monumental, decorative nymphaeum. The interior decoration can also be linked to these new spaces which are suspended midway between nature and artifice. The artists involved from 1655 included V. Castello, D. Piola and G. De Ferrari. Seriously damaged during the bombing raids of 1942-44, it is now used by institutes of the Arts Faculty. [G. S.]

60
Palazzo Reale (ex Balbi, Durazzo)
VIA BALBI 10
BUS 18, 19, 20, 30, 35, 41

The long, complex construction phases of the palazzo, once called Balbi, Centurione and Durazzo, began in 1643 when Stefano Balbi commissioned the architects F. Cantoni and M. Moncino with the project. In 1677, after belonging briefly to the Centurione family, it became the property of E. Durazzo, who acquired new buildings, amongst which the 17th-century Teatro del Falcone, and who had the new eastern wing completed. In 1705, Carlo Fontana was commissioned to provide a unified design for the whole varied complex. The excessive length of the façade was balanced with a decorative internal perspective: in the succession of hall, stairways opening on to broad loggias (closed off today), ceremonial courtyard enclosed by a backdrop of triple arches and hanging garden open to the sea, the architect made use of theatrical effects of perspective to broaden and deepen the space and provide astonishing effects. In the first half of the 18th century, the interior decoration was finished with frescos by L. De Ferrari, U. Aldovrandini, G. A. Boni and D. Parodi. The latter was responsible for the decoration of the Galleria degli Specchi in which painting and sculpture blend marvellously in a space multiplied an infinite number of times by the mirrors. In 1823, the building was acquired by the Savoy family, and under Carlo Alberto further decoration was undertaken with the design by M. Canzio. Since becoming state property, it has been used as a home for the Galleria di Palazzo Reale. It also houses the offices of the Soprintendenze. [G. S.]

61
Palazzo dell'Ateneo (ex Jesuit College)
VIA BALBI 5
BUS 18, 19, 20, 30, 35, 41

The history of the college begins in 1630 with a clear commitment between Stefano Balbi and the Jesuits for the construction of the schools. The site opened in 1634 for the construction of buildings designed by B. Bianco. By 1639, those facing the road had been completed, including the courtyard with coupled columns and the "hall for literary exercises", today the great hall. The unusual, difficult slope of the terrain made it impossible to base the Jesuit college on a typical Jesuit complex with several courtyards, one public for the schools, the other private for the religious. Instead, it had to rise vertically, with rooms for the Jesuits above the schools and a larger "domestic workroom" (now the Rector's floor) higher still, beyond the "little citrus orchard". Work was suspended several times due to lack of funds and construction was protracted. The façade was decorated in 1650 in an almost neo-Mannerist style, and construction of the church was completed (this still exists but is used as a storeroom for the State Library, totally preventing any other use). Only in 1672 did work resume to finish the courtyard on its uphill side with the airy staircase. Courtyard and stairs are the college's "public areas"; their highly refined nature puts them closer to courtyards in patrician houses than to monastic cloisters. The project finished in 1718 with the staircase that leads from the courtyard to the hall, designed by a set-designer, Domenico Parodi. Always used for study - by the university since 1775 - the palace has in practice never changed its role. [E. D. N.]

62
Church of San Carlo
VIA BALBI
BUS 18, 19, 20, 30, 35, 41

In 1629, thanks to a bequest from their brother, G. B. Spinola, the Chapter of the Discalced Carmelites were able to commission Bartolomeo Bianco to design a church on the uphill side of the new "Strada Balbi" in order to complete the monastic complex founded there in 1620. After Bianco left the project in 1631, at an advanced stage, the construction was continued without the presence of other architects and in line with the original project.

A wide nave covered by a barrel vault with lunettes and four chapels framed by robust piers is crossed by a transept and dome and terminates in a very deep choir. The overall design of the church, which shows the influence of Lombard examples evolving from Alessi's church of San Barnaba, reveals the re-use of a Counter-Reformation type, although modified by the deep choir to come closer to a centralised ground plan.

The façade is highly complex in design; Bianco had planned it to cover just the body of the church. It lay further back than today's and was linked to road level with two sets of steps. The present-day façade, planned and paid for by G. Durazzo in 1743-49, owner of the adjacent palazzo, to provide a scenic front on the road, saw two superimposed orders enlivened by rich stucco Rococo decoration in two colours. The lower storey opens on to a monumental arcaded portico which encloses the two staircases. [G. S.]

63
Palazzo Doria Pamphili
PIAZZA DEL PRINCIPE 4; VIA SAN BENEDETTO 2
BUS 18, 19, 20, 30, 32, 33

The building, known as Palazzo del Principe from the title of Andrea Doria, the powerful admiral of Charles V and Phillip II, has only in part preserved the imposing look recorded in 19th-century engravings and drawings. Built just outside Porta di San Tommaso to the west of the city, the palace stretched from the sea, where there used to be a mooring (today only the loggia of the landing stage survives below street level), to the Granarolo hill above which were terraced gardens on several levels (destroyed to make way for the railway, and later, the Miramare hotel). The ground plan is characterized by the exceptional length of the northern side which is not perfectly straight (partly as a result of later stages of building). At the end, it opens out into corner loggias with coupled columns and other buildings set at right angles to the main one in the gardens of the seaward end which give an asymmetrical disposition of the volumes. A. Doria summoned famous artists to work on the site: the extraordinary cycle of frescos can certainly be attributed to Perin del Vaga, as can the design of the northern gateway (which proved extremely important in the development of Genoese Renaissance gateways) and the project for the decorative sculptures (chimneys, fountains), executed by S. Cosini. The fresco decoration of the southern façade with its subjects drawn from Jason (painted by Antonio da Pordenone, D. Beccafumi, Perin del Vaga) has been lost. That on the landward façade was never realized although Perin's drawings for it survive. The project foresaw a high rusticated base fronted by ringed columns, and an upper order in which windows with triangular tympana and resting figures alternated with panels of figurative scenes. Above this was to run a continuous frieze with small windows topped by Ghibelline merlons. The reconstruction of the gardens is problematical; they were laid out on a regular plan on the seaward side, with geometrical flower beds and marble fountains. Uphill of the palace and beyond the road, an embankment supported a gallery, known as *la cuba*, with Doric columns alternating with pilasters and vases. The garden then rose up the hill with terraced areas, grottoes and plays of water, culminating in the collossal, allusive "Grotta del Gigante" (M. Sparzo) which was visible from the open sea. The complex was terminated at the behest of Gianandrea Doria (1566-94) and under the direction of A. Roderio and G. Ponzello. From those years date the fountain of "Triton" (Montorsoli), the eastern gateway (P. A. del Curto and B. and M. da Novi), the fountain of "Neptune" (T. G. and B. Carlone). Of the uphill complex, only the altered, suffocated remains of the Fonte Doria survives, an artificial grotto with an octagonal ground plan, covered with rich decoration of many materials by G. Alessi. The palace is private property and has now re-found its original fuction as an aristocratic dwelling. Connected to the residence is the little church of San Benedetto, once part of a Cistercian monastery (12th century), and altered to take on its present form by G. Ponzello (1593). [G. S.]

III.
THE CITY OF THE OLD WALLS: CONTEMPORARY AND PRESENT-DAY BUILDINGS
ENNIO POLEGGI

Following a precise format which has been adopted for each section of the city, it is worth recalling each town-planning period of the last two centuries together with the main spatial characteristics which resulted in changes in the area within the Mura Vecchie (the old city walls - an area of 150 hectares). Today, this area is completely built over and stretches between the railway station of Porta Principe, the Circonvallazione a Monte (the landward ring road), Acquasola, the Mura delle Cappuccine (Carignano) and the old port. The buildings mentioned are more for public than residential use because they were intended to qualify a completely central area in the wake of expansion beyond the walls. They lie along the "Strade Nuove" (new roads), built in the 19th century towards the east by Via XX Settembre or which turn off shortly before the little valleys behind the walls. However, they also lie along the coast, a result of commuting over the past century or two and which has only been blocked recently to the west by the opening of the San Benigno business centre which handles all requests for land originating from the old city centre.

RESTORATION (1820-50)

The city-state was given over to Savoy following the Congress of Vienna and its leading citizens, deprived of large sums of capital by the revolutionary events in Europe, watched passively as the first public buildings were erected by a foreign government: the Carlo Felice theatre (1828), the Accademia and the Civica Libreria (1932), and also a whole quarter planned by Carlo Barabino as part of a vaster town-plan for the increase in dwellings (1825) intended for the workers in the flat, outer area to the east, between the Mura Vecchie and the Mura Nuove, from San Vincenzo to Porta Romana. During this period, the civic centre built over the old site of San Domenico (the future Piazza R. de Ferrari) marks the overturning of the age-old limits of the original city towards the Bisagno valley. At the same time the ingenious urban plan, which reworked the solution of the Strada Nuova to "build along the flanks of a hill" an incredible city of serried ranks in regular lines placed as though on the flat, was put into practice by Barabino and his pupils.

FIRST INDUSTRIAL AGE (1875-1915)

Set between the contemporary adoption of plans for the new port (A. Parodi, 1875) and the Plan for the enlargement of the suburbs to the east (1876) and also the later plans for the tracing and creation of Via XX Settembre, the urbanization of the area of the Mura Vecchie was limited unless radical measures were envisaged such as, indeed, the excavation of the Sant'Andrea hill (1904) which served for the construction of Piazza De Ferrari and those deriving from the implementation of the Plan for the central zones (1931) which are described below. Before the buildings erected between the stations of Porta Principe to the west (1855) and Brignole to the east (1875-1903), which are a distant echo of Paris boulevards and still constitute the heart of the city today, there are a number of good, and sometimes exceptional buildings mentioned here, including Villa Mylius in Carignano (c. 1851) and the hospital of Sant'Andrea, built at the behest of the Duchi di Galliera (Cesare Parodi, 1875-84).

None of this altered the medieval layout of the city because it was mainly tangential to the edge of the historic centre, just like the reconstruction and extension of the port towards the west (1920). However, as in every new urban age, it instigated widespread, deep processes of changes in ownership and demography which bore on the traditional use and conservation of old residences and altered the collective identity of the city, leading to a loss of perception of its historic identity. The time had arrived when the contemporary city, which had turned its back upon its historic centre after the laying down of the Carlo Alberto road (including the southern part of Via San Lorenzo), was to become another city, one paradoxically closer to the outlying quarters which heavy industry led by Ansaldo had extended to the west, from Sampierdarena to Sestri and Bolzaneto.

This was an urban revolution governed by the public transport that could be built, also through the area of the Mura Vecchie, using modern techniques such as tunnels (1927-28), rack-railways (Granarolo, 1910), funicular railways (Righi, 1910) and lifts which relaunched the real estate business in the hills above our area which had first appeared in the mid 19th century along the straight roads in the valley bottoms.

FIRST AND SECOND POST WAR (1931-76)

Any architecture worth mentioning from this period in this zone is far rarer owing to the lack of suitable areas for profitable residential projects. Apart from a few 20th-century buildings dotted along the margins of the historic city centre at a cost of further demolitions, the last thirty years have been marked by large-scale public buildings, such as the museums by Franco Albini, the Teatro dell'Opera, the Faculty of Architecture at San Silvestro - in the "castle", cradle of the city - or more intrusive business centres such as those in Borgo Lanaioli, medieval heart of the textile industry, which was partly demolished in 1936-38 to build the "skyscrapers" of Piazza Dante and then pulled down completely to put up the Centro dei Liguri on the ancient traces of the Via Madre di Dio and Via della Marina.

ITINERARY

Since the topic in question is the 20th-century additions to the walled area, it is not possible to trace a continuous route; one must rather link the principal centres of today's city mentally.

SINGLE ROUTE: FROM PIAZZA CORVETTO TO PIAZZA COLOMBO

Start in Piazza Corvetto, the link between the walled area and the new hillside city built along the Circonvallazione a Monte. It is an elegant junction which connects the first straight roads (1851) with Barabino's parks of Villetta and Acquasola (1820). Pass through the Galleria Mazzini (c. 1871) which, through the hall of the Teatro dell'Opera (completed 1991), leads to Piazza R. De Ferrari which unites all the main buildings of the 19th-century, central renewal. Along Via XX Settembre, to the left of the Piazza, we pass all of the examples mentioned (which are of great interest for the rapid acculturation of the international building industry) as far as Ponte Monumentale and Palazzina Eridania (Via U. Foscolo). Continue and turn right and left towards the Mercato Orientale, Palazzo dei Giganti and Palazzo Zuccarino as far as the square, Piazza Colombo.

From here, one can proceed from east to west on quite long walks between one building and another, visiting examples on the Carignano hill, to the south of Via XX Settembre, to return then westwards along the coast as far as the Marina where one re-enters the historic centre which is currently being restored (from Piazza Sarzano to Palazzo Ducale). Finally, climbing sharply along the main road leading to the station of Porta Principe one has good views over the industrial port.

64
"E. Chiossone" Museum of Oriental Art Villetta di Negro
PIAZZALE G. MAZZINI
BUS 33, 34, 36

Completed for the City Council in 1971 but planned in 1949/53 after a long series of various problems, the Museum of Oriental Art falls within the scope of Genoese Rationalism of which Mario Labò was one of the undisputed leaders. His death in 1961 caused the alternation of two architects for the completion and setting up of the museum: respectively Giorgio Olcese (1963/67) and Luciano Grossi Bianchi (1967), thereby extending even further the time needed to finish a project whose design was already dated. The building forms a part of the Villetta di Negro, an 18th-century park and famous literary salon inherited and transformed by the City Council at the end of the 19th century, and once bulwark of Santa Caterina in the Mura Vecchie and thus dominating the historic centre behind the port. The ground plan is an elongated rectangle divided into two volumes: a low body covered with a terrace is set into the main part of the building of three levels. The structure is in reinforced concrete with exposed pilasters: the front overlooking the port is broken up with large windows, screened at ground level by wooden grills which run on rails; the other façades are blind and covered in tiles; originally these were plum-red but they have been replaced with a darker colour. Through the hall, one arrives at the large room which contains five galleries at different levels linked by slender metal and wood stairs, whereas the central, full-height space enables the distribution of the museum to be taken in in one glance.   [M. P. G.]

65
Church of Santa Croce e San Camillo
VIA PAMMATONE
BUS 15, 17, 18, 19, 20, 30, 36, 39, 40, 41, 4*

The little church is all that is left of the 17th-century complex of the Crociferi which was eventually demolished after an eventful history with the opening of Via XII Ottobre, an essential part of the radical transformations which involved the old quarter of Portoria in the sixties. Built at the behest of Camillo de Lellis to provide assistance in Genoa to the infirm offered by the order he founded, the complex was begun in 1604 and was built with public and private funds on a more strategic site than that of the Incurabili hospital (now Via E. Vernazzi) and that of Pammatone (in part of the present-day Courts). The approval gained during the outbreak of plague in 1657 led the Crociferi to build a new church from 1567, based on a design by the Lombard Carlo Muttone. Apart from the consolidation to the presbytery area, it corresponds to the present church and was frescoed during the first two decades of the 18th century. Suffocated by modern alterations, the little building still reveals the original, bare façade on two levels, with tympanum on a windowed attic and linking volutes and in which the rich entrance is prominently placed. The interior is of some interest, with a single hall with central dome above an octagonal space barely widened by the side chapels. The result is highlighted by the rich pictorial decoration whose composition is yet another confirmation of the influence of Lombardy which from the 15th century found expression in the culture of Genoa. [N. D. M.]

66
Galleria Mazzini
BUS 15, 17, 18, 19, 20, 30, 35, 36, 39, 40, 41, 41, 42

With the building of Via Roma (1860-77) - one of the largest projects of the 19th century - we see for the first time a bank acting as contractor combined with highly advanced procedures. The site was located at the margins of the working class area of the town where the monastery of San Sebastiano used to stand before it was closed in 1866. The block-like buildings along the road provide the basis for a glass-panelled passage which transforms the rears of the buildings, giving them two effective façades, and also providing a solution for those buildings without road access. The glass-covered metal roof, closed off by two colonnaded screens on two orders of serliana arches, includes a number of domes supported by large metal eagles at each junction. The decorative furnishings which are all based on lighting features (large lamps which hang from the top of the domes to beneath the piano nobile, and appliques at shop level) are thus integrated with the structure. The market atmosphere which soon arose derives directly from its nature as a passage and an attempt to create a place for elegant encounters with a choice of after-theatre cafés (the Teatro Carlo Felice is nearby), an "intellectually dangerous" place for Wagnerians and anti-Wagnerians to challenge each other and perhaps hold a duel. With the theatre closing after the bedlam of the last war, the passage became a backwater, hosting small exhibitions of books in an attempt to inject some new life. The reopening of the theatre now provides the Galleria with a new opportunity to provide a lively venue. [C. B.]

67
Piazza Raffaele De Ferrari
BUS 15, 17, 18, 19, 20, 30, 35, 36, 39, 40, 41, 41, 42

This is the junction around which all of Genoa's traffic revolves and which for its citizens is the city's "centre". The earlier Piazza San Domenico, whose buildings from the west side still survive (including the side façade of Palazzo Ducale, ancient seat of the Commune), was already modified in the first half of the 19th century with the construction of the Carlo Felice theatre and the Accademia di Belle Arti by the architect, Carlo Barabino. The present look of the piazza dates from the project for the new Via XX Settembre (1890) which required a partial razing of the Sant'Andrea hill to allow for expansion towards the south. Its final aspect was the result of numerous changes, first with the variant which included the arcades (1900), then, following a competition (1901) and several consultations, with the project from the City Council's technical office (1906). This last foresaw further excavation of the Sant'Andrea hill to the east, an area next to the church of Sant'Ambrogio and the opening of the first part of Via Dante.

With this, the piazza took on the look we see today, finished by the buildings at the end of Via XX Settembre, including the Stock Exchange. The area adjacent to the church was built upon only in 1920, when it was sold by the engineer Gamba, the architect of Via XX Settembre, to Navigazione Generale Italiana, together with a building project in an eclectic style which was the result of reworkings over several years. [A. M. N.]

Accademia Ligustica di Belle Arti

PIAZZA R. DE FERRARI 5
BUS 15, 17, 18, 19, 20, 30, 35, 36, 39, 40, 41, 41, 42

An initial project by Carlo Barabino in 1821 for the site (left empty after the demolition of the monastery of San Domenico) foresaw the construction of a barracks; work on this was started and an arcaded floor built. Protests from citizens prevented its completion and work stopped pending a decision as to its future use. In 1825, the Corpo Decurionale decided to complete the building and to house in it the "Library and Academy", turning the Piazza into a cultural centre and the city's showpiece. Built between 1826 and 1831, the three-storey building includes the arcades of the old barracks and has a textbook façade. The interior displays greater originality, as evidenced by the large octagonal hall and complex play of flights of stairs in the main stairwell set around a monumental empty space. Following the excavations needed for the building of Via XX Settembre, the palace, which was built against the Piccapietra hill, found itself isolated on all four sides and took on its present, block-like aspect, losing the "Rotonda" - a noted Neoclassical hall - on the way. The bombings of 1942 destroyed the second-floor salons which had been characterized by their even lighting, barely screened by a succession of internal columns. It is currently the seat of the Accademia Ligustica di Belle Arti, of the Museo dell'Accademia and of the Civica Biblioteca Berio. [I. F.]

69
Teatro Comunale dell'Opera
PIAZZA R. DE FERRARI
BUS 15, 17, 18, 19, 20, 30, 35, 36, 39, 40, 41, 41, 42

Arising from the competition arranged by the Genoa City Council in 1981 for the reconstruction of the Teatro Carlo Felice, the project by the group A. Rossi, I. Gardella, R. Reinhardt and A. Sibilla (1981/84) tackled a number of problems: the restoration and reconstruciton of what was old, the recovery of the decoration, the city-monument relationship and the inclusion of new elements in a context with strong historical features. The project was accepted after lengthy controversy, finally bringing to a close the debate concerning the reconstruction which had already led to an earlier competition in 1949 (the Chessa project won) and to a later commission for Carlo Scarpa to work on the project (1963/77), without, however, leading to any actual building work. The building combines three different volumes: the pronaos, restored together with Barabino's original arcades; the theatre, reconstructed as per the original; the stage tower, a new element in the composition which typified the whole. Just as in the Scarpa project, the confluence of the pedestrian ways in the external foyer took on an urban character, creating a link between the Galleria G. Mazzini and Piazza R. De Ferrari. Within, under a sky dotted with small lights, the auditorium opens like a vault towards the stage which is framed by two gigantic trunks of columns. Massive stone walls, with Genoese-style windows and doors set in them evoke an "outside" which is perhaps not Genoese. The intense use of decoration in the finishing materials of the auditorium contrast with the elegant simplicity of the internal foyer. [M. P. G.]

Stock Exchange
PIAZZA R. DE FERRARI 4; VIA G. BOCCARDO 1
BUS 15, 17, 18, 19, 20, 30, 35, 36, 39, 40, 41, 41, 42

The new stock exchange replaced the old one in Piazza Banchi at the end of the 19th century when the representative offices situated in the historic centre relocated. The area was acquired in 1906 by the Società Nuova Borsa, comprising powerful real estate agents and financiers, which commissioned a project from Dario Carbone with the collaboration of A. Coppedè for the interior decoration. The work was contracted to the Società Immobiliare Ædes in 1907 and finished only in 1912. The ground plan is arranged around an elliptical room in which four pairs of columns support the roof in which is set a decorated skylight, and the upper floors which house the offices in a double ring. A theatre was planned for the basement (it is now a cinema). The large windows were built in reinforced concrete by Porcheddu of Turin using the Hennebique system. The hall is impressive: the space looks as though it had been created from a mould, with heavy decoration covering every architectural feature. The rose-coloured façade, with its massive arcades echoed in the upper arches, is crowned by a jutting cornice which hides the fifth floor and an attic. The decoration, terminating in a sculpted group and four corner domes, is strongly sculptural in feel (defined as neo-Baroque at the time of construction) and reveals the skill of the industry involved in manufacturing artificial stone features.

[A. M. N.]

71
Palazzo degli Uffici Giudiziari (Legal offices)
PIAZZA PORTORIA 1
BUS 15, 17, 18, 19, 20, 30, 35, 36, 39, 40, 41, 41, 42

Located on the Colle di Pammatone in the working-class district of Portoria, an area radically changed by post-war building, the new Palazzo di Giustizia (a 1950s design finished in 1970) comprises a closed volume with internal courtyard which embraces the surviving remains of the old hospital of 1420 which had been greatly restructured in 1750-83 by Andrea Orsolino. Used until 1928, the hospital was then made over to the City Council's Demographic Offices. During the bombings of 1943, the palace suffered extensive damage: only the old portico in the courtyard survived, although in a damaged condition, and some parts of the basement; these were placed under a preservation order by the Soprintendenza ai Beni Architettonici.

In the reconstruction project, Giovanni Romano restored the porticoed courtyard and had a faithful reproduction of the mezzanine built, recreating the original look of the internal courtyard which was reached from the old staircase. The new structure, which encompasses the restored features, is instead completely unlike a philological reconstruction, and provides an example of an "ahistorical" architecture of technological stamp. Strongly characterized by the rhythmical modulation of the structural steel bracing, the interior and exterior skin of the building reveals an emphatic use of materials whose dimensions go beyond a structural or functional role to become part of the aesthetic work of the building. [M. P. G.]

72
Via XX Settembre
BUS 15, 17, 18, 19, 20, 30, 36, 39, 40, 41, 41, 42

A straight line 792 metres long, Via XX Settembre is the city's main street, a position it gained as soon as it was built between the 19th and 20th centuries, thanks to the relocation of commercial and representative offices which had hitherto been in the historic centre.

The project to widen the earlier road (Via Giulia), drawn up by the engineer Cesare Gamba, was accepted in 1887 by the City Council which commissioned two large credit institutions - the Banca Generale and Cassa di Sovvenzione per Imprese - to undertake the work. However, the plan was only approved by the central authorities in 1890, at which date the straight road was adopted. The road was built by the two banks which formed the Impresa di Via Giulia e Piccapietra for the project, with the assistance of a technical office directed by Gamba. After the bankruptcy of the concessionaires in the banking crisis of 1894, Gamba also took on the financial responsibility. The work on the road was contracted out in 1892 to Impresa Boggio e Rosazza, set up *ad hoc* by a Genoese engineer and a Turinese construction company. The lots were sold singly. Amongst the construction companies Carbone e Repetto stands out; this was founded by an employee of the Impresa di Via Giulia and it erected about a third of the buildings.

The project gave rise to a long-lasting building site (the last buildings were only put up at the end of the first decade of the new century) and provided the opportunity for a modernization of the whole building industry. Here, for example, we find the first use of reinforced concrete by the Impresa Porcheddu of Turin, Italian agent for the Hennebique system. The use of concrete was at first limited to the building of floors but was later also adopted for load-bearing structures. The work was undertaken in two phases: the first, from Via Cadorna to the Ponte Monumentale, was begun in 1892 and ended at the end of 1893. The second, from the bridge to Piazza R. De Ferrari, was begun in 1895 and opened in 1900. This second phase saw the introduction of arcades (1900) and taller buildings were also permitted. The constructions reflect this span of years. Those from the earlier phase reflect the historical eclecticism which sought to imitate the Italian town palace in different styles (see the so-called Florentine palace at no. 6 and Palazzo dei Giganti at no. 14). The second phase, on the other hand, is typified by the city's first essays in the new international Art Nouveau style and include features such as bow windows, mansard roofs and domes which were not yet allowed for in the regulations. The buildings were far more uniform in ground plan: the high-density use of the often irregularly-shaped lots is common, with a single staircase for many apartments. These, although equipped with the latest technological and design features, often reveal a poor distribution of space around dark inner courtyards. [A. M. N.]

73
Old Seminary
VIA PORTA D'ARCHI
BUS 15, 17, 18, 19, 20, 30, 36, 39, 40, 41, 41, 42

The seminary of the clergy, which owed its foundation to Cardinal Cipriano Pallavicino in 1575-77, gained its own quarters and a more functional organization thanks to Cardinal Stefano Durazzo. It was begun in February 1655, to plans by Gerolamo Gandolfo who, as site director, oversaw the construction rapidly concluded in two years, although structural problems appeared right from the start. Gio Batta Orsolino provided the marble for the colonnade. The whole was controlled by Emanuele Brignole who was then involved in the construction of the grandiose Albergo dei Poveri.

The palazzo tried to be both stately and severe at the same time. The façade recalls the bare, solemn examples by Bianco, but is marked by two slight avant-corps in 16th-century style which have no bearing on the ground plan. The entrance gives an impression of airiness and leads into the courtyard loggias, originally open in a U shape towards the gardens on the slopes of the Carignano hill. In 1840, Ignazio Gardella closed the courtyard with the addition of a fourth wing in which he placed the neo-Palladian chapel; a final enlargement was undertaken in 1890 with two new wings to the south designed by the engineer Massaro. Abandoned after the construction of a new seminary, it has now been restructured to house a bank in the monumental part and the Civica Biblioteca Berio in the 19th-century part. The project was by the architect Gambacciani. [E. D. N.]

74
Monumental Bridge
VIA XX SETTEMBRE
BUS 15, 17, 18, 19, 20, 30, 36, 39, 40, 41, 41, 42

As a result of the construction of Via XX Settembre, in 1893 it was decided to replace the old Porta dell'Arco ⁄ one of the gates in the 14th⁄century walls ⁄ with a "monumental" bridge reflecting the importance of the new road. This bridge would link the walls of Santa Chiara with Acquasola. The proposal was drawn up by the Gamba studio, the architect of Via XX Settembre, and was submitted to Delmoro and Camillo Boito who approved it, declaring that the project, comprising a depressed central arch with lateral arcades and a non⁄classical superimposition of orders, bore all the elements of a bridge, a gate and a triumphal arch together. The building work was contracted to the Impresa Calderai in 1893. Gamba supplied the structural calculations (with the assistance of eng. N. Ronco) and the executive project, to which he applied the construction system adopted for the building of the Busalla⁄Ronco railway viaducts: a load⁄bearing arch in brick covered with decorative architectural facing designed by the architect R. Haupt. This distinction between the structural and the architectural parts caused both Gamba and Haupt to declare themselves authors of the work. The planning paid much attention to the production requirements: the shape of the arch, for each of the roughly 7,500 wedges, and those of the wooden centering were all studied on a scale of 1:2 in the sets⁄room of the Teatro Carlo Felice and a number of models of the marbles were also produced, provided by the G. Novi company. The bridge was finished in 1899, but the sculptures were only terminated some time later. [A. M. N.]

75
Palazzina Eridania
CORSO A. PODESTÀ 2
BUS 15, 17, 18, 19, 20, 30, 35, 36, 39, 40, 41, 41, 42

The little palace, home of Eridania since 1931, is an interesting example of a not-infrequent practice in early 20th century architecture, that of superimposing a false stylistic and historical identity on an earlier building. It was built in the 19th century on a bastion of the 16th-century walls and has been restructured several times. When Eridania acquired it in 1913, the ground plan was T-shaped with the shorter side on Corso Podestà, and it had two floors, with another two in the central part. The company had work done on it twice, first between 1913 and 1915, then again between 1923 and 1926, both times employing R. Haupt as architect.

The earlier work consisted in inserting lifts and the stairwell, in raising the wings and renewing the façade. The new staircase, supported by fluted marble piers and of clear monumental intent, pierced the earlier structure to reach the piano nobile under a lunetted and grandiosely frescoed vault. The lower floors of the front remained substantially unchanged whilst the upper central part was topped by a façade in eclectic style with tall, flat pilasters and rich friezes. The new wings with high loggias were added and these reveal themselves as later additions in the cornices set at different levels.

The second phase of the work included the construction of a wing towards Acquasola, backing on to an internal courtyard, whose façade takes up the motif of the loggia, although closed with glazed windows. [A. M. N.]

76
Palazzo dei Giganti
VIA XX SETTEMBRE 14
BUS 15, 17, 18, 19, 20, 30, 36, 39, 40, 41, 41, 42

The palazzo was built partly on the basis of building permission granted in 1895 for a design by the architect D. Carbone and the engineer Carlo Fuselli, partners with the Repetto brothers of the company of the same name which had already put up the buildings at nos. 4 and 6, but it presents some stylistic and structural innovations. The use of reinforced concrete for floors for the first time in the city in an apartment block (laid down by Porcheddu of Turin using the Hennebique system) made it possible to have large rooms on the ground floor and vast underground storerooms. It is also perceptible in the façade (there is a very thin floor between the ground floor and the mezzanine). The ground plan reveals a high-density use of the site (seven apartments per floor). The large courtyard was divided into two by a transverse wing housing the marble stairs on load-bearing, shaped iron beams and was adorned with a finely-worked cast-iron handrail. From this, one reaches the side apartments along the corridors which divide the internal volume into two once again. The building is crowned by a terraced roof and has six floors: the mezzanine and last floor, made to look smaller on the façade so as to imitate the hierarchical layout of an aristocratic palace, actually have rooms of the same height as the others. The eclectic façade is decorated with a rich series of ornamentation and from it emerge four imposing piers highlighted by richly sculpted groups, the pairs of giants from which the palazzo takes its name, executed by M. Sansebastiano. [A. M. N.]

77
Palazzo Zuccarino
VIA A. M. MARAGLIANO 2
BUS 15, 17, 18, 19, 20, 30, 36, 39, 40, 41, 41, 42

The palazzo was built by Giovanni Zuccarino, one of the most important building contractors at the turn of the 20th century, and was designed by Gino Coppedè with the collaboration of the engineer Predasso for the structural elements. Building began in 1906 and was finished the following year.
Located on one of the roads crossing Via XX Settembre made after the old lunatic asylum was demolished, the palazzo boasts a highly visible position and this is given visible expression in Coppedè's classical style with a rich fabric of projections and interlacements of unusual forms interposed with a rich pictorial decoration which is now lost (probably by E. Bifoli). The effect is almost grotesque, especially as the decoration ends up by being more prominent than the overall composition which is quite weak.
The façade is rusticated along the ground floor (given over to shops) and portioned and plastered on the upper floors. It is richer towards the centre of the piano nobile and expands upwards towards the wings, terminating in balconies with loggias which go around the corner, over which a sloping cornice projects. The ground plan of the building does not reveal any great originality; there are two apartments per floor with a central antechamber and bathrooms towards the courtyard. Of some interest is the frescoed hall with grandiloquent subjects; here a marble arch frames the access to the stairs and lift, slotted into a wrought-iron cage. [A. M. N.]

78
Mercato Orientale
VIA XX SETTEMBRE
BUS 15, 17, 18, 19, 20, 30, 36, 39, 40, 41, 41, 42

Intended for the sale of vegetables and fruit and various other products, the market is located on the site of the old monastery of the Consolazione and was built by the F. Risso company and designed by Veroggio, Bisagno and Cordoni, all City Council engineers (1898-99). It was opened with an exhibition of flowers. This was the first building to be made of reinforced concrete in Genoa and one of the first in Italy to be built completely in this way, with the relevant work undertaken by Porcheddu of Turin using structural calculations supplied by the parent company, Hennebique, patent-holder of this technique. After having been satisfactorily inspected by the City Council, it led to the company undertaking other work in Liguria.

From the earlier building on Via XX Settembre against which the entrance portico was placed, one reaches the market, comprising an arcade with coupled marble columns which stretches around the square building, separated by a road open to the sky. Slightly raised from ground level as a result of the underground storerooms, this is formed of a gallery around the side next to a central raised area closed off by glazed windows and covered by a roof supported by a criss-cross of beams. A large skylight is set into this roof. The original structure is rather difficult to discern today because the central portico has been filled in and stalls built against it. The internal street has been covered with metal beams and corrugated plastic roofing. [A. M. N.]

79
Piazza Colombo
BUS 15, 17, 18, 19, 20, 30, 36, 41, 41

In 1825, in his project "to increase the number of homes within the city", Carlo Barabino picked out the flat areas of Pace and San Vincenzo next to the main roads into the historic centre as suitable zones for expansion for residential and commercial property, and he proposed the Neoclassical idea of a square piazza to be its central point.
In the 1840s, G. B. Resasco constructed the four palazzi, creating large arcades of simple and monumental design, and preserving the sense of importance of the crossroads between the straight roads with long perspective views.
In 1861, the fountain of Ponte Reale was recovered from the harbour and placed at the centre of the piazza; the large basin with its curved and straight lines had been made in 1646 by G. B. Garré and commissioned by the Protettori of the Banco di San Giorgio to provide water for the vessels moored by the Ponte Reale. The group of dolphins whose tails support the four naiads holding a smaller basin is by G. B. Orsolino. [E. D. N.]

80
Hospital of Sant'Andrea (Galliera)
VIA A. VOLTA
BUS 35

The complex appears stately and well-integrated into the landscape and has become an image of respect in the psychology of the Genoese who still think highly of its tradition of care. It was built between 1876 and 1884 at the behest of Maria Brignole Sale de Ferrari, Duchess of Galliera, and was designed by the engineer Cesare Parodi with the intention of providing a highly modern hospital on European standards for the city which was at that time caught up in the whirlwind of industrial modernization. Designed as a series of separate pavilions linked by airy loggias in imitation of hospitals just built in Paris and London (1854-71), it made Genoa the only city in Italy with two hospitals built *ex novo* in the 19th century, including the psychiatric hospital designed by C. Barabino in about 1840 in the form of a *panoptikon*. The formal qualities of the façades and the public areas of the interiors, directly copied from local 16th-century examples, is echoed by the completely innovative functional layout which from the start made use of avant-garde features for a hospital, such as a *decauville*, lifts and a special air-conditioning system. [E. P.]

81
Yacht Club
VIA DEI PESCATORI
BUS 12, 15, 32

Located in a small area squeezed in between the sea and the embankment of Corso Aurelio Saffi, the clubhouse of the Yacht Club Italiano has been since the sixties even more hemmed in by the adjacent flyover which almost touches the roof. The square structure, designed by Giuseppe Crosa di Vergagni in 1928, has an imposing presence thanks to the bare walls pierced by the pointed arches of the windows which are reflected in the water of the little yacht harbour, today swallowed up by the commercial port. The view from the sea adds to the sense of monumentality. Within, the double-height hall creates a luminous gathering point which the rooms on the mezzanine overlook. With its succession of single and double flights, the scissors-shaped staircase provides a scenic route between the three levels of the building. Based on a local neo-Gothic style, the building seems to seek a link with the tradition of the place through the repeated use of historical elements. In reality, Crosa di Vergagni falls comfortably into the provincial, conservative taste of the city, for which he set himself up as the arbiter within a group of patrons largely drawn from the aristocracy of Genoa. His designs developed into a 20th-century style which found fruit in many public commissions made the easier as a result of his position with the architectural association. Amongst his most interesting works are the main offices of Ilva in Via Corsica, the Opera Nazionale Balilla in Via Cesarea, Palazzo Terzano in Piazza Dante and the fountain in Piazza R. De Ferrari. [M. P. G.]

82
Church of San Giacomo di Carignano (Sacro Cuore)
PIAZZA R. PIAGGIO
BUS 35

The refurbishment of Via Corsica ⁄ a popular 19th⁄century destination for a stroll ending at the "rotonda" with its splendid view over the Ligurian gulf ⁄ led at the end of the 19th century to the demolition of the medieval church of San Giacomo on the heights of the promontory. Authorisation for the construction of the new church designed by Luigi Rovelli was requested in December of 1890. The detailed, refined drawings show a neo⁄medieval church with nave and two aisles, round⁄headed arches and a women's gallery and ample light entering from the upper part of the three⁄mullioned windows. The transept is crowned by a very high spire. In 1892, work began with the construction of the crypt (now used as a theatre) which extends underneath the church and carries it to the height of Via Corsica. After this first phase, work halted for many years and the crypt itself was used as a church. The construction which finally took shape does not reflect Rovelli's initial project; only the ground plan corresponds with any degree of accuracy. The neo⁄medieval coherence was replaced by a modernist style which was monumentalist and geometrical and rich in original features. Except for the care taken over the altars ⁄ produced in the thirties by Piero Barbieri (high altar) and Rovelli's son, Antonio ⁄ and the paintings by P. Dodero, M. Traverso and very fine ones by G. Chini, the church remained bare. An attempt to finish it in the '60s with marble cladding and large capitals and bases for the coupled columns remained yet again unfinished. [E. D. N.]

83
Villa Mylius
VIA MYLIUS 9; CORSO A. SAFFI
BUS 35

Although it is no longer possible to see the entrance façade as intended, this is a rare, well-preserved example of neo-Gothic architecture, similar to the contemporary Villa Serra Gentile, built in the mid 19th century by the architect Cusani in Comago-Manesseno di Val Polcevera.
The villa was built for the Swiss, Federico Mylius, on an extremely panoramic site along the sea-walls which defended the crags of the Cava di Carignano (16th century), but the view was soon obscured by large marine pines and hedges planted to ensure an understandable desire for privacy. This hideaway was home to rich art and archeological collections to which the owner, a building contractor, added using the carts which transported the stones from the refurbished districts. The view over the sea and harbour, which the visitor can still enjoy from below along Corso A. Saffi, was made grander at the start of the century by the new owner, Fiagri, who added a neo-Gothic loggia on two levels in terracotta and marble next to a bold, overhanging structure in reinforced concrete. [E. P.]

84
Palazzo Ilva
VIA CORSICA 4; VIA ILVA 1
BUS 35

With this 1929 office building, Giuseppe Crosa di Vergagni deliberately sought a monumental effect with Neoclassical features in the provincial, conservative taste of the city. In so doing, he demonstrated a certain skill in blending a modernist style with the Genoese classical tradition, to which he made more explicit reference on other occasions.

The building has a rectangular ground plan and stands on a lot stretching from Via Corsica to Via Ilva on to which open the two main entrances. The impressiveness of the entrance on Via Corsica and the magnificence of the hall behind seem to provide a perfect combination of the political aspirations of the period and the importance and prestige of such a large industry as Ilva. The main façade, which is regular, features a series of windows of differing height on the various floors and is largely faced with dark grey marble slabs, alternating with smooth plaster work. The top of the building is unusual in having an overhanging cornice with a pseudotympanum above, repeated on the three main fronts. These are strongly hierarchical and are notably differentiated, almost as though to give more importance to those next to the main roads. The front on Via Ilva differs from the main one only through the presence of a central feature containing the stairwell which can be seen through the windows. [F. G.]

85
Tower Blocks of Piazza Dante
PIAZZA DANTE 9-11; PIAZZA DANTE 8
BUS 15, 17, 20, 32, 35, 36, 41, 41, 42

The 1932 town-planning scheme allowed for no less than four tower blocks in the area left empty by the demolition of the old Lanaioli quarter and the flattening of the Morcento hillock. The two eventually built, towards the end of the '30s, became the standard-bearers of the loudly-proclaimed yet debatable renaissance under the Fascists and the symbol of the city's growth. The northern tower, designed by Giuseppe Rosso and built between 1935 and 1937, comprises an arcaded base with 7 floors and a tower of 14 floors. Quite apart from its formal interest, the significance of this building lies in the technological solutions adopted which were at the forefront for the period (such as, for example, the use of variable-velocity lifts).

Of slightly later date (1937-41) and better known because it is still the highest in Italy, is the southern tower, built by the engineer Invernizzi, who designed it in collaboration with Marcello Piacentini. The latter abandoned the use of arches and columns and turned instead to American examples made known in Genoa by Renzo Picasso. The reference point was above all the skyscrapers of New York, built in the second phase of their vertical development (1921-31), and of which our skyscraper constitutes an original interpretation. The building comprises an arcaded base with two bas-reliefs by Guido Galletti (Christopher Columbus to the left, the Balilla at Porta Soprana to the right), and a tower of 23 floors which are stepped as it rises. [L. D.]

86
Madre di Dio Business Centre
PIAZZA DANTE; CORSO M. QUADRIO
BUS 15, 17, 20, 32, 35, 36, 41, 41, 42

The last project of the 1931 Fascist urban renovation programme was completed in 1966 with the special plan for Via Madre di Dio which saw the demolition of the entire medieval Lanaioli district and Marina. The rebuilding began in the '70s using the already outdated model of the high-density office district, and it reveals all the limits of the flawed urbanisation strategy which emerged after 1965 in the revision of the Town-planning Scheme. The lack of a pedestrian outlet capable of encouraging through streams of people and the attempt to create a naturalistic open space in which Barabino's admirable basins (1798) were placed willy-nilly without making them the fulcrum of the composition, marginalised the public area - if not more - which should instead have been a gathering point. The eastern block (designed by Marco Dasso) derives its inspiration from the English late brutalism of the '60s and advances in steps from Piazza Dante towards the sea without presenting any sort of urban front. Facing it, the L-shaped block (designed by F. Albini and F. Helg) closes the side of Piazza Dante overlooking the sea and blocks the Piccapietra/sea axis suggested by the short archway of Via Ceccardi. The effects sought are repeated to the point of banality and the architectural motif is reduced to an alternation between filled bands (rose-coloured artificial stone panels) and transparent bands (ribbon windows). [M. P. G.]

87
Sant'Agostino Museum
PIAZZA SARZANO 21
BUS ~~15~~, 17, 20, 32, 35, 36, 41, ~~41~~, 42

The recovery of the monumental Sant'Agostino complex and its transformation into museum and cultural spaces falls into the programme set up by the City Council to improve an area of the city which was potentially rich in areas and buildings of some architectural interest but which was falling into decay, a process started by the bombings of the Second World War. A good part of the square cloisters of Sant'Agostino had survived, as had two damaged sides of the triangular cloisters, the bell tower (although with cracks and some problems of stability), and the deconsecrated church which had already been opened as a museum of Genoese architecture.

With later accretions removed, the recovery programme (1963/79; F. Albini, F. Helg, A. Piva, M. Albini) ran along parallel lines: the radical demolition and replacement of the square cloisters, the restoration of the damaged triangular cloisters and the *ex novo* construction of upper floors, built with floors and load-bearing supports in steel along the lines (in terms of height and ground plan) of the original building. The nature of these operations is clearly visible in the features of the building both on the inside, which is of great geometric rigour, and on the exterior surface which is deeply marked by the insertion of the new structures. With the overall intervention finished, the Museum of Ligurian Architecture and Sculpture, the church has also been transformed into an auditorium for symphonic and chamber music. [M. P. G.]

88
Faculty of Architecture
STRADONE DI SANT'AGOSTINO 37
BUS 15, 17, 20, 32, 35, 36, 41, 41, 42

The special Plan for San Donato and San Silvestro (1972; Ignazio and Jacopo Gardella, S. Larini, G. Nardi, D. Vitale) provided for a university centre for the humanities faculties in that part of the historic centre which had over the years provided a home for the early medieval religious and civil authorities, the "sacred" city of the later medieval great monasteries and, after the suppressions (1798) and the confiscations (1855), the segregation of certain civil services then crowned by war damage and civil neglect. The plan thus seemed to provide an excellent means of linking this neglected area again to the town around it and offering chances for exchanges between the old and the new. However, it was not realised for 15 years, during which time the concept itself of reclamation had changed, while the modified requirements of the Humanities Faculties meant that only the Architecture Faculty was in need of reshaping. Contracted out in two lots, the first saw the building of the new block of lecture halls, finished in 1989 (design I. Gardella and A. Malaponti, 1st ed., 1976-77), which rises on the area within the ex-church of San Silvestro, and restoration of the church's bell tower. The second phase of the work, completed in 1991 (design L. Grossi Bianchi), saw the library and rector's offices built inside the restored 17th-century monastery, while departments and laboratories with more lecture halls were inserted into the old Bishop's Palace, incorporating the preserved remains of early medieval towers and walls. [M. P. G.]

89
Urban park (Expo '92)
MOLO VECCHIO; PIAZZA CARICAMENTO
BUS 1, 2, 3, 7, 8, 12, 15, 32

The old port, chosen as the venture for the Columbus anniversary exhibition, is the cradle of Genoa's economic and settlement history. 1988 saw the foundation of Ente Colombo '92 (formed from different local bodies) which was responsible for the exhibition and realisation of the work (Italimpianti-Iri). This company delegated the architectural design to Renzo Piano, employing him direct or on a consultancy basis for the structures and layouts, and contracting out the execution of the work to two consortiums (Molo Vecchio, general contractor for works on that site; Cogeco, cooperatives, and Gepco for the works on the Spinola bridge). From east to west the project provided for: Molo Vecchio, total reuse of the "Magazzini generali" (1898-1901, eng. L. Timosci) for exhibition spaces and a large congress centre. To the rear and on other lots, there were to be service buildings, a car park and the harbour office; new layout of the 16th-century Porto del Molo area, with an open-air theatre and restoration of the historic quays; reuse of the Mandraccio basin for spectacular events, with the large "Bigo" structure in steel rising above it symbolising and imitating ships' loading cranes. This supports a panoramic lift and a large, teflon canvas above Piazza delle Feste (bridge G. Embriaco). A series of flagstaffs with moving canvas parts emphasise the shape of the quay; reuse of the "Deposito franco" (17th-18th centuries) for offices, meeting halls and services for the district. Only some pavilions remain after construction of the flyover in the 1960s and these were restored and the roofs rebuilt in slate; the Milo area, built at the beginning of the century, was reduced to its original dimensions for exhibition and didactic spaces, a bookshop and restaurant on the ground floor; the Caricamento archeological park showing the underground bridges of the port, extremely rare medieval structures which integrate the arcading of the Ripa, but this has been partially destroyed by the excavations for the motor underpass (above the underground) introduced, paradoxically, to make the most of an urban experience that is unique in Europe; the Spinola bridge, once housed the Italian exhibition pavilion, today made up of a long building suspended on a central spine, where the extremely popular Acquarium has been sited, now extended to the floating section in the form of a ship. The Porto Antico company, a joint venture set up in 1995 to manage the 70,000 square metres (35,000 of which are covered) given to the City Council by the State in 1993, has assumed or integrated initiatives and definitive use of, for example, the congress centre, the Padiglione del Mare e della Navigazione, the very modern, interactive children's city and the multi cinema, with the idea of transforming Expo '92 into a great urban park; a park which is so necessary for putting the old city back onto the waterfront again. The overall layout is still unfinished today, especially Piazza Caricamento with its role as central hinge between the contemporary city and the old port. [E. P.]

90
Museo del Tesoro di San Lorenzo
PIAZZA SAN LORENZO (CATHEDRAL)
BUS 12, 15, 15, 17, 19, 30, 41

The underground museum, designed by Franco Albini between 1954 and 1956, holds the collection of disparate, precious objects such as the "Holy Basin", 14th and 15th-century tombs, reliquaries and an 18th-century statue of the Virgin, which form the Cathedral's "Tesoro" or Treasure. The display is by Caterina Marcenaro. Every sort of image has been evoked to define the museum: "metaphysical space", "informal space", "cavern", "Lascaux caves", "the Curia's basement", "treasure of the Atridi", "reliquary", "baroque pearl". The limitations for the project were various. The Tesoro's collection was unlikely ever to grow, since it comprised sacred objects whose liturgical requirements were such that there had to be a direct link between the "museum-warehouse" and the Cathedral in a complex relationship between exhibited objects, new architecture and ancient forms.

After a number of hypotheses, Albini made use of the area between the foundations of the Archbishop's residence, with public access from the sacristy of San Lorenzo. The declared intention of creating an environment rich in "analogical memory" with the crypts and catacombs determined the form of the composition, which is articulated into three circular spaces of varying diameter covered with domes, *tholoi* linked and pierced by a hexagonal space and another, smaller *tholos* at the entrance, with floors and walls in Promontorio stone, in accordance with Genoese building tradition. [I. F.]

91
Portello-Castelletto Lift
PIAZZA DEL PORTELLO; BELVEDERE L. MONTALDO
BUS 18, 19, 20, 30, 33, 34, 37

The lift, a convenient link between the city and the hills above, starts from Piazza Portello, with which it is connected by a tunnel enlivened by polychrome Art Nouveau tiles. It rises 57 metres to the L. Montaldo belvedere on the esplanade of Castelletto. The first project for a lift dates from 1900 and was produced by the engineers Sertorio and Selingeri; it was a mixed mechanism in which a tram was raised by a lift. However, authorization for the construction and running of a pair of lifts dates from 1906 and was granted by the City Council to S. A. Lig. Lifts (later to become Soc. Lig. per Impianto ed Esercizio Ascensori). The machinery was electric and comprised two cabins in wood and glass built by Stigler. The lift was running by 1910. The original cabins were kept until 1990, when the plant was modernised.

From the Castelletto esplanade, there is a magnificent view over the historic heart of the city. It was built on the site of the old military headquarters built by the French in 1401, which had been demolished and reconstructed several times up to 1820, and a number of working-class houses (1849-55) were also constructed which have since become highly sought-after.

The arrival station of the lift, a glazed platform around the cabins is an excellent belvedere: linked to the esplanade by a walkway, it has the form of a tapering bulb surrounded by windows and is one of the finest examples of Genoese Art Nouveau architecture.　　　　　　　　　　　　　　　　　　　　[A. M. N.]

"G. Garibaldi" and "N. Bixio" Portello-Zecca Tunnels

LARGO ZECCA; PIAZZA DEL PORTELLO; PIAZZA E. CORVETTO
BUS 18, 19, 20, 30, 34, 37, 39, 40, 41

The opening of the tunnels under the hills of Castelletto and the Villetta Di Negro made it possible to create a ring road through the centre whose utilitarian role is highlighted by the lack of any formal features. A first tunnel was cut at the end of the 19th century by the Soc. di Ferrovie Elettriche e Funicolari for the tramline between Principe and Brignole, but the present tunnels, which are larger and open to private traffic, date from the '20s. The first of the tunnels to be built was the Zecca-Portello (then Vittorio Emanuele III and now Garibaldi), using plans produced by the City Council's technical office and especially by the engineer T. Badano, who, with the engineer M. Braccialini, directed the works which were contracted out in 1922. The roof of the tunnel was made from waterproofed rough plaster (recently replaced with a covering in line with present regulations) with occasional decorative pilasters placed along a base of Karst stone. The tunnel was inaugurated in 1927, although the entrances were still to be finished (faced with squared ashlar stone and marble inserts, and topped with a balustrade and groups of statues). At the same time, the lift for Castelletto and the link with Piazza della Meridiana were added in mid-tunnel. 1928 saw the inauguration of the curved Portello-Corvetto tunnel (then Regina Elena, now N. Bixio), accepted by the City Council administration in 1923 with a project from the City Council's own technical department; its arrangement is identical to the other tunnel. [A. M. N.]

93
New City Council Offices
VIA GARIBALDI 9
BUS 18, 19, 20, 30, 32, 35, 36, 41, 41, 42

The complex of new council offices designed by Franco Albini (1952-59) is a happy example of a type of stepped building with hanging gardens which one can find in various Genoese constructions of this century. Such examples include the houses with courtyards backing on to the Staglieno hill or the more recent stepped condominiums by Daneri (1952-55) at Quinto. Built in two parallel blocks which drop regularly floor by floor, the City Council's offices stretch over the steep Castelletto hill, occupying the gardens of Palazzo Tursi. The twelfth-century church of San Francesco used to stand on the site, but it was more than half demolished in 1820, leaving only the left-hand aisle in Palazzo Galliera behind Palazzo Bianco and the adjacent Palazzo Tursi, now seat of the City Council Administration, with which the new block of offices is connected via a network of routes. The stepped section of the new building blends naturally into the slope of the hill and retraces the line traced by 19th-century building as it moved up the city's hills. The light colour of the facing on the walls and the dense division of windows at full height lighten the overall volume of the building and enable the rooftop gardens to be seen as single, emptied floors.

Within, the fulcrum of the building lies in the council chamber, situated in the basement; its circular skylight rises above the internal courtyard created by the gap between the old Palazzo Tursi and the new block. [M. P. G.]

94
Zecca-Righi Funicular Railway
TERMINUS VIA C. TARGA; MURA DELLE CHIAPPE
BUS 18, 19, 20, 30, 34, 37, 39, 40, 41

The funicular runs from Largo Zecca to the Mura delle Chiappe, partly through tunnel and partly in the open (length: 1,520 m., difference in height: 278.58 m.). It has a single track with a passing place at San Nicola and provides a rapid, comfortable means of transport. It also provides a magnificent view over the city from the top station.

The project was drawn up by the engineers L. Mignacco and C. Pfaltz, and was presented in 1891 by the Swiss Società di Ferrovie Elettriche e Funicolari. The agreement for its construction and operation was approved the following year and was taken over as work proceeded by a financial group headed by Aeg, which in 1895 formed Uite (Unione Italiana Tramways Elettrici); this became a municipal body in 1964. The funicular operated in two separate sections; the upper part was finished in 1895, the lower in 1897. The railway stimulated the spread of the town into nearby areas, although this started slowly despite the parcelling up of land (exceptions to this are the Art Nouveau houses on Via Piaggio). In 1959, a project was drawn up by the engineers Mor and Sibilla to join the two sections (work completed in 1964), and to modify the route and replace the machinery, which was renovated by the company Agudio and Ansaldo in 1991. [A. M. N.]

95
Castello De Albertis
CORSO DOGALI 18
BUS 33, 39, 40

This massive construction dominates the city and harbour from the Montegalletto hill, emerging from the park's mass of vegetation with the sharp profiles of its "slender, crenellated" towers. Built between 1886 and 1892 for Captain Enrico De Albertis on the remains of ancient fortifications from which it takes its ground plan, the castle constitutes an important example of historicising neo-medieval taste. The Romantic desire to relive the pomp of the old Commune within the walls of the castle (as documented by erudite quotations - the Embriaci tower, the loggia of Palazzo San Giorgio, the mullioned windows of Corrado Doria's palazzo, the cloisters of San Colombano in Bobbio) and the intention of reusing the forms of the earlier fortifications induced the patron to entrust the work to two engineers, M. Graziani and F. M. Parodi, assisted by the archaeologists and restorers G. Campora and M. A. Crotta (A. D'Andrade's 'pupil'), and the sculptor, Allegro. Surrounded by a vast park, the main mass of the castle is open to the south, with two towers to the sides - a square, massive one to the west, and another more slender and round one to the east. The building is divided into various loggias and defined chromatically by the contrast between the red of the bricks and the white of the lintels and little marble columns. Donated in 1932 to Genoa City Council, after the death of the captain, together with his collection of nautical instruments, antique arms and curios, it has been made into a Museum of Ethnography. It has been restored and is now being fitted out. [G. S.]

96
Porta Principe Railway Station
PIAZZA ACQUAVERDE
BUS 3, 18, 19, 20, 30, 32, 33, 34, 35, 37, 38, 41, 54

The station of Piazza del Principe was inaugurated in 1854 after the construction of the Turin-Genoa railway between 1846 and 1853. The station (1855-60) is earlier than that of Porta Nuova in Turin (1866-68) and has remained virtually unchanged; it is the earliest example of important railway architecture under the Kingdom of Sardinia. Given their experience with smaller buildings along the Turin-Asti line and with the station of Alessandria (1849-50), the railway terminals were entrusted to the engineer Alessandro Mazzuchetti (Biella, 1824-94), director of the Ufficio d'Arte delle Strade Ferrate. For Porta Nuova, he was assisted by the architect Carlo Ceppi (1829-1921). If the southern wing (demolished in the '30s) is included, the station of Genoa perfectly illustrates the demands of a project on an urban scale and a layout which was able to allow for considerable differences in land level. The complex reveals a skillful integration of the articulated but symmetrical travellers' area with the 10 platforms at a 30° angle. These were already covered by a single curved roof, whose centering had been constructed in the Orlando factory with advice from Professor Giovanni Ansaldo. At a higher level the building opens out on to Piazza Acquaverde and the monument to Christopher Columbus (inaugurated in 1862); the façade with tall granite columns, which was already documented in a plan by A. Mazzuchetti in 1857, provides an echo of a Genoese classicism which could have been produced by a local hand (G. B. Resasco?), a point reinforced by the subjects of the sculptures and the pictures by F. Gandolfi. [E. P.]

97
Grain Silos
CALATA S. LIMBANIA
BUS 30

The silos were inaugurated in 1901. An area of land and adjacent harbour were granted in 1898 to the engineers A. Carissimo, G. Crotti and G. B. De Cristoforis for the construction and operation of granaries. They formed a new company, S. A. dei Silos di Genova, largely with German capital. The building has a long front towards the sea in eclectic style and is of great interest above all from a structural point of view since at the time it was the largest reinforced concrete building in the world, and the only one with fixed fittings in the same material. Planned by Hennebique, the work was undertaken by its representative for Italy, Porcheddu of Turin.
The building (originally 140m long, then extended to 212 and raised several times) comprises two wings which contain cells ending in hoppers ⁄ the actual silos ⁄ whilst the higher central part houses the areas for the technical apparatus (the original equipment is now lost) with which the grain was sucked up from the holds and sent to the warehouses or for shipping. The plant was also equipped with a quay at which ships could berth, with suction towers and machinery for transporting the grain to the warehouses.
The building now belongs to Ceres Cereali Silos of the Ferruzzi group, and there is a project to transform it into a hotel, drawn up by G. Polastri, F. Tomasinelli and M. Ferralasco.   [A. M. N.]

The Old Port —
Projects for Reusing the Infrastructures

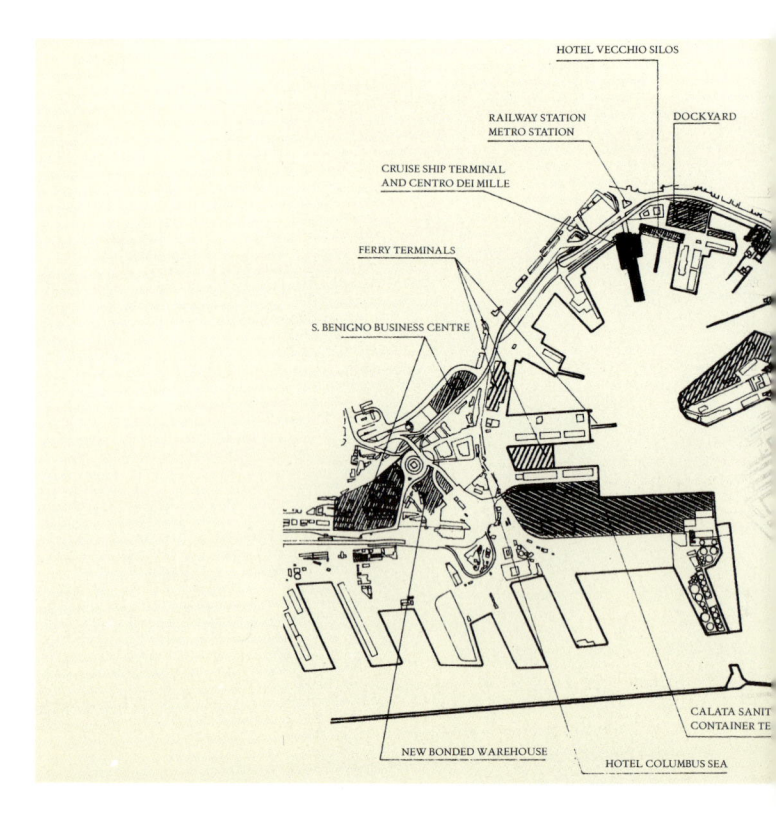

After years of progressive commercial decline, the old port — between the Molo Vecchio and the Sanità quay — is the subject of a long conversion of its first reorganisation due to Parodi's project of 1876-82. After having relocated industrial functions elsewhere (1984), the Consorzio Autonomo del Porto (Cap), together with the Region and City Council, approved a change in the port town planning scheme in 1987 to introduce mixed urban and harbour uses to the area. In the meantime, operational projects in the individual plots were begun (by joint ventures between Cap and private firms) then approved separately by the Conferenza dei Servizi, the new, parallel organism created under a 1989 law for projects connected to the football World Cup.
From east to west, the following projects were earmarked, as well as Expo '92: yacht harbour (finished), with shops and services for leisure craft, arranged in a fan-like array along projections which mimic the quays (client Porto Storico spa, a joint venture between Cap and Fortune-Gadolla, today Zerbone; designed by Gambacciani, Ciruzzi and Garibaldi). Since its presentation in 1984, the project has been subjected to changes among which a controversial proposal for a very high, cone-shaped tower with a platform on pilotis in the water (arch. Portman); recovery of the dockyard (under way), coordinated by B. Gabrielli and carried out by the Consorzio di recupero della Darsena (a pool of building contractors working for the City Council), provides for the

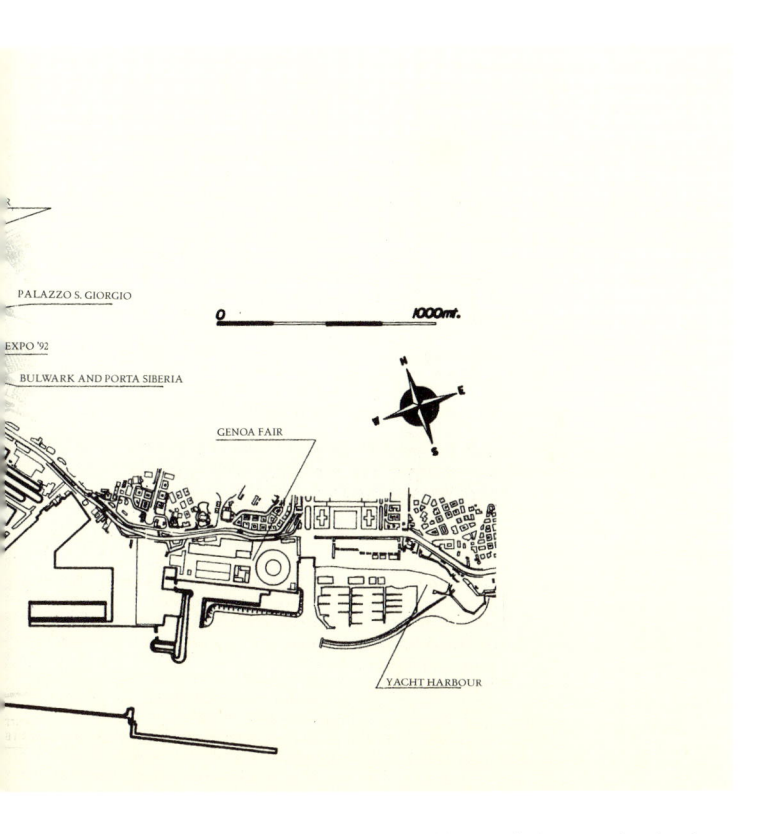

creation of public buildings in the various "districts" the complex has been divided into, entrusted to the same number of architects. Seeing that the sewage purification plant for the historic centre (project Intertekna) and the Faculty of Economics and Commerce (A. L. Rizzo and Seicom) have only just been terminated, the broad range of uses and buildings planned seem to realise a unity which is merely virtual. In fact, the National Library (project G. Spalla), the Nautical Institute (Seicom and Sogedil), a multi-purpose centre (M. Semino and G. P. Bartolozzi), the functional recovery of the Sauli drydock (A. Orazzini and A. Armanino), university residences (A. Sibilla and Seicom), the relocation of the Piazza Statuto market (L. Fontana and S. Filippini) are still only on paper; the grain silos of Calata Santa Limbania (1901, rebuilding project) with doubt as to their final use between a hotel or the Faculty of Engineering; cruise terminal (completed) with up-dating of the maritime station (1928) and new ferry terminals (constituted by Cap, Sci and Costa Crociere, designed respectively by the architects Polastri, Tommasinelli and Ferralasco and A. Pino and A. L. Rizzo); container terminal of Calata Sanità (completed), with a project by Cap's technical office. This is the only transformation project which, set on the borders of the old port, preserves an explicitly productive function for the quay. [E. P.]

IV.
THE CITY OF THE NEW WALLS
EMMINA DE NEGRI

The construction of the Mura Nuove (New Walls) and the Molo Nuovo (New Wharf) were large-scale projects of the 1630s and 1640s commissioned by the government of the Genoese Republic. The speed with which they were built and the involvement of all the citizenry were a clear indication of the will to assert the power of the city-state in a European context. From Punta della Lanterna, the jetty stretches out to protect the harbour from the libeccio (south-west) wind, whereas the walls rise up to Monte Peralto (512 m), the highest point of the limestone cliffs which enclose the basin in which the city grew.

Between the walls, which in 1536 had largely redefined the limits of the medieval city and the extensive sweep of the new ones, there had been few nuclei to stimulate building and development. Nor, between the 17th and 18th centuries, do we find projects for a new urban expansion into the area which the new walls annexed to the city. For this reason, the area was used solely for the construction of isolated villas or family houses which were traditional alternatives to a city dwelling.

Thanks to its strategic position overlooking the sea and the access road, the area to the west of the city was chosen by Andrea Doria in the 1520s for the construction of his palace - a princely mansion - with a private mooring by the sea and a relationship with the landscape which was "more of control than enjoyment" (Poleggi), despite the broad sweep of gardens.

The land towards the hills no less than by the sea saw the sprouting of houses which rose in the 17th and 18th centuries to reflect the living habits of a small emerging class which invested its capital in prestigious buildings.

Until the 19th century, the territory was arranged along the lines of the crôse (narrow alleys between the high walls of the houses) which, starting from the gateways of the walls or the jetties and coast road, rose from the city towards the hills. Along them, we find the occasional monastery, the only structures to date back to medieval times. It is impossible now to recognize the simpler houses which rose alongside the crôse behind the high walls which hid them from curious eyes. We can only see here and there some large suburban houses which are still recognizable thanks to their setting in the landscape. The greatest of these is Andrea Doria's house and, in the same area of Fassolo, that of Di Negro "dello scoglietto" with the gardens that used to stretch from the seashore almost to the top of the hill. Further uphill are Villa Pallavicini called "delle Peschiere" in Via San Bartolomeo degli Armeni, Villa Balbi (later renamed Villa Groppallo) at Zerbino and Villa De Mari (later renamed Villa Gruber) next to the Circonvallazione (ring road). This last is a museum and the house and gardens are open to the public. These are houses which survived intact thanks to their precious and exceptional nature; more modest houses were eventually restructured and poor town and country dwellings were simply pulled down.

It is only in the mid 19th century that the city began to expand towards the hills. The growth of the merchant class echoing the city's economic revival, the propensity towards investment in real estate and the consequent need to find new areas for houses lie at the origin of this process. The new roads (Via Assarotti and Via Caffaro were approved in 1851, Via Palestro in 1859) which climbed the mountain from the edge of town and were flanked by regular, monumental blocks of houses were used exclusively for residential use. Only exceptionally would a lot beside a road be destined for a non-residential function, but this was usually a church (such as the Immacolata in Via Assarotti) or a theatre (the Paganini in Via Caffaro) and thus meeting points for communion or culture; all commercial ventures were excluded. The palazzi adopted a classicizing style and were regular and symmetrical in plan, in conformity with that air of decorum which typifies in a positive manner so many 19th-century towns.

By the end of the century, the increase in population imposed the adoption of new models. The breakthrough came with the Circonvallazione a Monte (upper ring road), one of the most important and successful achievements of the urbanisation of Genoa. Houses were to have been built only along the uphill side of the ring road. An aim for a still classical unity inspired the careful regulation of the road. The continuous rows of trees, the public gardens, the squares and the belvederes complete the impression of a "local" road open to the view over town and sea. Even though it was not created just to link up various points of panoramic interest with a romantic itinerary (as in Florence's contemporary Viale dei Colli), and even though it does not aim to mark the flight of the city into the country, the special location and panoramic qualities make it into a feature of great landscape interest.

The character of the buildings reflects the taste of the period in which they were built. Those in the first stretch (1865-80) were more modest and preoccupied with the general "decorum" of the road than the individuality of the single house. Those of the second phase were more the expression of a revival in eclecticism with highly ornamented buildings. Here, alongside architects of renown such as Coppedè, we find the work of such as Riccardo Haupt who was more closely inspired by Renaissance models, or the numerous examples of work by Giuseppe Tallero whose buildings are marked by a dignified eclecticism which was up to any situation. It is the same entrepreneurial middle class, involved in service industries or shipping, which sees a safe investment for its capital and so pushed for the development of areas further uphill from the start of the 20th century, often adopting the formula of building cooperatives. However, the absence of a new project for the city, and the rebuttal of suggestions to build another corniche road to add to the Circonvallazione, caused the growth of the city to become ever more chaotic, without the formation of new urban focal points and the destruction of old routes.

The new houses on the ridges loom overhead more than the ancient "Castelletto". And yet disdain for the casermoni or barracks destroying the profile of the ridges underlies the construction in 1886 of Captain De Albertis' castle on the remains of the bastion of Montegalletto. The regret for the beauties of medieval Genoa which were little by little disappearing from the memories of its citizens, and the almost Romantic desire to transfer symbols loaded with history to the new house were at the base of this project. Set in a dominant position on the edge of a ridge, Castello De Albertis and, later, Castello Mackenzie rose above the surrounding houses and took on a status as a symbol and a benchmark for the design of the whole city.

This does not intend to be a nostalgic call for unrealizable revivals; the aim is simply to underline the need for the relationship between architecture and land and for care to be taken over the "place", especially in Genoa where this had been done positively in the past but which in recent expansions had been blithely ignored. The expansion of the city and the construction of roads in this century have altered the original urban pattern more radically along the sea and in the Fassolo quarter than in the higher parts of the city. Behind Palazzo Doria, the recently widened Via San Benedetto preserves the marks of the old road (only really usable by traffic from the 19th century; before this, even passengers were moved by boat through the port). The construction of the Genoa-Turin railway (1854) brought about the first large-scale damage, particularly destroying important gardens.

Grandiose projects such as the excavation of the San Benigno hill (1930) for a more direct link between the city and the west, the widening of roads and the construction of the maritime station, have definitively altered the physiognomy of the zone and made it harder to gain a sense of continuation between past and present because of the excessive contrasts between the two.

ITINERARY
FIRST ROUTE: FROM PIAZZA CORVETTO
TO THE CIRCONVALLAZIONE A MONTE (UPPER RING ROAD)

Created in 1873 and the meeting point of the new roads, Piazza Corvetto is happily dominated by earlier gardens: to the west lies Villetta Di Negro, built in the 19th century with little waterfalls and artificial grottoes, as befitted an important "literary garden"; to the east the esplanade of Acquasola. Despite the traffic, one can perceive the successful integration with the landscape and the lively theatrical setting of the buildings.

From Piazza Corvetto to Piazza Manin. Along the line of Via Assarotti, there is a view of the medieval tower of Palazzo Ducale. Thus begins a vision of the city which is completely the opposite to that offered from the sea (or from the flyover).

The Circonvallazione a Monte (ring road) begins in Piazza Manin and follows the sinuous movement of the promontories and valleys. It is linked to the city by lifts and a funicular railway and is important for its panoramic viewpoints. Although planned in 1865, the stretch from Piazza Manin to San Bartolomeo was only built in 1880. It required more excavations and so higher embankments which interrupted old routes, but it was indispensable for linking up with Via Assarotti and the gateways of the city towards Bisagno.

With small detours from the ring road, one reaches charming points along the old crôse - Salita Multedo, Salita San Rocchino and Salita Sant'Anna - which survived at the edges of the modern districts. Here, it is still possible to admire the beauty of drystone walls, the disposition of bricks in the passatoie of the crôse, the details in some plaster work, in fountains, in iron handrails: materials in which time has impressed its mark in a unique, irreproducible manner.

A fundamental viewpoint is that of the "Castelletto". It is no longer a 15th-century citadel, demolished and rebuilt so many times to dominate the city, but an esplanade with regular, 19th-century buildings, and a belvedere (Belvedere Montaldo, top station of the lift from Portello) with a magnificent view over the medieval town gathered around the inlet of the harbour and buzzing with movement amongst the luminous greys of the slate roofs, and over the modern town.

The more recent part of the Circonvallazione starts from Castelletto and stretches to Castello De Albertis, with important detours to take in 17th-century monasteries. From the castle, descend into the Valle di Carbonara to the Albergo dei Poveri, a monumental 18th-century building of great architectural interest.

THE FORT ITINERARY

Another fundamental itinerary is that of the Forts, from Porta di San Bartolomeo, near Piazza Manin, to the San Bernardino Tower and as far as Fort Sperone on the top of the Peralto hill, which reveals splendid architecture and at the same time the urban systemization of the walls.

99
Church of Santa Maria Immacolata
VIA ASSAROTTI
BUS 33, 34, 36

Pietro Gambaro, involved in the construction of the first stretch of Via Assarotti which began in 1852, decided to leave one lot aside for a church rather than a dwelling. In 1856, he commissioned the design from Domenico Cervetto who planned a church similar to that of the Gesù: a basically centric structure with a high dome and a façade of clear Neoclassical style. Construction was interrupted by the death of Gambaro and Cervetto, but began again in 1864 with plans by Maurizio Dufour. The purity of the Neoclassical forms were replaced by elaborate neo-Renaissance decoration which gradually became ever heavier in an attempt to gain greater monumentality, all of which contrasted with the lack of sense of space and the relationship with the road and adjacent buildings.

The church opened for worship in 1873. At the beginning of the 20th century, the façade was still being built, following yet another variant to the design by B. Pesce. The interior was also richly decorated.

The chapel of San Giuseppe, to the right of the transept, was still that designed by Dufour. Other parts, such as the presbytery or the Cappella del Rosario, at the end of the left-hand nave, were decorated with precious marble, semi precious stones and bronze. [E. D. N.]

Villa Pallavicino delle Peschiere
via San Bartolomeo degli Armeni 5
bus 33, 34, 36

This suburban residence of Tobia Pallavicino was built in about 1556. The house, surrounded by a vast park which was cut up in 1880 to open Via Peschiera, formed a unified complex with an axis of symmetry aligned with that facing the sea. In the design of the scenic terraced garden, where the rich nymphaeum and grotto with mosaic of many materials can be seen, we can see the hand of G. B. Castello, 'il Bergamasco'. The house clearly echoes Peruzzi's Farnesina and appears the product of an encounter by the patron and architect with Roman culture. Its closest relation in the Genoese context is Villa Giustiniani Cambiaso in Albaro, from which it differs in its greater articulation of the ground plan.

The division of the fronts into three which is typical of Alessi is clearly stressed in the north façade through the extension of the wings to the point that they become two avant-corps. In the south façade, on the other hand, the sides project slightly. The interior layout is articulated around the loggia-hall-loggia model on the ground floor and loggia-salon on the piano nobile. The decoration, produced by il Bergamasco with some work by Luca Cambiaso is one of the most significant examples of Genoese fresco of the 16th century. Restored by Michele Canzio in 1848, it was damaged in the last war and restored with the roof being renovated using reinforced concrete. [I. F.]

101
Gioventù del Littorio School (Faculty of Arts)
CORSO MONTE GRAPPA 39
BUS 49

Built by the engineer and speculator C. Nardi Greco and designed by L. Castello, the building was erected in 1937, following a series of interesting projects from the family firm for holiday camps provided free (1934-37) and a commitment to build homes.

The regime's commission enabled the planners to produce an elegant compromise between Rationalism and Art Deco. The highly regular V-shape which separates the boy's and girl's sections of the school is characterized by the concave fronts facing the road which highlight the convex form of the terminal hall. The latter is glazed to its full height on the short side and is the most important aesthetic feature of the structure. The layout seems to recall the basilica form where the hall corresponds to the apse.

Of some interest is the careful use of light. The cold light that penetrates from the high translucent windows seems to arrive to the observer via a series of parallel lines traced on the floor (originally of linoleum - the furniture, too, being faced in the same material). An overall examination of the project cannot ignore the relationship with the agricultural and sports equipment below which integrated with the educational scopes of the regime. [C. B.]

Castello Mackenzie
VIA C. CABELLA 15
BUS 64

One of Gino Coppedè's earliest and most well-known designs, the castle was built between 1896 and 1906 for Evans Mackenzie. "A king's caprice" or "architectural dream", it magnificently and eloquently revealed the elements which make its author easily recognizable and succinctly termed "Coppedè's style" by his contemporaries. In strict accord with the patron's desire for self-celebration, and permeated with admiration for medieval and Renaissance art, the architect, "poet of architecture, lord of decoration", became the "resuscitator of ancient castles", reinterpreted in a free, skillful manner free of any philological intent.
Surrounded by a park and protected by a perimeter wall with crenellated towers, the castle, which is in part a rebuilding of an earlier house, comprises a central part of three floors with a juxtaposed wing, surmounted by a tower which recalls the Torre del Mangia in Siena. A masterly play of evocative effects, a succession of pinnacles, walkways with embrasures, loggias and a thick weave of decorative elements embrace the building without any sense of uniformity, whilst in the interior, frescos, designs, majolica and wrought iron seem to remove the walls altogether in a sort of fantastic *horror vacui*. Sold by the heirs in 1939, and used for the most varied roles, after years of neglect it became the property in 1986 of the Novecento Corporation; it is now being restored and will be used as a museum and exhibition space. [I. F.]

103
Villa De Mari Gruber (American Museum)
CORSO SOLFERINO 27
BUS 33

Bearing many marks of later additions, the house was built in the second half of the 16th century for Stefano De Mari and was perhaps designed by Giovanni Ponzello. The original structure, of which only the small tower and the nymphaeum-basin remain unchanged, featured a U-shaped layout. In order to adjust the hall, stairs and garden to the various levels of the uneven terrain, use was made of other examples of contemporary buildings on the uphill side of Strada Nuova. The layout of the rooms did not differ from that used traditionally, with the central room used as hall on the ground floor and as a salon on the piano nobile. Towards the end of the 18th century, the first important modifications were made to bring the house "up-to-date". Within, there was the creation of the so-called *sala delle colonne* (hall of columns) - a very high room illuminated by ten thermal windows - whereas on the outside the present neo-Palladian façade was built. Passing into the hands of Adolfo Gruber in 1856, the house underwent further transformations which compromised all of the already altered 16th-century layout. The most evident changes were the replacement of the masonry stairs with others in wood and the creation of a heavy coffered ceiling in the piano nobile salon. The addition of the two glazed side-wings on the first floor date back to the first decade of the 20th century (the house then belonged to F. M. Perrone), as does the construction of the elegant marble staircase which leads from the garden to the piano nobile. [L. D.]

104
Church of Sant'Anna
PIAZZA SANT'ANNA 8
BUS 33

This is the church of the first Discalced Carmelite monastery to be built outside Spain and was founded in 1584 on the Bachernia hill by Father Nicolò Doria. The church dates from 1586 and faces a small square filled with trees, with cobble and brick paving reached from a *crôsa* (narrow alley) and a set of steps which start from the Circonvallazione a Monte (upper ring road).

The façade rises to a single point and has a large white marble entrance surmounted by a bas-relief depicting the "Holy Family". The rich fresco decoration, recorded until the beginning of this century, has been lost; it used to imitate a rusticated surface, metopes and volutes framing the Cross.

The original interior layout with a single nave and altars set against the side walls was radically altered in the first half of the 17th century with the construction of new chapels and the replacement of the wooden trusses with a barrel vault. Of the interior decoration undertaken in two phases - in the mid 17th century and in the mid 18th century - stucco rocaille motifs still survive in the side chapels, but most was covered in the 20th century with fresco. The high altar, commissioned by the Cattaneo family from the workshop of Francesco Schiaffino, is surmounted by a sculpture of "Saint Anna and the Virgin Mary as a child". [I. F.]

105
Ponte Caffaro
VIA CAFFARO; CORSO PAGANINI
BUS 33, 76

The bridge spans the valley of Bachernia between Corso Paganini and Corso Magenta with a grandiose central arch and two smaller lateral arches. Via Caffaro below, like Via Palestro, another valley-bottom road, climbs to the ring-road level with two long, symmetrical sets of stairs, which provide a dramatic setting for the city as it rises.

The Bisagno aqueduct passes above the arches on the Via Caffaro side. Built as a canal and almost entirely on arches, the old aqueduct was already functioning in the 12th century and was extended and repaired over the years, becoming an integral part of the urban scene.

The construction of the Circonvallazione (ring road), whose surface followed the old aqueduct, resulted in the destruction of much of the old structure, although this was partly rebuilt at the heads of the valleys. Other parts were swallowed up by the urban changes which followed, but sections of bridges, canals and traces of the conduit are still visible behind San Bartolomeo degli Armeni, in Passo dell'Acquedotto and in Salita San Gerolamo. The new bridges partly reproduce the effect of the old aqueduct. [E. D. N.]

106
Sanctuary of the Madonnetta (Santa Maria Assunta)
SALITA MADONNETTA
BUS 377

The church, better known as "La Madonnetta", stands alongside the steep *crôsa* which links the city and the 17th-century walls. Founded in 1695 by P. Carlo Giacinto di Santa Maria, a Discalced Augustinian and "inexhaustible bastion" of the faith, it was planned by A. M. Ricca (1660-1725), the most original and creative member of a dynasty of master builders originating from Imperia and working in and around Genoa between the end of the 17th and the start of the 18th century. The building was consecrated, though not yet complete, in 1706; its exterior reveals a simple, spare design with only the façade showing any trace of fresco decoration, namely *trompe l'œil* architectural motifs. The ground plan is an extended central octagon with a lowered dome and is divided into three chapels on each side, the central one of which stretches to full height. The large, luminous main space ends in a spectacular play of steps leading to the presbytery which is raised higher than the level of the church itself and to the polygonal area below (frescos in the vault by B. Guidobono, 1707). At an even lower level, finally, one finds the chapel of the Pietà, a small crypt decorated with elegant Rococo stucco; this can also be seen from an opening set into the floor of the church itself. The churchyard, paved in black and white cobbles based on the design of the octagon and designed by B. Storace, was laid out in 1732. In the first half of the 18th century, the internal decoration was completed. [G. S.]

107
Sanctuary of Nostra Signora di Loreto
PIAZZA OREGINA
BUS 35, 40

The earliest settlement of the Observant Minorite Fathers on the Oregina hill almost certainly dates back to 1635. The construction of the monastery church can be dated to 1650-55 and is laid out around a small chapel, later encompassed within the building, which reproduced the Santa Casa di Loreto (demolished in 1928) on a smaller scale. It was probably because of this earlier structure that it was decided to adopt a central ground plan (extended octagon) which results in a large, luminous space roofed with a pendentive vault which shows clear analogies with other contemporary Genoese examples.

The façade is unusually tall in order to reflect the dominating position of the sanctuary in the urban landscape and was built in 1707. The search for spectacular effects is underlined by the increase in decoration in the upper level, pierced by a large serliana flanked by paired Corinthian pilasters which frame semi-circular niches and ending in a scalloped pediment. Within, flat Doric pilasters are placed regularly along the walls and extend into the arches of the smaller vaults.

Of particular significance is the bond between the sanctuary and the town, renewed for many years by the annual ceremonious visit of the Doge, in memory of the liberation from the Austrians in 1747 thanks to the intercession of the Virgin; this costume ritual was brought to life again during the Risorgimento and is still observed by the mayor every 10 December. [G. S.]

Albergo dei Poveri
PIAZZALE E. BRIGNOLE 2
BUS 39, 40

The edifice rises at the centre of the Carbonara valley which it blocks off with its bulk. The origins of the building, significantly recorded in documents as "impregnable fortress", "basilica of mercy", "palace of compassion", lie in the tradition for private, lay charity which developed between the 15th and 16th centuries, then institutionalized in the Ufficio dei Poveri in 1539. The project itself was begun at the behest of the Genoese aristocrat, E. Brignole, with the intention of gathering together into one large building all of the town's various institutions, which had by then become insufficient. Traditionally, the design is attributed to a collaborative effort by four local architects (G. Gandolfo, G. B. Ghiso, P. A. Corradi, G. B. Torriglia), but S. Scaniglia, who produced some drawings, must not be excluded either. The ground plan - a large square enclosing four courtyards - culminates at the centre in a church, the architectural and spiritual fulcrum of the building ("soul of the whole complex"). This was not an innovative solution as it was representative of other hospital architecture as typified by the 15th-century Ospedale Maggiore in Milan by Filarete, who was also connected with the project for the Escurial in Madrid (1586); thanks to the close links between Genoa and Spain, the project for the Escurial proved to be the closest example for the Albergo. Building began in 1656 and continued in various phases until the beginning of the 18th century when the plan of the western part was modified with the reduction of the two courtyards to rectangles. The imposing front, closed off by massive corner towers (the one on the left dates from 1835), reveals a central part in which six pairs of giant Corinthian pilasters "in verdigris colour" supported by a rusticated base, bear a high entablature which is interrupted at the centre by a small pediment with frescos (now lost) by G. B. Carlone (1665). Two sets of stairs with three flights each located at the sides of the hall within (with a tent vault) lead to the spectacular upper hall from which the long corridors running parallel to the front of the building lead off. The large, grandiloquent statues of the founders and benefactors, commissioned from the Lombard G. B. Barberini, transform these solemn, severe spaces into an impressive, thrilling theatrical set which sumptuously celebrates the *erga pauperes* charity. The church is set in line with the hall; it is not a chapel reserved for internal use but a grandiose building which had parish functions from 1668. It is flanked to right and left respectively by the oratories for women and men. Under the dome, to crown a sumptuous altar by F. M. Schiaffino (1751), stands the statue of the Virgin executed by Puget (1666-68) for E. Brignole and given to the Albergo by him. At present, it is only in part used by the Istituto Brignole which continues the work of the old Albergo, and in the future it is intended for use by the university (project, E. D. Bona) which will respect the original layout and revitalise this area. [G. S.]

109
Andrea Doria Maritime Station
VIADOTTO C. IMPERIALE
BUS 1, 2, 3, 7, 8, 18, 19, 20, 30, 34

The station was commissioned in 1933 from Luigi Vietti by the Consorzio Autonomo del Porto to provide a suitable landing stage for the new transatlantic liners. It is only slightly later in date than the nearby Ponte dei Mille (inaugurated in 1930) to which it is linked by the viaduct and with which it comprises an overall unity only in terms of function; in terms of style, they are very different. The Andrea Doria station adopts an explicitly avant-garde style which is stressed by the widespread use of "modern" materials such as reinforced concrete, glass and concrete-framed glass blocks. The building has two storeys and features a main entrance protected by a projecting cantilever roof to shelter any motor vehicles arriving. Inside, the hall leads into the waiting room and passport control offices; from here, one passes into a broad corridor and onto the landing terrace, connected by a spiral staircase to the upper terrace. The simple, sober furnishings were also designed by Vietti whose care for details is made evident in the colours used to decorate the various rooms which varied according to class of travellers, and in the flooring, on which are indicated lines to guide the pedestrian traffic. The building summarises and reproposes features which are typical of the European Rationalist school. In particular, the elliptical tower which crowns the main structure and the series of piers projecting along the landing terrace recall the architecture of ships in using one of the metaphors most used by Rationalist architects. [L. D.]

110
Ex Municipal Technical Offices
VIA AMBA ALAGI 3/5
BUS 1, 2, 3, 7, 8, 18, 19, 20, 30, 34

The building designed by Robaldo Morozzo della Rocca (1952/58) and originally intended for use as a hotel, closes off the triangle created by the junction of Via San Benedetto and Via Adua and defines the end of the Palazzo Doria garden at Fassolo. The structure comprises one central element which is slightly convex to the west and a lower arcaded element to the east which is not aligned to the main front but constitutes another front for the road.

The main body is irregular and long in shape and comprises a block of three floors above ground (and another three basement floors which to the west form a front giving on to the lower Via Mura degli Zingari). Faced in Finale stone, it presents a regularly-placed series of windows which maintain the sense of continuity of the wall surface. On the other hand, the two top floors present an alternation of solids and voids: the plastered wall with small vertical windows gives way to over/sized loggias with deeply-inset glazing.

Within, the design of the two identical, spiral staircases seems to break free from the rational rigour of the overall project to provide a personal expressive feature to which Morozzo always paid particular attention. [M. P. G.]

111
Villa Di Negro Rosazza (lo "Scoglietto")
PIAZZA DI NEGRO 3
BUS 1, 2, 3, 7, 8, 18, 19, 20, 30, 32, 34

At the end of the 15th century, the Di Negro family owned a house at the foot of the "Scoglietto" hill. This was later enlarged and further refurbished between the 16th and 17th centuries by Orazio Di Negro with decoration by Andrea Ansaldo and Agostino Tassi. By then the property of Gio Luca Durazzo, the house was completely restructured once more in 1787 with a design by E. Andrea Tagliafichi. The 16th century house was almost a cube in form with loggias at the corners and a richly decorated façade. Tagliafichi's design, one of the most important examples of Neoclassicism in Genoa, saw the filling in of the loggias and a radical change in the main façade, with a central, slightly projecting element crowned by a tympanum supporting slightly projecting statues and wings set much further back. Tagliafichi also redesigned the park uphill and the garden, with natural backdrops, niches, fountains and a celebrated astronomical observatory.

Within, some obvious irregularities in the ground plan reveal the successive rebuilding of the house. From the salon on the piano nobile, one reaches the 16th-century nymphaeum of considerable beauty. After passing through the hands of Rolla Rosazza, it became the property of the Genoa City Council and now houses offices. The garden on the seaward side was reduced to allow for the passage of the railway, altering the famous relationship between house and landscape; the park on the uphill side survives as a public park. [I. F.]

112
Houses of the Opera Pia De Ferrari Galliera
VIA VENEZIA 40/50
BUS 32, 38

These three groups of working-class homes formed part of a larger series of philanthropic initiatives promoted by the Duchi di Galliera in Genoa. These were built in Via della Fenice, Via del Lagaccio and Via Venezia and they became the prototypes for many later, similar projects in Genoa and elsewhere. Designed in 1873 by Cesare Parodi, university lecturer, politician and later designer of the Ospedale Galliera, the houses were probably built between 1875 (Via della Fenice) and 1879 (Via Venezia). In order to assess the buildings, it is important to refer to the context of a period in which the idea of working-class housing provoked considerable controversy. They were built after a long period of debate and administrative measures which for a long time produced no results and then saw the rise in growth of cooperatives. Each group of houses comprises two long wings varying in length from 62.5 m (Via della Fenice) to 72 m (Via del Lagaccio) and in depth from 10 to 12 m, each separated from each other by long courtyards closed off at each end by portals resembling city gates.

The ground plan of the apartments is everywhere identical; each is separated into four rooms (plus kitchen and tiny lavatory) and prefigures a sort of *existenz minimum ante litteram*. The layout of the stairs is interesting as it subdivides the whole block into smaller, more distinct units. [C. B.]

113
Church of San Marcellino
VIA BOLOGNA
BUS 32

Located in a densely populated area on the hills behind San Teodoro, the markedly 20th-century church of San Marcellino (designed by L. C. Daneri, 1932-35), contrasts sharply with the religious architecture traditionally built in Genoa in the adoption of a central ground plan.

Situated on one of the bends of Via Bologna, the base of the church levels out the contours of the hillside and provides a surface for the church itself whose main entrance is on the upper square. A brief flight of steps leads to the full-height pronaos, defined by eight piers stretching up to the level of the base of the dome which is a thin membrane of reinforced concrete produced by P. L. Nervi, crowned by a small stone lantern. The almost cylindrical main structure features a series of concave and convex, load-bearing niches with the wall being faced in white Finale stone and the windows stretching to full height.

The interior is sombre and almost bare, with no frescos or other decoration. A tall, wooden crucifix, suspended above the main altar against the light which enters from the apse window, provides a sense of drama. The bell tower, located on the square near the main body of the church, was only finished in 1953. A prism with a rectangular base, it has a smooth surface pierced only by thin, elongated windows which are repeated rhythmically on the four sides and provide the decorative feature of the uppermost chamber. [M. P. G.]

114
Sanctuary of San Francesco da Paola (Sailors' shrine)
SALITA SAN FRANCESCO DA PAOLA
BUS 1, 2, 3, 4, 32, 38

The origins of the sanctuary, situated on the upper slopes of the Caldetto on the Granarolo hill, go back to the 15th century when a community of Padri Minimi built a monastery and church dedicated to Mary and Christ. In the second half of the 16th century, the church was rebuilt larger and dedicated also to San Francesco da Paola, patron saint of sailors. Further internal restructuring concerning the presbytery and choir was undertaken in the 17th century by Pietro Antonio Corradi and Luca Carlone at the behest of Veronica Spinola.

The body of the church faces east-west and opens on to a tree-lined square offering a wide view over the city and the whole gulf of Genoa; this has always been a famous viewpoint used by landscapists.

There is no main façade because of the presence of a projecting element which functions as hall and which preserves a rich collection of seafaring *ex votos* evidencing centuries of worship. The interior, with nave and two aisles and no transept, has maintained its 16th-century layout. Only the nave (with barrel vault) provides passage as the raised aisles were transformed into a series of independent chapels roofed with hemispherical domes. The chapel dedicated to San Francesco da Paola, built around the middle of the 18th century, is one of the most noted works by the sculptor, Francesco Schiaffino. [I. F.]

115
Villa Tomati
SALITA DEGLI ANGELI 70
BUS 66

Located on the Angeli hill near the old road linking the coast with the Valle del Polcevera, the villa finds itself today in an area marked deeply by recent, untidy speculation. It is an imposing building of late-Gothic taste (15th century), and is considered an almost unique example for understanding the development of Genoese family houses between the Middle Ages and the present day. It preserves the original body of the building: a massive element with an external side loggia of double height which, set asymmetrically, constitutes the main feature of the whole structure and represents one of the first cases of mediation between building and environment.

On the ground floor, the loggia features pointed arches and cross-vaulting whereas, on the first floor, it has black-and-white banded columns with square capitals and an exceptional wooden roof of pyramid shape with traces of painted decoration on the beams.

The house underwent some restructuring in the 18th century; the salon being affected, a chapel also built and the interior decoration enriched. Frescos were added in the mid 19th century. [I. F.]

Fort Diamante
FUNICULAR FOR THE RIGHI

Fort Diamante is the highest fort in Genoa, being located at 670 m above sea-level on the most elevated point of the ridge between Val Polcevera and Val Bisagno. It was designed in 1747 after Austrian troops had occupied the summit in the assault on the Mura Nuove.

No less than nine years of controversy and changes passed between the engineer Jacques De Sicre's initial plan and the actual building. Work finally began in 1756 at the behest of the Magistrato delle Fortificazioni, thanks to a donation from Giacomo Filippo Durazzo, and lasted until 1758, when the fort was completed with some modifications agreed between De Sicre, Pierre De Cotte and the marshall, Frederic Flobert.

It was in practice a barracks on several floors set within a star-shaped rampart. In 1800, the fort was besieged by the Austrians and defended by General Bertrand who also had under his command the poet, Ugo Foscolo, who was wounded there. Later, the fort was enlarged and reinforced with a further rampart by the Genio Militare Sardo (Sardinian Engineer Corps) in the years 1811-20, and the barracks covered with a flat roof able to provide further firing stations. A few decades later, once it had lost its strategic importance, the fort was abandoned. [M. M.]

117
Fort Sperone
FUNICULAR FOR THE RIGHI

The fort rises from the northern end of the Mura Nuove on Monte Peralto at a height of 512 m, and at the point of intersection between the two main lengths of wall which follow Val Polcevera and Val Bisagno. This was the site of a *bastida* (1319), and of a later fortress built in the 16th century together with its neighbours, Castellaccio and Rocca delle Forche (now the Torre Specola). Later again, there was a reinforced bastion with watchtowers and embrasures and a single fortified barracks on three floors with barrel vaulted ceilings and a ditch and rampart next to the Mura Nuove (1633).

The fort was enlarged during the Napoleonic years and under Sardinian rule, becoming an autonomous element in the outermost defensive system of the city, together with the Diamante, Puin and Due Fratelli forts. From 1826, it became a large barracks with defences able to withstand cannons, boasting ten strong, square casemates. Later, further casemates and watchtowers were added with loopholes and embrasures, giving it its present aspect of articulated masses converging upon the stepped towers set against the ancient bastion. [M. M.]

118
San Bernardino and Quezzi Towers
VIA CARSO; VIA L. LORIA
BUS 64

Going from Porta di San Bernardino towards Fort Sperone, on the ridge one comes across the San Bernardino Tower beneath the bastion of the same name (see photograph). This is one of the towers planned for the perimeter of the western walls by the Genio Militare Sardo (Sardinian Military Engineers) after 1818, forming part of the new "isolated towers" defensive scheme proposed by such military engineers as De Sicre, De Cotte, Matteo Vinzoni, Michele Codeviola and others following the experience of the Austrian siege of 1747. Built of stone in 1821 with a diameter of 12 m and a height of 14 m in the form of a steeply tapering cylinder pierced by long, slim embrasures, it is divided into three floors for clearly defined defensive purposes and with specific openings for each firearm. Perfectly preserved and restored, with its clearly geometric lines, it stresses the expressiveness of functional architecture.

Torre Quezzi is the only eastern tower and rises on a plateau at 321 m above sea-level about 700 m from the fort of the same name. It was built around 1822 and designed by Colonel De Andreis. It shares the same characteristics as the San Bernardino tower: a cylindrical, tapering body here measuring 15 m in diameter and 17 m in height. [M. M.]

V.
VAL BISAGNO
PAOLO CEVINI

The Bisagno valley cuts deeply into the Appenines (as far as Passo della Scoffera, some 30 km from the sea) and in its lower stretch (Foce) defines the historical limits of the eastern side of the city. In the present administrative division of areas, however, the Foce quarter belongs to the Levante borough and not to Val Bisagno, almost as though there were an intent to mark the continuity between the walled city and its "natural" expansion. This was initially extended to the alluvial plain on the left bank of the Bisagno torrent, along the old road of Ponte Pila (corresponding to the line of Via XX Settembre and Corso Buenos Aires). Further south, it developed in line to an orthogonal grid set out in the Town-planning and expansion scheme drawn up by the City of Genoa (1877).

Uphill from the railway (built towards the end of the 1860s), which cuts a swathe through the built-up area and across the valley, are the densely-populated quarters of San Fruttuoso and Marassi. Here, urbanization came later than at Foce and was more episodic to start with, first developing along the inner Corso Sardegna (around 1890) and then moving up the eastern slopes of Paverano (Via Contubernio G. B. D'Albertis). During these same years, Piazza Manzoni was being rebuilt, taking its tone from the civic dignity of the façade of the municipal palace, and from here building spread up the left bank (Via del Piano), occupying the narrow plateau of Marassi and little by little nibbling at the slopes of Quezzi, which were surrounded by building along the Fereggiano. The services for this new urban area also came to be more closely defined in these years with a view to ever closer metropolitan integration. This had already been anticipated before 1874 (the year the six boroughs of the Bisagno were annexed: Foce, San Francesco di Albaro, San Martino di Albaro, San Fruttuoso, Marassi and Staglieno) with a series of projects, some of them of architectural importance, such as the large cemetery (designed by Barabino, 1837), or of strict utilitarian significance, such as the hostel for the poor and the prison (Marassi), the gasometer and tram repair yard (Gavette), the rifle range (Quezzi) and rubbish dump (Volpara). Other vital structures associated with the provision of foodstuffs, including the vegetable and fruit market of Corso Sardegna and the slaughterhouse of Ca' de Pitta were to follow later in the 1920s, thereby confirming it as the city's traditional source in this field. Although some important examples of residential building must not be ignored, especially in the lower part of the valley (the most famous example being Villa Imperiale di Terralba, and nor must we overlook the 16th-century Centurione Musso Piantelli and Saredo Parodi at Marassi and the 17th-century Borsotti Ayroli Franzone at San Fruttouso), the pre-industrial landscape was marked above all by intensive agriculture (kitchen gardens, together with soft fruits in flatter areas and orchards, vineyards and stock farming on the slopes). All was geared to the local Genoese market, and the valley was the city's main source of food. A. Giustiniani described the Bisagno in his Descrittione of 1537 thus: "it enjoys a positive position in relation to the sun and pleasant, salubrious air. Its men are strapping in body and lively in spirit; it yields excellent wine, perfect milk, various, precious fruits, all of which [...] appear as nothing in comparison to the convenience of washing laundry white and drying them which the valley provides the city with and the reception of all the refuse which comes from building sites, of which the town is full." Thus, even in the 16th century, this dependence upon the city is shown not only by the provision of labour and products of the earth, but also with the supply of services such as the washing and drying of laundry and the preparation of tips for refuse from the town's building sites. As well as this, the valley has always been an important link with the hinterland (with Val Trebbia and Piacenza), even though clearly less so than the main roads to the west of Voltri (Valle Stura, Novi and Alessandria) and, above all, that of Polcevera (Valle Scrivia, Tortona and Milan). The historical "exit" from the town in the Val Bisagno area is still clearly recognizable near Brignole, although in transformations made from 1867, with the construction of the railway and Stazione Orientale in Piazza Brignole, and then with the opening of Via De Amicis (1907) and the erection of the new station in Piazza Giuseppe Verdi. The ancient road of San Vincenzo led through Porta Romana to the medieval villages outside the walls - to the Incrociati on the right bank and to Sant'Agata on the left bank - both of which had monastery-hospitals (of the Crucifers and Cistercians respectively, of which there is mention in 1191; traces of the second survive in the complex of the Augustinians of Sant'Agata). From Borgo Incrociati the road to Oltregiogo began: little more than a little track along the bed of the Bisagno, it was only improved for wheeled traffic by the Napoleonic authorities in 1809 (and extended to the Scoffera in 1850). The "Roman" road, on the other hand, crossed the Bisagno via the long bridge of Sant'Agata (medieval, originally with 28 arches, many of which were washed away in the floods of 1970) and so arrived at Sant'Agata and proceeded eastward via San Fruttuoso.

One structure which might be taken as representative of much of Val Bisagno's history thanks to its importance, and which provides a summary of the valley's landscape with its unified character, size and scale is the town's aqueduct. Mentioned in 1232, and since then extended and broadened in successive phases, it follows a route halfway up the hill some 20 km long from Via Burlando to the Presa, near the confluence with the Lentro. The structure shows that it was built using criteria and solutions that were avant-garde for their time, and it provides a benchmark for the best, most up-to-date technical culture over a period of centuries; almost all of the most famous local architects were at some point involved with the aqueduct: from Giovanni Aicardo to Giovanni Ponzello, from Pier Antonio Corradi to Andrea Vannone, Bartolomeo Bianco, Giacomo Brusco and Abbot Ximenes (the latter being involved in the complex building of the siphon bridge on the Geirato between 1770 and 1777, for which project even Vanvitelli was summoned). In the 19th century, it was Barabino and Resasco who were to finish the last great work: the aqueduct bridge over the Veilino at Staglieno.

ITINERARY
FROM BRIGNOLE TO STRUPPA

The visit begins in *Piazza G. Verdi*. High in the railway park of Brignole, one can see the 17th-century *Porta della Pila* (1633; uncertainly attributed to B. Bianco and moved here as a result of the building of Via XX Settembre). Immediately to the west of the station, take the underpass leading to *Borgo Incrociati*. Although in a deplorable state of neglect, the medieval features of the buildings are easily recognizable, and here and there are a few 16th-century houses. The itinerary continues along the route of the old, eastern "Roman" road which used to cross the bridge of Sant'Agata to reach the village of that name on the left bank. Today, the scene has changed dramatically following major work in the 19th and 20th centuries (Piazza Manzoni, Corso Sardegna, Piazza Giusti), but the continuation of the road can be seen in Via De Paoli. Alongside this stands the *church of Sant'Agata* (rebuilt in the 16th century and later modified again) next to the convent which was first Cistercian, then Augustinian and now belongs to the Maestre Pie di Sant'Agata. Still following the old road, pass through Via Toselli and Piazza Martinez to reach Via San Fruttuoso. To the left the "new" road starts climbing to Nostra Signora del Monte which rises above *Villa Borsotto Ayroli Franzone* to reach the *sanctuary of Nostra Signora del Monte*, which is notable above all for the roughly 6 hectares of woodland surrounding it - a real oasis in an area which is densely populated.

The monastery has kept its original 15th-century aspect, although the church itself is 17th-century and designed by G. B. Ghiso (1654-58). Returning to Via San Fruttuoso, still on the left there is the entrance to Villa Imperiale di Terralba, which is also immersed in what is left of its park. Return to Corso Sardegna and, passing from the San Fruttuoso district to that of Marassi, turn left into Corso De Stefanis. On the uphill side, at the top of Via Casata Centuriona stands the 16th-century Villa Saredo Parodi (the main façade overlooks Via Marassi behind).

On the opposite side, next to the Luigi Ferraris stadium (recently rebuilt to a plan by Gregotti Associati), rises the most important house, the 16th-century Villa Centurione Musso Piantelli (corner loggias and internal frescos by Semino and B. Castello). Go along Via Bertuccioni and Viale Centurione Bracelli to climb the slopes of the Quezzi and so reach the Ina Casa estate ("Biscione"), planned by Daneri and others from 1956. Following Via Loria, one can climb to the eastern fortifications (the Quezzi, Ratti, Richelieu and Santa Tecla forts, all of the 18th-19th centuries).

Return to the right bank of the Bisagno and climb the Montaldo stairs to reach Via Burlando; here, outside the walls of San Bartolomeo, runs the Genoa-Casella railway. At the end of Via Burlando begins the interesting and impressive acqueduct itinerary which follows the whole length of the structure (21 km, with the only interruption being the unusable bridge over the Geirato at Molassana) as far as Presa, near the confluence with the Lentro. Alternatively, take the road along the valley bottom (Via Bobbio) to arrive at the cemetery of Staglieno (G. B. Resasco, to an initial design by C. Barabino). Taking the form of the most typical "romantic" classicism, and decorated with much varied statuary, it provides one of the grandest expressions of the city's self-celebration.

Proceed along the right bank taking Via Piacenza to reach Molassana. Here, the recent building has filled the small area on the Bisagno and pushed against the hills to climb in a disorderly fashion up the valley of the Geirato (however, this last valley is still dominated by the grand siphon-bridge of the aqueduct, 1770). Midway and towards the top, the original rural layout has been preserved in the villages of San Gottardo, Pino Soprano, Pino Sottano and San Giacomo. Continuing along the bankside road, one finally arrives at Struppa. Standing at the confluence of the Rio Torbido, to the left can be seen Via di Creto which climbs to the abbey church of San Siro, the important medieval parish at the crossroads of the mountain routes for Valle Scrivia (which can be reached by following Strada di Creto) and for Val Trebbia (from Scoffera, along main road no. 45).

119
Fishermen's Houses
VIA DEI PESCATORI 1-11
BUS 12, 15, 31

Completed in 1938, the building takes its name from the original reason for the project, namely to provide homes for the families of fishermen who had traditionally always lived in the area of the Foce. The project, commissioned by the Istituto Fascista Case Popolari from the City Council's chief engineer, Mario Braccialini, for the technical part and from the architect, Luigi Vietti, for the architectural aspects, was realized in the area running from the covered part of the Bisagno (now Viale Brigate Partigiane), the embankment wall supporting Corso A. Saffi and the beach.
In this case, Vietti distanced himself from his early attachment to rationalism to give a more personal, almost rural touch to the working-class homes, a feature accentuated by the yellow and pink tones of the rustic plaster work. The building has just one volume and is today heavily compromised by the passage of the nearby flyover (1962-65) which interrupts its original relationship with the sea. The main façade is symmetrical with a series of arches along the ground floor alternating with massive buttresses. The three higher floors have apartments with three to five rooms and feature gallery balconies and a series of rhythmically interspersed windows.
The secondary front gives on to Via dei Pescatori and provides access to the building; here, the same sort of balconies are repeated. [F. G.]

Fiera del Mare

PIAZZALE J. F. KENNEDY; FOCE
BUS 12, 13, 31

In 1958 the Ente Autonomo della Fiera del Mare commissioned L. C. Daneri (with C. Chiari and M. Braccialini) to prepare a study for a fair complex to be built in one large operation on an artificial patch of land obtained by filling in part of the coast to the west of the mouth of the Bisagno. This was an area which had already hosted some exhibitions in the past (the Esposizione Colombiana in 1892 and the Esposizione di Marina e Igiene in 1914).

This thin sliver of land taken from the sea, which links the mouth of the Bisagno to the port, is today defined by the pillars of the raised highway and, enclosed by the customs area, it is filled with industrial activities associated with shipping and the harbour and is still somewhat separated from the rest of the city. Daneri's commission foresaw the planning of sketched out blocks and the unified design of the spaces within the fair grounds, whereas the architectural definition of each single building was left to the results of national competitions (some of which were disregarded in the event, as happened to Daneri and Nervi's project for the Palazzo dello Sport). During building and in the following years, many changes were made to the original project.

The plan divided the area into five main sites: the Palazzo dello Sport, of circular form; pavilion "D" which was square; pavilion "B" which was an elongated rectangle overlooking the sea, and pavilion "C", a modular building, set further inland below the embankment of Corso A. Saffi; to the west the Palazzo dei Congressi was built closing off the site towards the port, and a small square boatyard for leisure craft, to be used for marine exhibitions and today enlarged.

The ticket offices, also designed by Daneri and still in use today, define the perimeter of the area to the east.

The small pavilion designed for Iri by A. Mangiarotti dates from 1963, a year after the rest of the complex; it stands close to the Palazzo dello Sport. A light roof in sheet metal lies on four tapering columns to cover the slightly raised free exhibition space; beneath, there is a small auditorium. [M.P.G.]

121
San Pietro Restaurant
VIALE BRIGATE PARTIGIANE 19/21 A/R
BUS 12, 13, 31

This is one of Mario Labò's most noted and appreciated buildings, being enthusiastically described in its time in reviews such as *Casabella* and *Architettura*. Built between 1935 and 1938 for the Società Immobiliare San Pietro alla Foce, it was part of the development of the area after the Bisagno was covered over (1928/34), culminating in the building of Piazza Rossetti (1934/58). It is to this work by Daneri that the building is closely tied with its adhesion to the Rationalist school, as evidenced in its clear composition, in the care taken in selecting colours and materials and, above all, in its relationship with the surroundings, in this case, the sea. With the San Pietro restaurant, Labò came closer to organic architecture, despite his clear rationalist intent. The geometric rigour of the fronts are, in a certain sense, merely ideal: the façade is interrupted by two jutting terraces and long, sliding windows. Within, the light rooms, the staircase enclosed between two windows (recalling those at the Viipuri library by Aalto) and especially the central salon, set at a higher level than the side rooms, contribute to giving an idea of movement in the order. Unfortunately, many of these features are no longer visible today because of the changes wrought in the '60s with the opening of the raised highway. The ground floor, which once housed the bar and was, perhaps, the most carefully designed area, has been transformed into a petrol station. [L. D.]

122
Casa del Mutilato (Hostel for the Disabled)
CORSO A. SAFFI
BUS 12, 13, 15

The Casa del Mutilato and home to the Civico Museo delle Guerre d'Italia (Museum of Italian Wars; 1937-38) sprang from a concrete requirement from the Associazione dei Reduci Minorati and to render eternal the value of the "supreme sacrifice". For these "noble" causes, the Casa del Mutilato was financed by various associations, and the City Council itself provided the land for the building, an area to the south of Piazza della Vittoria, along the first part of Corso Saffi. It is set back from the road and behind it rises the green slope leading up to the walls of the Cappuccine. The construction company was Garbarino-Sciaccaluga, and the designer and director of works the Genoese architect, Eugenio Fuselli. The arrangement of the front overlooking Corso Aurelio Saffi reveals the various roles allotted to the rooms within. To the left, the Casa del Mutilato has four floors of rectangular windows set back from the line of the wall and enclosed in marble jambs in the same way as the main entrance which runs to the full height of the building. The surface of the walls feature bands of light and dark marble (red marble from Levanto). To the right, the façade is in grey stone and screens the administrative functions on the ground floor and the Museo delle Guerre d'Italia on the upper floors. A memorial in bronze representing the "Disabled" by E. Baroni stands in an open space to the left against a backdrop of green. [L. C.]

123
Piazza della Vittoria
BUS 15, 18, 19, 41, 42, 44, 48

Overall, this is the most important project of the Fascist era in Genoa. It is located between Via XX Settembre and Corso Buenos Aires. The Piazza is a large rectangle at the centre of which stands the Arco dei Caduti (Memorial Arch to the Fallen), surrounded by gardens. On the long sides stand eight symmetrically placed palazzi whilst at one end there is the green slope which rises with flights of stairs to the Mura delle Cappuccine. The project for the laying out of the Piazza formed part of a vaster town-planning scheme and was drawn up by Marcello Piacentini who won the competition proclaimed by the City Council in 1923. The eight palazzi overlooking the Piazza were not all by this architect, who nevertheless remains the real "set" designer for the whole complex. The first building to go up (1929-36), designed by Cristoforo Ginatta, was Palazzo "Nafta" at the north-west corner: this provided the point of reference from the point of view of regulations for all the others built successively, whereas the Palazzo dell'Inps, designed by Marcello Piacentini (1936-38) in the opposite north-east corner provided the architectural model. The last two palazzi on the southern corners, and those at the centre were designed at the end of the '30s by Beniamino Bellati on the west side and by Giuseppe Tallero on the eastern. All the palazzi are connected by a long arcade which gives a sense of overall unity and have features which confer a monumentality on the Piazza as a whole. This is most in evidence in the use of heavy volumes and the general facing in travertine. [L. C.]

124
Arco dei Caduti
PIAZZA DELLA VITTORIA
BUS 15, 15, 19, 41, 42, 44, 48

The Arco dei Caduti (Memorial Arch to the Fallen) is located at the centre of Piazza della Vittoria. Construction began in 1927 and ended in 1930, when the memorial crypt was included into the initial project for the monument. The commission was given to Marcello Piacentini in 1925 following a national competition launched by the City Council on 9 May 1923.
The edifice was in fact the starting gun for the construction of the whole Piazza della Vittoria. It made use of all the elements which were typical of Roman triumphal arches: an extremely simple structure with columns and pillars supporting the roof and the central, square space surrounded by arcades covered by sail vaults. The celebrative aspects of the arch, representing aspects of war and the eternal remembrance of the fallen, is given to the sculpted elements. The sculptures on the arch are by Arturo Dazzi and those in the crypt by Edoardo De Albertis. [L. C.]

125
Corte Lambruschini
CORSO BUENOS AIRES; CORSO E. F. DUCA D'AOSTA; VIA TOLEMAIDE
BUS 12, 13, 15, 18, 19, 20, 30, 36, 41, 43, 44

Started in 1981 and now completed, the Corte Lambruschini complex provides a centre for offices, commerce, tourism and hotels on a site which required the demolition of a large, decayed 19th-century housing area with courtyards and the ex Flower Market, a rationalist building of some significance in Genoa. The project was commissioned by private enterprise and the City Council from P. Gambacciani & Associati and took the form of two distinct themes which do not come together to create a single entity: the massive presence of the tall buildings, set on the diagonal axes of the area of land, contrasts with the town, whereas the dense, lower structure underlying them is supposed to reforge the links with the surroundings.

The elongated volumes of the high blocks are rich in geometric forms and impose their presence on the compact city beneath. The smooth vision of the towers is characterized by the contrast between the visible, structural cement elements and the reflective skin. The base, on the other hand, revolves around the union of low elements which hide their function as supports for the towers. Joined together to form a front overlooking the road, they define routes and squares within, some of which are intended for shops but which have not yet come into their own. Moreover, the materials used for the lower elements, in particular the theatre, create a sharp contrast with the vision of the tall blocks, suggesting that a unity in the project was lacking.   [M. P. G.]

126
Porta della Pila
VIA MONTESANO
BUS 49

In 1632, during the brief period of the construction of the Mura Nuove, Ansaldo De Mari proposed building a gate to the south, an intuitive idea in view of the future development of the town on the Porta d'Arco-Porta Pila axis, along Via Giulia (now Via XX Settembre). Tradition attributes Porta Pila to Bartolomeo Bianco, and this seems to be confirmed in the side fronts and in the general plan although the rampant lions, the rustic order of the two side-windows and central arch and the rusticated columns do not betray a single unity of style.

According to a 17th-century print, the interior comprised a central hall and two narrower passages at the ends. The gate underwent major restorations in 1772 under the direction of Michele Codeviola. After the construction of Via XX Settembre at the beginning of the 20th century and the demolition of the screen of "low fronts" which faced the east, the gate remained isolated for some time, and was then moved to the Mura di Montesano where it remained until 1940. At the end of the last war, it was rebuilt on Via Montesano which once again isolated it from the walls (1951). [M. M.]

127
Villa Imperiale di Terralba
VIA SAN FRUTTOUSO 70
BUS 18, 46, 67

Built at the end of the 15th century for Lorenzo Cattaneo at Terralba, along the old "Roman road", it seems to have only just been finished in 1502 when Louis XII of France stayed as a guest. The elongated main element, placed along the contour lines of the hill, with corner loggias with characteristic ringed columns of Lombard origin, is harmoniously integrated with the landscape and is one of the most representative examples of the Genoese country house. A corner entrance portico featuring many elements drawn from high Gothic is the oldest part of the house.
Radical changes were made in the middle of the 16th century when a loggia was added to the rear and two wings which changed the house in a U-shape, an unusual format in Genoa. The façade was transformed by G. B. Castello, called il Bergamasco. The layout of the rooms is governed by the strict symmetry of the 16th-century ground plan. The frescos in the salon on the piano nobile, executed between 1560 and 1570, are among the most noted in the œuvre of Luca Cambiaso. In the 18th century, it became the property of Salvago and then of Imperiale di Sant'Angelo until 1920 when it was purchased by the City Council. At present, it houses a crèche and a nursery school, and the park is open to the public. [I. F.]

128
Sanctuary of Madonna del Monte
SALITA NUOVA NOSTRA SIGNORA DEL MONTE

Built on the "Monte", as the wooded hill dominating the valley of the Bisagno and the eastern part of Genoa has always been known, the sanctuary comprises an ancient, constant topographical point of reference in the image of the city. It was one of the first centres of Marian worship in Genoa, which a rich collection of *ex votos* bears witness to; a chapel was first built in 985 and a church constructed by the Mortariensi followed (first mention in 1183) next to which was built a monastery. The present complex comprising church and monastery and accorded the title of sanctuary since 1230, is the partial enlargement of the Mortariensian priory. This work was undertaken by the Franciscan Observants who had acquired the monastery in 1443 through cession of Eugene IV. The 15th-century structure is still discernible in the monastery whereas the church, after some changes, was completely renovated in the 17th century. Initial work commissioned by Giacomo Saluzzo was undertaken around 1630 and involved the choir and crypt; sculptures by Giovanni and G. B. Orsolino were added. Between 1653 and 1658, the restructuring was completed by Giovan Battista Negrone with a design by Giovanni Battista Ghiso. The interior with nave and two aisles and side chapels features a raised presbytery and choir and its corresponding space beneath. The vault of the crypt was frescoed by Giovanni Andrea Ansaldo and houses the 15th-century Sienese statue of the Madonna del Monte. [I. F.]

129
Luigi Ferraris Stadium
PIAZZALE MARASSI
BUS 12, 13, 14, 48, 80

The Luigi Ferraris stadium was rebuilt for the 1990 World Cup with a considerable increase in capacity and improvement in technical aspects over the old stadium. The decision to keep the stadium in town and indeed in the densely built-up area of Val Bisagno meant that the old site had to be closely adhered to and, consequently, that the increase in crowd capacity had to be won without enlarging the ground plan. The design (1986, V. Gregotti & Associati) enclosed the pitch and public areas within a compact, symmetrical structure with cutaway corners forming four squares characterized by the technical towers supporting the roof over the tiers. The main front, next to the square covering the Bisagno torrent, includes the original entrances which were restored and displays a renewed 20th-century taste in which the contrast created by the use of colour highlights the separation between old and new. The lateral façades, flat surfaces pierced by wide openings revealing the interior corridors, define a single structure which gives some sense of monumentality able to provide a vision of urban order. [M. P. G.]

Church of the Sacra Famiglia
VIA BOBBIO; VIA L. MONTALDO
BUS 12, 13, 14, 34, 48

The church of the Sacra Famiglia (1956-59, designed by L. Quaroni with G. de Carlo, A. Mor and A. Sibilla), located in a neglected zone on the outskirts of the city, represents a fundamental element in the process of review and self-criticism started by Quaroni after the Ina Casa project. The special conception of the religious context and the siting in a neglected, peripheral location (as in the case of the unrealized San Gottardo church), represent a strong social attention which has taken form in architecture: slipped into a narrow area snatched from the surrounding buildings and overlooked by a tall wall, the church constitutes an element of continuity in the urban fabric. Overshadowed by a solid tower with a deep cut in one corner, the main body of the building has three floors linked together by a continuous flow of stairs connecting Via Bobbio and Via Montaldo which are at different levels. The church is thus placed at a junction, and the passer-by is invited to pass through the church itself. The light is used to create a strong mystical effect and cuts the continuity between tower and roof of the church which is supported by slender pillars. The cleft which has remained open was supposed to have been closed off with an iron grille, but this was never produced. [M. P. G.]

131
Houses for tramway employees
SALITA CROSETTA
BUS 12, ~~13~~, 14, 34, ~~34~~

This unusual type of stepped building in the form of a horseshoe, based on Milanese or Turinese models, is completely unlike traditional Genoese housing making this complex at Staglieno, in fact, unique. The dwellings were to be built on a steep area to the right of the Bisagno torrent, and were designed by B. Pesce Maineri in 1904-06 for the Società Cooperativa "L'Economica". The result of research into urban forms best able to satisfy its role as homes (a form which the architect abandoned in later projects), the complex is built like a citadel in which the community aspect of the residence is given precedence over that of the private aspect. Although revealing particular care over the interior spaces and in the integration of the complex with the surroundings, the Salita Crosetta project reveals an essentiality of form which was probably conditioned by the business aspect of the commission and by its intended use as working-class dwellings. The project thus radically differs from the later neo-Renaissance designs of the architect, revealing a sort of fracture between cultural forms, stimulated in part by the collaboration with Boito and the professional results of the designer. [M. P. G.]

132
Cemetery (Cimitero Monumentale)
PIAZZALE G. B. RESASCO (STAGLIENO)
BUS 12, 13, 14, 34, 34, 48, 48

In 1835, C. Barabino selected a sloping site suitable for a cemetery in Staglieno, which was separate from places of worship and far from residential areas. He drew up a square site dominated by a chapel built on the side of the hill. The project was relaunched in 1840 by G. B. Resasco who closed off the area with a monumental gallery and linked it with a system of stairs rising to a classicizing temple with a dome. The cemetery immediately found favour and from the 1850s private funerary monuments began to appear, reflecting the society of the time. It became a "museum" of Ligurian sculpture with classicizing and purist styles alongside more up-to-date Romantic and naturalistic forms, soon to be followed at the turn of the century with Symbolist and Art Nouveau examples. In 1903, the City Council launched a competition to enlarge the cemetery in the valley of the Veilino torrent. In Coppedè's unrealized project, the valley was conceived as a grandiose "sepulchral city", a sort of "countermelody to the great building taking place in the city at that time". In 1904, Coppedè produced a plan for the English Cemetery. Little by little, private chapels appeared, first of all in the "irregular wood" and in neo-Gothic style, such as the Cappella Raggio del Rovelli of 1890, which seems to compete with the spires of the Duomo in Milan. These were followed by neo-Egyptian, neo-Renaissance and Art Nouveau forms such as the Cappella Canali de Althans by Coppedè. [E. D. N.]

133
Forte Quezzi Housing Estate
VIA L. LORIA
BUS 356, 383

The Quartiere Forte Quezzi was commissioned by Ina Casa and designed by a group of architects, including Fuselli, Andreani, Morozzo della Rocca, Pateri, Pulitzer and Sibilla, coordinated by L. C. Daneri.
Built in 1956/57 on the hill behind the Marassi disctrict, it comprises five curved buildings set at 150 to 185 metres above sea level and follows the natural lie of the land. In this, they contrast with the traditional layout of blocks in Genoa as characterized by the high/density building immediately below.
Next to the main façade of each building is the road. The "biscione" / the longest of the five buildings and designed exclusively by Daneri / has one further unusual feature: it has an internal pedestrian street in the form of a terrace and loggia which creates a shadow halfway along the façade and recalls Le Corbusier's famous Unité (Marseilles, 1947/52). Indeed, this seems to have served as a model for Daneri's "brutalist" façade design which just has pillars framing the terraces of the apartments.
The site represents one of Daneri's most complex and controversial building projects, especially in view of the high density of homes squeezed into a very small number of buildings (the residents planned for numbered 4,400) and lack of services and green areas. [L. C.]

134
Church of San Siro di Struppa
VIA CRETO 64
BUS 12, 13, 474, 475

The medieval parish church of San Siro di Struppa (first recorded in 1025) stands close to the old junction between the roads for Montoggio, Valle Scrivia, Scoffera and Val Trebbia. It was erected by Bishop Landolfo and dedicated to Siro, bishop of Genoa, who was born in Struppa in the 4th century. The church preserved its medieval characteristics until 1582 when, with the pastoral visit of Monsignor Bossio, changes were made to the altar and the position of the holy water stoups; in 1658, the wooden roof of the nave and one aisle was replaced with vaults. The apse was also restructured in a plainly Baroque style, and the new sacristy was built behind this.
With the restorations of 1921-27 and 1957-64, the church was returned to the early Romanesque aspect it was presumed to have had: the façade, divided into three elements by pilaster strips with a central rose window and blind arches, is the result of the restoration, as are the three-mullioned openings at the top of the bell tower, copied directly from those of the last bay in the right-hand aisle; these are one of the main features characterizing the church.
In the interior, the wooden tie beams, newly redone in the roofs of the nave and aisles which end in apses with hemispherical vaults, do not reduce the rhythm of the block columns and the powerful spherical-cubic capitals. In the latest restoration, the altar frontal of the high altar was created using an architrave from a 16th-century Genoese palazzo. [M. M.]

135
Fort Ratti
MONTE RATTI

The fort is located at 564 metres above sea level on a ridge of Monte Ratti which acts as a watershed for the Bisagno valley, towards the Bavari saddle to the east of the city. The site, comprising two old redoubts, captured first by the Austrians and then by the Franco-Genoese in 1747, took on increased strategic and defensive importance with the advent of the Sardinian Kingdom. In 1818, this latter had already commissioned Colonel De Andreis to draw up two towers based on the Quezzi and San Bernardino models. The first effective plan (1830), inspired by a project for a barracks by De Andreis to be located lower on the slopes of Monte Ratti, was built between 1833 and 1837; one of the earlier towers was included in the structure and later demolished at the start of the 20th century.

In terms of style, the building derives from the four-sided bastions of the Genoese forts of the 18th century, the result of plans combining elements from French fortifications and innovations of the mid 19th century. Because of its size and extension, the Ratti cannot be compared with nearby forts: the long front of the barracks on three floors, with its uninterrupted sequence of openings in the southern wall, reaches the considerable length of 260 metres and is an imposing, majestic presence in the Genoese landscape, even from a distance. [M. M.]

136
Fort Richelieu and Fort Santa Tecla
VIA BERGINI; VIA AL FORTE DI SANTA TECLA

The two forts were designed by Sicre in 1747 during a brief interval in the siege to provide dry-stone redoubts in case of an enemy offensive aimed at the Albaro hills which dominated the gates of the city walls at their weakest point. During Napoleonic times, both forts, together with the Quezzi, underwent their first rebuilding (1799-1812) with stone bastions, an enlargement of the internal courtyards and the erection of small barracks for their garrisons. Under the Genio Militare Sardo (Sardinian Military Engineers, 1815), the works were completed, resulting in the forts we see today.

Fort Richelieu (415 metres above sea level) takes its name from Maréchal Armand Duplessis de Richelieu and replaced its earlier name of "Redoubt above Camaldoli". It underwent several changes between the 18th and 19th centuries which altered its perimeter walls, added the central barracks and enlarged the rectangular block. Fort Santa Tecla (180 metres above sea level, illustrated) was rebuilt several times after 1747, and yet again by the Genio Militare Sardo between 1814 and 1833, with the creation of a barracks, the restructuring of the walls and the consolidation of the bastions resulting in the fort which survives today. During the last decade, it has been restored by the Soprintendenza ai Beni Architettonici, but is awaiting a new role and is at risk of renewed decay. [M. M.]

VI.
ALBARO AND THE EASTERN SUBURBS
CARLO BERTELLI

Eastern Genoa has a distinct character in the spread of the suburban villa, a fashion which for a long time had been a part of the customs of the governing classes of the Republic and was an integral part of the city, just as the various means of transforming the city centre were.

Looking east from Piazza R. De Ferrari one can still see, framed by Corso Buenos Aires, the traditional outline of the Albaro Hills, with Villa Saluzzo Bombrini. This view has always loomed large in the Genoese's image of the city, an image once connected to the culture of the villa seen as the main way of experiencing life in the suburban countryside, and is today linked above all to a privileged milieu, reflecting the centuries-old social divisions in the city.

The eastern part of the town, from the Bisagno torrent to Nervi, has managed to retain its characteristic features: Foce, San Francesco and San Martino d'Albaro, added in 1876, have become the subject of intense building speculation, while Sturla, Quarto, Quinto, Nervi and Sant'Ilario, independent until 1926, have developed their tourist potential and residential developments have been added only recently. The central valley of the Sturla has retained certain aspects of a mountain way of life in its increasingly marginal agriculture and uncertain suburban status. In contrast, the Foce area has always been more integrated into the life of the modern city. The building of the Corte Lambruschini office block and above all the growing importance of business locations, related to the increasing use of space by financial and government institutions, is tending to boost the areas developed in the nineteenth century.

Albaro was one of the favourite sites for residential building and a preferred area for experimenting the most up-to-date building trends of the 20th century, and reveals close connections to the inherited tradition of villa landscapes.

A feature of these villas is that they were large enough to accommodate a working farm, as well as a landscape designed for gracious living. They were organized in such a way as to combine the entrepreneurial and business activities of the owner of the property and of the farm to produce an elegance far removed from feudalism.

As the meeting point between the demands of running a farm and the attractions of an urban lifestyle, the villa has often provided the opportunity for the introduction of innovative architectural styles. In modern times (with such examples as Villa Giustiniani by Alessi and work by several other local architects of equal importance) the suburban family home experimented with new building styles which were only later transferred to the fully urban environment of Strada Nuova.

The area to the east of Genoa was also on the ancient route leading from the city to the sea and has never fully come to terms with the commercial requirements of modern times. San Francesco d'Albaro is crossed only by Via Pisa, a road halfway up the hill, introduced by a steep ascent, from which the crôse *(narrow alleys between the high walls of the houses) branch out at right angles to the sea, on the ridges of the hills. The villas are arranged herring-bone fashion on these, so as to provide courtyards giving onto two valleys which their fronts overlook, while the rear of the houses face the road, with high walls revealing public and private relationships closely connected to the property relations be-*

tween families. There are many examples of extended families living in the same house in a sort of modern version of a feudal arrangement (e.g. the Saluzzo, Brignole and De Franchi families). The present perception of the villa seems to be the result of an explicit historical selection, in which the importance of property can be seen. The plots are in general of average size and were largely in the hands of the nobility until recently. The villas were thus passed down to the present century generally untouched by the bourgeois alterations of the early nineteenth century designed to render them more efficient. Elsewhere at this time the agricultural crisis and the break-up of large estates, partly due to the dissolution of religious orders, led to the growth of small and medium-sized businesses.

This backwardness could have led to an even quicker dissolution of the villa way of life if the expansion of the eastern communes had not been designed to provide dwellings for the well-to-do.

This was an opportunity which the Ædes building company was quick to take up, making use of the existing villas in the development of the new residential district. The firm was set up at the beginning of the century to build a seafront promenade (which was to become the present Corso Italia) and in the end constructed the entire road network in the southern part of the city on behalf of the municipality, at the same time acquiring a huge amount of real estate.

The incorporation of this cultural heritage thus meant a virtual redesigning of the whole role of the villa, whether those owned by the building company and involved in speculation, in which the land was divided up in order to build small blocks of flats, or those of greater architectural merit, which remained isolated so as to take advantage of their monumentality, or even the minor "picturesque" architecture, like the fishermen's houses of Boccadasse.

Although Ædes's approach was undoubtedly elitist, it was still nonetheless an adaptation of the aristocratic villa tradition to the bourgeois housing market, which has played such an important part in the evolution of the eastern section of the town. In effect it anticipated the zoning of the city, which saw Albaro and the surrounding areas become elegant suburbs with sports and tourist facilities. A leisured lifestyle was thus combined with the parcelling out of land for the erection of blocks of flats and houses where architectural eclecticism was everywhere apparent (Villa Raggio, Castelletto Türcke, Villa Canali).

This model was to be taken up in the late 1920s through the Fascist regime's housing policy and the various projects submitted by private individuals on the basis of the 1914 town-planning scheme. The erection of smaller, new "Rationalist" houses made use of areas left unexploited by the original speculation and led to substantial overcrowding of the area. This area continued to be the favourite residential quarter of the well-to-do, so its inherent qualities as a residential area has led to the development of a very varied housing stock from the Middle Ages to the present day.

This stratification is still apparent today, both in the metaphorical and physical sense - through the house market and the linking of the coast road to the main road to Nervi - for all of this side of town. This has been a very effective instrument in the development of the town and was repeated in the 1960s and 1970s with the building of the road at the foot of the hills (Corso Europa).

This salubrious area, with its greenery and sports facilities, has also been chosen as the site for the major health facilities and scientific research establishments. This was the ideal context for the regional hospital of San Martino, which makes use of several pavilions and is closely integrated with university faculties, and the Gaslini pediatric hospital, which was built largely thanks to private donations.

ITINERARIES

There are two possible itineraries, which can be combined into a single one, concentrating on the development of the country house villa from early modern times to the present day. One explores the changes in contemporary architecture, with buildings by Carbone, Coppedè,

Daneri, Michelucci, Morozzo della Rocca and Caniggia (A). The other is based on the more important Genoese villas of the fifteenth and sixteenth centuries, concluding with the great botanical tradition of the eighteenth-century Genoese nobility in the gardens of Nervi (B).

FIRST ITINERARY (A)

Built in the 1930s by covering over the Bisagno torrent, Via Brigate Partigiane leads in the direction of the sea to the trade fair district and Piazza Rossetti. The flat area of La Foce is dominated by the parish church of San Pietro, next to which stands Villa Ollandini, in Via San Vito. The promenade of Corso Italia begins in La Foce and winds its way along the coast following the lower contours of Albaro. On the uphill side there are buildings from various periods, including neo-Gothic villas (Canali Gaslini), houses from the 1930s and buildings erected after the war. On the seaward side there is a series of bathing establishments, the most noteworthy being the Lido, dating from the beginning of the century. Only the abbey of San Giuliano (c. 1240) remains of the ancient buildings. From the Lido climb up Via Don Minzoni to Via De Gaspari, which bisects the hill horizontally and contains a block of flats by G. Michelucci and the swimming pool.

Climbing Via F. Cavallotti, one arrives at Piazza Sturla and the 'N. Bonservizi' Fascist meeting house and, along Via Sturla, to the Bernabò Brea public housing estate, which dates from the 1960s. Returning to the square, follow Via dei Mille up to the Gaslini hospital and turn into Via Carrara and Corso Europa up to the Quarto motorway toll gate, which is close to the modern Costa degli Ometti public housing estate. Return towards the centre until the hospital of San Martino is reached at the end of Corso Europa.

SECOND ITINERARY (B)

Starting from Piazza Verdi turn into Corso Buenos Aires, which was built in about 1820 over the alluvial plain of the Bisagno and the small market garden which then existed, and continue up to Piazza Tommaseo (see no.2 in Via Montevideo).

Looming over Via F. Pozzo is Palazzo Saluzzo Bombrini, which is followed by a series of family homes. These are arranged along the traditional crôse running vertically up the hills. In Via San Nazaro stands Villa Raggi, one of the few remaining Renaissance houses, and the seventeenth-century Villa Brignole-Sale. There are other interesting examples on the parallel Via Parini, which begins in Piazza Leopardi, which also contains the medieval church of Santa Maria del Prato and the parish church of San Francesco, which dates from the fourteenth century. Opposite lies the garden of the sturdy, sixteenth-century, Palazzo Giustiniani Cambiaso. Piazza Leonardo da Vinci stands at the start of the ancient Via San Giuliano, with the seventeenth-century Palazzo Airolo Franzone, one of the best-preserved houses of the period.

Continuing along Via Pisa, one comes to Villa Franchi-Raggio, the symbol of the nineteenth-century reinterpretation of the country house, like the contemporary neo-Gothic Castelletto Türcke, which from the cape of Santa Chiara dominates the ancient quarter of Boccadasse (at the end of Via Cavallotti).

Follow the road by the sea as far as Nervi. The Anita Garibaldi seaside promenade begins at the little harbour of Duca degli Abruzzi and from there one climbs up to the park of Villa Serra Groppallo.

137
Residential Complex
PIAZZA R. ROSSETTI
BUS 20, 31

Now entirely residential, it was originally intended also to include businesses, hotels and exhibition halls. In 1931, the area was vacated by the Odero naval shipyard and included in the 1932 town-planning scheme and a competition for its development was announced in 1933, but the winning project was shelved and the contract was awarded to L. C. Daneri in 1936.

The plots were assigned to private firms: 6 out of 8 were acquired by the Città Nuova building contractors, founded by Daneri himself, and building was carried out by the firm of Garbarino e Sciaccaluga. In 1938 the eastern block was completed and the western begun, although work was only resumed in 1949 after being interrupted by the war and finished in 1955. The block at the back was developed in the 1950s, with Daneri acting as consultant.

Daneri took up the U-shaped design of the town-planning scheme but raised the overall height with volume compensation: the façades of the buildings are lightened by the continuous balconies and are set back above the mezzanines, retaining a single unifying arcade on the ground floor. The model for the design is the lamellar tower-house which was much discussed at the international architectural congresses of the time. The layout and technological details of the buildings have been carefully thought out and each block has two or three flats per floor, with the servants' quarters and kitchen situated at the rear and the living quarters and bedrooms at the front and sides. [A. M. N.]

138
Casa Ollandini
VIA SAN VITO
BUS 31, 36

Built on the site of the nineteenth-century Villa Ollandini (destroyed in bombing during World War II), the elegant block of flats in Via San Vito (1956, R. Morozzo della Rocca) has an original shape, being on a square plan with one corner cut off by a curved line. The volume developes consistently, counterbalancing a dihedron-enclosed within a ribbed, stone surface - with a glassed wall created by the curves of the projecting floors.
The architect has been remarkably successful in combining his desire for a formal arrangement with the constrictions of an irregularly-shaped site.
The design is thoroughly rationalist in its internal layout and the vertical elements are designed to recall the kind of damage caused by war. [M. P. G.]

139
Eastern Seafront
from corso G. Marconi
bus 31

The seafront promenade from the Bisagno to the Sturla, which was a key feature of the town-planning scheme for Albaro designed by the architect D. Carbone in 1892, was very different from the present one. There were to be two separate carriageways, one at the original height of the land (thus well above sea level) and one following the contours of the shore, with small houses and recreational facilities in between.

The main road which was in fact built is the result of a combination of the building policy of the Ædes company, founded in order to carry out this project, and the plans of the town council, for which road access was a top priority. Building took place over a long period (1905-09 for the central section, 1911-18 for the opening Foce section and even later for the final portion).

The comparison between the central section and the original project is particularly instructive, as it includes the big Lido bathing establishment (today without its typical wooden 'Moorish' superstructure), taken as a model for various other similar establishments along the coast.

Enlargement of the pedestrian area was needed for 1992, carried out under the direction of the architect, B. Gabrielli. [c. b.]

140
Villa Canali Gaslini
CORSO ITALIA
BUS 31

Situated on Corso Italia the house was originally built for the Canali family and today houses the Gaslini Foundation, whose property it has been since 1942. It was designed by the architect G. Coppedè and the engineer Predasso on land aquired from C. Raggio in 1918/19 and one of its features is the relationship it establishes with the landscape and the road through the porter's lodge and the main house.

Thanks to its position on a rather reduced site on a small hill, the perspective effect is such as to suggest the existence of a wooded park (almost a wood) and a monumental entrance with an avenue, which seem much larger than they in fact are.

We have little information on how it was in fact built. The first design for the porter's lodge in 1921 suggests Coppedè constructed the main building (whose design dates from 1924, with alterations in 1925) over an earlier structure, as often happened. The ground plan is elaborate and broad on the ground floor on the side facing the sea, while the floor above is smaller (a square almost in the shape of a Greek cross) and contains the sleeping quarters. [C. B.]

141
Block of Flats
VIA O. DE GASPARI 21
BUS 42

This building was designed by Giovanni Michelucci in 1948-50 with a C-shaped ground plan and a marked difference in style between the internal and external façades.

The edifice stands on a rusticated base and is marked by the interplay of pilasters and string-course bands. The external faces project over the base with the extra volume created by balconies and present a juxtaposing series of solids and voids. The modular composition of the façade is highlighted by the string course bands and the contrast between the different materials used to set off the alternation of formal elements (stone-faced parapets, fine iron railings, plastered divisions, extensive use of glass in the wood-framed windows). The series of slim cement pillars running along the surface of the external faces become the ribbing of the projecting cornice. The internal façade has less formal detailing and reveals the building's open plan.

The glass-faced stairwell juts out from the main body of the building in the rear courtyard, while the entrance hall is on two floors connecting the main entrance in Via De Gaspari to the mezzanine with a flight of stairs, from where the stairs and lifts depart. [M. P. G.]

142
"Piscine di Albaro" Council Swimming Pool
VIA O. DE GASPARI 39
BUS 15, ~~18~~, 41, ~~41~~, 42, 43

The pool is certainly one of the most emblematic examples of Rationalist architecture in Genoa, at least among those built by council designers (1934, eng. Paride Contri), whose works were built by the Mantelli e Corbella firm. It is clear that a good deal of thought and care went into the project, which was thought out and built along the most up-to-date organisational criteria as regards division of routes, internal services, technical and dimensional standards, in its efforts to be one of the best Italian examples of the period.

The debt owed to European rationalist canons is clear in the design of the railings, the futuristic aerial tower and the light and graceful awning supported by metal pilotis, which gives depth to the structure with its shade. From the architectural point of view the main, glass-fronted central section, which faces south, has two symmetrical semi-circular blocks with ribbon windows at either end.

The building has three entrances, the main one being on the western side in Via D. Guerrazzi. In addition to the covered swimming pool, the facilities also include three outdoor swimming pools: one shell-shaped for children, an Olympic-sized pool complementing the one inside and a third one for water-polo. [F. G.]

143
New Lido at Albaro
CORSO ITALIA

In 1987, the Milanese architect, Luigi Caccia Dominioni, was commissioned to recover the old bathing establishment of the Lido at Albaro which was situated along the seafront promenade of Corso Italia. The project was part of the group of great works for the Columbus anniversary celebrations and initially provided for a radical rebuilding and enlargement of the derelict Art Nouveau building, built in 1908 by the architect, Dario Carbone, into a hotel. Public and critics had always liked the old building for its sophisticated architectural elegance - the "dashing Moorish construction" recalled "the appearance of a great fairy palace" - united with its most rigorous functional characteristics answering "all the modern requirements of comfort". Caccia Dominioni's project, finally completed after a long and tormented rebuilding of the old establishment, proposes an "up-dated" version of the original Art Nouveau building in a multi-functional hotel complex with exhibition and conference rooms, a bathing establishment with adjoining swimming pools, shops and car parks. Made up of two superimposed blocks of four storeys above ground, the building is quietly sober on a formal level (note the use of prized materials in the external facing of red Verona marble and multi-toned yellows of lithoceramic tiles), but this betrays a certain rigidity in the gratifying reproposal of late historical elements (from the classical mouldings to the eclectic paired windows). [R.F.]

144
"Nicola Bonservizi" Fascist Meeting House
PIAZZA STURLA 3
BUS 15, ~~18~~, 31, 43, 45

Designed as the meeting house of the Sturla Fascists and commissioned by the Federazione Genovese, the building was completed in 1938.
It is one of the best-known examples of Rationalist architecture in Genoa. The architect, Luigi Carlo Daneri, cleverly overcomes the problems inherent in the site (which is 11 metres below the level of the square) by dividing the building into two at street level. The lower part is on three floors and contained the less important offices while the floor above the offices was more important. The top section stands on the bottom as if it were simply the base and is visible from the square as a separate entity. It is supported by slim pilotis recalling those of Le Corbusier's Villa Savoye, as do the ribbon windows on the façade and the ellipsoid stairwell. This glass and concrete structure is set between the two sections and has an almost monumental appearance on the roof, underlined by the bell tower. However, taste for quotation remains restrained and does not degenerate into an excessive pompousness which the purpose of the building might have justified.
The internal layout is very simple, with evenly-sized rooms finished with standard materials. The structural features in reinforced concrete are equally simple, but neat and effective (the hollow pillars contain the pipes). [A. M. N.]

145
Bernabò-Brea Housing Estate
VIALE BERNABÒ-BREA
BUS 41, 41, 45

The estate, housing 1,800 people, built for Ina Casa by the architects L. C. Daneri and G. Zappa, in collaboration with the engineer L. Grossi Bianchi, was accepted by the city council in 1951 but only received approval from the ministry in 1957. Critical opinion has it that this is one of the most successful low-cost housing schemes, particularly with regard to its relationship to the surrounding environment and the unitary nature of the flats. The fourteen buildings contain 371 flats and are arranged along a north-south axis down the hill, following as far as possible the ancient byways of the area and preserving as much of the wooded park as possible. Only two blocks, one a "bridge" block with a road at the first floor level, which was to have been a shopping area, do not follow this pattern. A series of paths connects the various blocks. The buildings are reasonably low and the concrete façades have alternating solid/void sections provided by white panels and balconies set flush with the walls, with brightly coloured backgrounds.

There are 17 different types of flats of differing sizes, going from just one room for singles to flats with double bedrooms . The layout inside is extremely simple and connecting spaces have been done away with so that one enters directly into the living room, which is separated from the front door only by a folding door. [A. M. N.]

146
"Istituto Giannina Gaslini" Paediatric Hospital
LARGO G. GASLINI 5
BUS 15, 15, 31

This is one of the best paediatric hospitals in Italy and was founded in 1917 by the Senator Gerolamo Gaslini in memory of his daughter, who is also remembered in a memorial. The present complex was designed between 1926 and 1928 by the architect A. Crippa in accordance with the strictest criteria in health care and built from 1932 to 1938. The 17 buildings are arranged within a very steep site of 45,000 sq.m. and connected by tunnels and thus constitute an intermediate stage between a single building and a pavilion system, providing for the maximum separation of the departments while maintaining the functional link. In the centre of the complex stands the 'scorpion-shaped' department of general medicine, with its state-of-the-art operating theatres. Along the eastern side of the site the isolation pavilions were set, one for each disease (tuberculosis, whooping cough, measles, etc.), and on the western edge the pavilions housing the foundling hospital and the boarding school and the independent heating plant. Inside, the wards, with all the most modern technology, were carefully designed to provide the greatest practicality with an eye to sensitive social questions (illegitimate children were separated). The entire complex is made of reinforced concrete in a Rationalist style, which is evident already in the monumental entrance tower - a self-conscious declaration of modern efficiency in the accepted monumental form which this style had in Italy after it had been officially sanctioned by the Regime. [A. M. N.]

147
Costa degli Ometti Housing Estate
QUARTO ALTA
BUS 17, 512

Within the overall development of Quarto, which is designed to house 8,000 people and is mainly directed towards private enterprise (with 1,028 cooperative and 403 privately-owned flats to 1,860 council flats), the Costa degli Ometti share, near Quinto, makes up a large proportion of the cooperative flats and certainly has an unusual appearance. Abitcoop Liguria, from the association of cooperatives, and Coopcinque have built this block using a design by the technical department of the developers with G. F. Caniggia and others as consultants. The 500 flats are of various sizes, mono or multifamily (60%), in smallish blocks in the line type (40%) with several flats on each floor or the terraced, or adjacent, type following the medieval custom and are built up the hillside in accordance with the local tradition. At the centre of the development is a square containing the social services and shops, where the highest density housing is located. This development offers an alternative to the designs proposed by the municipal low-cost housing schemes, making use of a vernacular style and a simplification of the tradition mentioned above (producing an effect not dissimilar to that of tourist developments of the late 1970s). Its most important feature is its relatively small size, with paired duplex flats giving onto two sides. [C. B.]

Acuti Hospital Block
CITY HOSPITALS (SAN MARTINO); VIA F. MOSSO; SALITA SUP. SANTA TECLA
BUS 17, 18, 44, 45, 86, 87

Located near the old hospital of San Martino, this building is a self-sufficient unit within the hospital complex, which was originally designed for "acute" illnesses only requiring brief stays in hospital (1958, L. C. Daneri, A. Bagnasco, E. Fuselli). The building is a lamellar block over 180m long and includes 12 floors above ground, with three linear bodies at a slight angle to one another, thus tracing the characteristic shape of the San Martino hill. As occurs in the Forte Quezzi estate, the great mass of the building appears to rest lightly on the natural contours of the land, giving it a strong link to the mainly horizontal lines of the façade.

The clean expanse of the façade of horizontal lines is a play of solids and voids, creating a chiaroscuro effect accentuated by the materials used: concrete for the supporting walls, prefabricated concrete slabs for the dividing walls and glass and anodized aluminium for the frames.

The internal layout goes beyond the normal concept of the hospital ward and incorporates all the latest international theories in hospital design. [M. P. G.]

149
Block of flats
VIA MONTEVIDEO 2
BUS 17, 43, 44, 45

The building was erected by Angelo Crippa on a design dating from 1915 and is one of the best examples of Art Nouveau in Genoa.
The strict geometric design, carried out using neutral-coloured materials, brings out the richness of the monochrome sgraffito decorations on all the peripheral walls of the building, which include geometric designs and human figures. The play of light and shade created by the decorated surfaces on a dark background is reinforced by the protruding cornices, and simple capitals and concrete architraves outlining the windows, dividing the façades and framing the decorations.
On the fourth floor, framed by a cornice linking all the windows, can be seen a fresco of an "Allegory of War", painted by G. Saccorotti with cartoons by E. Bifoli.
The body of the building is made up of two identical sections, with symmetrical main entrances in wood carved with geometrical designs, and separate flights of stairs with the original wrought iron railings. The façade lends harmony to the building as a whole. [M. P. G.]

150
Villa Saluzzo-Bombrini (il "Paradiso")
via F. Pozzo 28
bus 15, 15, 41, 41

The villa stands in a superb position overlooking the Bisagno plain and was built for the Marquesses of Saluzzo at the end of the sixteenth century, perhaps by A. Vannone. At present it is owned by the Bombrini family and is one of the best preserved villas of the period. The building manages to combine a monumental appearance with a sensitive relationship to the surrounding environment. Indeed, the traditional corner loggia on the main floor exploits the spectacular view of the city by being substantially larger than normal, fully justifying the name of "Belvedere" or "Paradiso", as it was already called in the seventeenth and eighteenth centuries. Of marked longitudinal development, the façade presents unusual excess decoration, terminating in a severe balustrade. Inside, the rooms are laid out in two long series divided by a wall running the length of the building with, at right angles, the hall and staircase. The latter has a single flight and leads directly to the loggia, with the huge drawing room behind, a common feature in Genoa, and the east loggia on the opposite side of the building.

The house also contains fine seventeenth-century paintings by G. A. Ansaldo, B. Castello and L. Tavarone in the hall, the west loggia and the drawing room. The grounds are interestingly laid out and include a terraced Italian garden, a wooded park and a cultivated area, which has perhaps been altered over the years.

[A. M. N.]

151
Villa Raggi
VIA SAN NAZARO 19
BUS 15, ~~18~~, 41, ~~41~~, 42

The house is situated on a *crôsa* overlooking a valley laid mainly to vines; in the late nineteenth century it was taken over by the nuns of Saint Dorothea, who turned it into a school, greatly altering its setting. In spite of the seventeenth-century rebuilding and the modern additions, the house is still one of the best surviving examples of a sixteenth-century villa. The seasonal retreat to the suburbs, often copying the living arrangements and family alliances of the city, led to an elegant landscaping of the hills surrounding Genoa and has ancient origins, playing a part in the development of the city quite as important as what took place within the walled area.

As is typical of the period, the house was conceived as a single large structure, with a late-Renaissance decoration on the south façade appearing to divide it into three, which is characteristic of an Alessi design. Of the original internal layout there remains the vaulted hall supported by corbels, with the vaulted staircase in the loggia style (such as is commonly found in the courtyards of the town houses of the period) leading up to the drawing room on the main floor. The decorations include fifteenth-century slate work but there used to be fine seventeenth-century furnishings on the piano nobile with architectural views on the walls and frescoes on the ceilings which were destroyed by bombing in the last war. [A. M. N.]

152
Church of Santa Maria del Prato
PIAZZA LEOPARDI
BUS 15, ~~18~~, 41, ~~A1~~

The monastic complex of Santa Maria del Prato (the field ⸗ *prato* ⸗ is the present Piazza Leopardi) was built in the late twelfth century and substantially rebuilt over the following centuries and is today a fine example of renovation by analogy. It is one of only two churches in Albaro (the other being San Nazaro) and in the Middle Ages it was the home of the Mortariensi congregation, which held the priorate until its dissolution, subsequently becoming an ecclesiastical commendam for important Genoese families (Cybo, Raggio, De Fornari).

The church, comprising a crypt and upper presbitery of nave and two aisles, remained virtually unchanged until the seventeenth century. It was completely rebuilt in the following century and the pillars and walls were plastered, the apse moved back, the crypt eliminated and a new vault installed.

The building was occupied by Napoleonic troops and turned into a stable but was later restored to its proper use and in 1880 it was taken over by the Clarisse, who ceded it to the Immacolatine in 1936. In 1940 the convent was destroyed and subsequently rebuilt and the church was put in the hands of the *soprintendente* C. Ceschi, who worked to restore it to its original condition, as established in research by D'Andrade and De Marchi. He removed all the plaster, excavated the crypt and pulled down the apse and roof. However, work was then held up until 1947 and not completed until 1952. [C. B.]

153
Villa Giustiniani-Cambiaso
VIA MONTALLEGRO 1
BUS 15, ~~18~~, 41, ~~41~~, 43

Built by Galeazzo Alessi for Luca Giustiniani from 1548, the house stands in a little valley of the same name in the middle of a huge estate. It was sold in 1797 to the Cambiaso family, who in turn sold it to the local authorities in 1921; at present it houses the Faculty of Engineering. It is one of the best Italian interpretations of the villa residence in a monumental sense and became the model for several town houses and prototype of Alessi's architecture.

It is a compact building, with a pitched roof. The façade has very slightly projecting wings and is surmounted by a large cornice in the classical style. It has two superimposed orders with a piano nobile-mezzanine rhythm and the division into three sections is underlined by the loggia on the ground floor, which lightens the volume of the building, while providing an opening onto the external environment. Although the architectural decoration is strictly classical in style, there are also some Mannerist elements. The three sections on the façade are reflected in the plan. The double-apsed loggia gives onto the hall and the staircase, which leads to the other loggia at the rear of the main floor, as is usual. This then gives access to the drawing room which takes up two floors on the façade. Much of the decoration was damaged in the last war but one of the features is a series of stuccos by T. Orsolino and G. Lurago and lunettes with fresco decorations by L. Cambiaso and G. B. Castello in the vault of the upper loggia. [A. M. N.]

154
Villa Airolo Franzone
via della Sirena 8
bus bus 15, 18, 41, 41, 42

The house was built in the late sixteenth century for the Airolo family but was sold at the end of the eighteenth century to the Franzone family. A section was then sold separately before the whole building was recomposed in the present century by Count Raggio.

The imposing and austere structure has two lower wings and the only projecting feature is an elaborate portal. The lack of any architectural detailing on the façade is made up for by painted architectural panels of tall painted figures framed by rusticated pillars and coupled pilasters.

The internal layout is very simple, with two long series of parallel rooms and a large hall, from which the staircase leads to the loggia at the rear, giving onto the large drawing room at the front of the house. The main feature of the house is its relationship with the landscape: there are wonderful effects at both the front and the back of the house. From Via San Giuliano one reached the square in front of the building down a long arboured avenue, with two little towers at the end, from which one went down to an Italian garden on two levels.

The original complex is now virtually illegible but a view remains painted by M. P. Gauthier (1832), which is perhaps a little fanciful in its ebullient use of architectural details and elaborate pergolas, but nevertheless gives a tantalizing idea of the magnificence of the original effect. [A. M. N.]

155
Villa De Franchi-Raggio
VIA PISA 56
BUS 15, ~~18~~, 41, ~~41~~, 43

This palazzo in Via Pisa was rendered accessible by the building of Via F. Pozzo and had acquired great importance by the end of the last century. It remained the property of the De Franchi family from at least the end of the eighteenth century before passing into the hands of the Brignole Sale, the Melzi d'Eril and finally the Pallavicino-Grimaldi. The last person to buy it was Armando Raggio, one of the new generation of financiers. The original, probably late medieval building, then a monk's residence and later oratory, was partly renovated in 1817. Its last owner thoroughly rebuilt it for entertainment purposes. The design by the engineer G. Tallero and the architect R. Haupt set out to cover the existing structure with a layer of eclectic references, while the internal layout pivoted around an enormous hall and a staircase in two flights with coupled red marble columns at the rear of the building. For its new nature as a villa residence this work was certainly not negligible and from a functional point of view these alterations made a big difference to the villa as a means of offering hospitality thanks to technological improvements to the domestic economy but considerations of style were even more striking. In his memoirs Haupt says that the new architecture of the palace reflected "the taste of the late nineteenth century with Garnier's French influence", correlating this building with the opera house. It was to provide the impetus for the renovation of the entire district, as can be seen in the last part of Via XX Settembre. [C. B.]

156
Castelletto Türcke
VIA AL CAPO DI SANTA CHIARA 246
BUS 15, 18, 31, 42, 43

Giovanni Türcke was one of the Swiss immigrants who came to Genoa at the end of the nineteenth century. He was not only an engineer employed as director of the Officina Elettrica Genovese (electricity company), a subsidiary of Aeg, but also the managing director of Uite, the public transport company, which was backed by German capital.
In 1897 he bought a house at San Luca d'Albaro and two years later he acquired land on the eastern slopes of the cape of Santa Chiara and asked Gino Coppedè to design a small villa for him in 1903. The slope was quite steep so a strong retaining wall was added and a little castle with towers was built on a square plan, simply divided into four rooms per floor. The castle is reached by a footbridge in the form of a drawbridge at the corner of the building.
Of the huge number of small houses built by Coppedè and the engineer Predasso in the form of castles, Castello Türcke is perhaps the most interesting in its relationship to the site, which is at first sight unsuitable for the type of building designed for it.
But one can almost believe that this castle really was built for defensive purposes on this outcrop and, indeed, even the land registry office describes it as a "medieval castle with drawbridge, tower and garden". [C. B.]

157
Boccadasse Village
CORSO ITALIA, JUNCTION WITH VIA F. CAVALLOTTI
BUS 31, 42

The village is now a regular destination on tourist itineraries and even at the start of the modern period it stood out from the surrounding area. The Napoleonic land registry for San Francesco d'Albaro (c. 1810) describes the ownership of property in the area as heavily fragmented, belonging largely to families of fishermen named Dodero, in a zone characterized by large villas set in extensive grounds.

For this reason, and on account of its position on the southeastern tip of the promontory, the village was spared when the modern road network in Albaro was built at the beginning of the century. The position was important when the rocky, jagged Ligurian coastline came to be seen as the typical romantic Mediterranean landscape. But quite apart from the tourist stereotype, Boccadasse was in fact the first of the small villages around Genoa to acquire this picturesque reputation (in the late nineteenth century). The very uniformity of the village is itself partly the result of the demolition of eighteenth-century accretions in order to build the Lido. Its great attractiveness as a fishermen's village very soon became just a question of appearance as others quickly moved in to take the place of people who had made their living from the sea.

The houses are probably late-medieval in origin and, although there have been several alterations, largely connected to the high cost of property in the area, they mostly retain their original character. [C. B.]

158
Villa Serra-Gropallo
VIA CAPOLUOGO 3
BUS 17

In 1927-28 the Town Council acquired Villa Gnecco-Serra (originally Saluzzo) and Gropallo, to which Villa Grimaldi-Fassio was added in 1979, whose contiguous gardens (although smaller than their original dimensions) were to become an attractive focal point for tourists and citizens in a city which is today wholly devoid of any sort of public parks.

This complex lies just outside the centre of Nervi and covers almost 10 hectares from Via Capuluogo to the "Anita Garibaldi" seafront promenade, with a garden which is a fine example of late eighteenth-century botanic taste, with trees and shrubs typical of the flora of the Mediterranean, as well as several species of well-acclimatised exotic plants. The most important building is Palazzo Serra, which now houses the city modern art gallery, and the adjacent chapel. The house was probably built in the third quarter of the 17th century and is now made up of a central section with six series of windows, although two wings were probably added later. The south-facing side was substantially altered by Serra, who added a projecting terraced porch in the centre. It is not likely that the eighteenth-century statues on the parapet of the main entrance are part of the original design either, but probably reflect the antiquarian taste of one of the previous owners. [C. B.]

VII.
SAMPIERDARENA AND THE WESTERN SUBURBS
PAOLO CEVINI

The division of the city into five large urban areas, Central, Eastern, Western, Valpolcevera and Valbisagno, which seems natural today, originally came about in 1926 with the formal incorporation into the city of Genoa of the 19 suburban communes. In greater Genoa the Western area stretches from the mouth of the Polcevera (Sampierdarena is held to be part of the Central region) to the western edge of the city, with a linear development of seven kilometres overall and a surface area of just under 10,000 hectares.

This area has undergone widespread industrialization, including land reclamation for the enlargement of ports (the Sampierdarena harbours, Cornigliano steelworks and port and airport of Voltri) over the past two centuries with the consequent extension of the road and rail networks, as well as messy and unregulated residential developments. In some cases these have led to a deterioration of the environment which appears irreversible, but overall they have not been so drastic as to submerge the material traces of the culture and identity of the area.

By tracing the routes of the ancient roads, mostly Roman (although some attributions are doubtful, even though the names have been handed down to the present), one can build up a picture of the earliest urban developments along the coast between the hills and the sea, as far as Voltri. Right from the outset this town's function as a secondary port had to combine with its much more important role as a manufacturing centre (steel, textiles and paper) and road junction. Voltri is the starting point of all the most important roads heading inland, after those of the Polcevera: the ancient salt route, which climbs along the watershed between the Leira and the Cerusa basins and was abandoned in the 19th century in favour of the new Turchino pass road, the steep railway line passing through Oviada and Alessandria (1898), and the modern motorway of the 'Tunnels'.

In the organization of the medieval parishes, which frequently followed the Roman civil and administrative boundaries, the central and outer western sections fell under the jurisdiction of the parish of Voltri (with its seat in Palmaro) and its dependent rectories of Multedo, Pegli, Voltri, Crevari, Mele and Arenzano. The territory from Sestri to the Polcevera came under the parish of Sestri (Borzoli). Civil affairs were also centred on Voltri and Sestri. Voltri was the seat of the podestà *from the 13th century, with its jurisdiction extending as far as Cogoleto (the western boundary of the present province of Genoa) up to the Polcevera, and later of the captainship up to the end of the 18th century. Sestri was the seat of a captainship, with jurisdiction over the territory from Pegli to the Polcevera, in the early 17th century.*

Naturally, the relationship with Genoa was extremely close, at least politically. The organs of government and of the judiciary were stipulated by the Senate just as the offices were normally reserved for a narrow circle of the nobility of the city. Besides, the ties the nobility had with their original feudal lands were very strong and were expressed in many different ways: from the ownership and more or less direct involvement in agricultural or manufacturing activities to the practice, which became a fashion, particularly in the 16th century, with remarkable cultural and artistic implications, of residing permanently in luxurious villas expressly designed and built for them.

Towards the middle of the 19th century the final steps were taken which would prepare the ground for the great changes which were to take place after the unification of Italy. In 1842 the new coast road was laid out as an alternative to the old "Roman" road. Although it had been rebuilt and made suitable for wheeled vehicles in 1808, as part of the extensive public work schemes of the Napoleonic administration, this road had become insufficient for the growing volume of traffic following the establishment of the first industries (textile manufacturing, tanning, foundries, shipyards). These were being set up in the plain at the foot of the hills between the new road and the sea and taking the place of the market gardens, farms and gardens; they were gradually undermining the typical pre-industrial "villa" landscape.

1856 saw the opening of the Genoa-Voltri railway line, whose initially insignificant commercial role was to be made up for by its usefulness to the tourist industry, serving resorts such as Cornigliano, Sestri and Pegli. Thus it was that this coast was "discovered" and half of the aristocracy of northern Europe swept down to enjoy it, and the country houses of the Genoese nobility, which were beginning to fall into disrepair, were often converted into hotels or in any case adapted to accommodate this élite tourism. The best known of these were Villa Doria and Villa Lomellini at Pegli and Villa Durazzo at Cornigliano.

However, the factor which had the greatest influence on the overall appearance of this western area was the growth of heavy industry and it is no accident that it came to be concentrated around Sampierdarena, Cornigliano and Sestri in a few decades between the late 19th and early 20th century. Among the companies most active in this process which brought to this area levels of industrial concentration found with difficulty at this date in Europe, were Ansaldo, owned by the Perrone family, which made the most of special privileges granted by the State in the years just before the First World War to exploit to the full the potential of "vertical" integration of the steel cycle (from mineral extraction to blast furnace to cannons, ships, vehicles and armour-plate).

This landscape of the modern industrial city dear to the iconography and literature of the period, poised between the Futurists' paean to progress and the suspended atmosphere of the 20th century, still in some sense applies. Even so, signs of the crisis of modern industrial society are all too apparent, with closures announced regularly and derelict factories looming as evidence of the end of a cycle in which the industrial city was the paradigm.

While earnest discussions are held and tentative plans made for a possible "post-industrial" role for this western sector, based on the development of the electronics and service industries, one cannot help noticing traces of an earlier way of life among the relics of a dying industrial civilization. Several are of some importance, a few from the distant past, but they all send out confused, contradictory and even embarrassing signals as testimony of the uncertain fate of the city.

ITINERARY
FROM SAMPIERADARENA TO VOLTRI

The itinerary begins in Piazzale San Benigno. The area straddles the Promontorio, which used to mark the western boundary of the city, and is the result of the excavation of the hill of San Benigno. This was done in various stages, the last of which, in 1938, was carried out to lay down the dual carriageway and junction. Turn from Via Francia and the new business centre (with the Northern Tower behind and the World Trade Centre on the left), which has taken the place of the old Coscia quarter, into Sampierdarena (Via Dottesio, Via Daste), lined with splendid 16th-century houses (including the Grimaldi "Fortezza", the Imperiale Scassi "Bellezza" and the Sauli "Semplicità"). Head towards the sea along Via Giovanetti and cross Via Buranello. On the left, in the middle of the old village of Sampierdarena, is Santa Maria della Cella. Further on is the old town hall and then, in Piazza del Monastero, Villa Centurione "del Monastero". The area is characterized by the classical taste which predominated in its various forms from the 16th to the 19th century. Slightly inland, in a widening of the road giving onto Via Buranello, stands the Gustavo Modena theatre (A. Scaniglia, 1833). However, the zone also has its fair share of buildings influenced by the more modern styles of the beginning of the 20th century, such as the Excelsior cinema in Piazza Vittorio Veneto. Going further inland, across Via Cantore (built in the 1930s as the first stage of the city's expansion towards the hills) one comes to Corso Martinetti (Palazzo "dei Pagliacci") and from here one reaches the Belvedere (N. S. del Belvedere, medieval, rebuilt in 1680), the focal point of the city's defences in the 19th century. Continuing across the Polcevera, with the huge Ansaldo Sampierdarena works on the left (the interesting late 19th-century "Fiumara" building is worth a pause), one comes to Cornigliano. To seaward, and facing the ex-Italsider blast furnaces, stands the 18th-century Villa Durazzo Bombrini. From Piazza Massena, a little inland, the main road leads to Coronata (18th-century oratory of the Assunta and the Santuario di Santa Maria Incoronata), with a fine view of the Polcevera.

Returning down Via Cornigliano, on the right stands Villa Serra (E. A. Tagliafichi, 1787) and just beyond it starts the old "Roman" road (Via Cervetto), leading to the villas of Cornigliano. This takes us to Capo Sant'Andrea (the ancient border between Sestri and Cornigliano), but now completely unrecognizable owing to land reclamation (Italsider, Cristoforo Colombo Airport) and a messy road network. However, in the midst of all this lies the old Cistercian nunnery of Erzelli, rebuilt in a neo-Gothic style at the end of the 19th century. Continue down Via Siffredi and Via Giotto past the 17th-century church of Santa Maria di Castiglione and into Sestri, with its series of streets running parallel to the coast. Of these Via Paglia is clearly of medieval origin.

Passing through Piazza Micone and Piazza Baracca (church of Santa Maria Assunta), the itinerary turns towards the sea and the 19th-century quarter (the elegantly arcaded Via Biancheri and, parallel to the east, Via Caterina Rossi, with its typical "workers" houses). Then, continuing along Via Soliman (19th-century tobacco manufacturers' building) and Via Merano and crossing the railway line one finds the huge shipyard stretching ahead. On the seaward side of Via Multedo di Pegli stands the 19th-century iron foundry.

On one side of the pleasant 19th-century station square in Pegli is the entrance to Villa Pallavicini; further up the hill stand the house and park of the 16th-century Villa Doria. Continuing through Prà (with the new port taking up part of what was the old village and the ugly low-cost housing development further up the hill) the road finally reaches Voltri, where the main thoroughfare (Via Chiaramone, Via Guala and Via Cerusa) reveal the high quality of life attained over recent years. From Via Guala a steep climb leads to the Santuario delle Grazie (of medieval origin and rebuilt in the neo-Gothic style in the 19th century), and the Palazzo and huge park of Brignole Sale.

159
Industrial Port
FROM LANTERNA WESTWARDS

In spite of all the works carried out as a result of the Galliera donation, the port was already showing serious inadequacies in the 1890s. Inglese, an engineer, decided to tackle the requirements of the new forms of goods transport in 1905 by extending the offshore breakwater by 1,500m in the direction of Sampierdarena and forcing a passage through the Galliera jetty. In 1912 work was begun on the Lanterna dock, which was completed in the late 1920s and was designed for coal transport, while the new offshore breakwater, begun in 1916, was not completed until 1932.

Once this was in position, the expansion along the Sampierdarena coast could go ahead. This was based on plans drawn up in 1919 by the engineer Coen Cagli and this so-called Port of the Empire was reserved for goods and had four angled jetties (Ethiopia, Eritrea, Somalia and Libya), while a fifth (Canepa) was added after the war based on the British dock system.

Other modern industrial developments at the mouth of the Polcevera and along the coast from Cornigliano to Multedo (for the manufacture and transport of steel) are virtual continuations of the same area, as are the C. Colombo airport, the Sestri shipyards and the oil port of Multedo. [C. B.]

160
Sampierdarena Town Hall
VIA SAMPIERDARENA 34
BUS 3, 8

Built on the ruins of the old castle, some traces of which remain on the seaward side, the Sampierdarena town hall bears all the symbols of a middle-class town. It was designed in 1852 by Angelo Scaniglia, an academician of the Ligustica and follower of Barabini, and is a fine example of traditional classicism. It is situated between the royal road for Turin (Via Aurelia, to seaward) and the road leading to the nobility's villas (Via D'Aste, inland), but today it is rather decentralized with respect to the urban layout of modern Sampierdarena. The rapid urban development resulting from the construction of the Genoa-Turin railway (1853) and the parallel Vittorio Emanuele royal road, as well as the siting of industrial plants along the coast, led to the drift inland of the town's commercial interests.

The building is C-shaped, with a central section and two wings. As is suitable in a town hall, the façade is adorned with solemn decorations, giving the structure the necessary monumentality. The wings are altogether lighter and more restrained and form a courtyard set back from the road. The main staircase is set in the hall and projects from the rear of the building leading up to the council chamber on the first floor. The two wings are reached by an arcaded corridor, now with windows. [M. P. G.]

161
San Benigno Business Centre (North Tower and Wtc Tower)
SAN BENIGNO
BUS 3, 8, 10, 34, 90

Begun in 1977, the design for the Business Centre was the result of a variation in the town-planning scheme providing for a special scheme for the San Benigno area, in the port near the Lanterna. The sections which have been completed (supervised by Seicom), as well as the more recent ones, reveal very little sensitivity to the character of the area and a strong attachment to the American model of progress and modernity, which had already been introduced into Genoa by Piacentini in the 1930s with the skyscrapers of Piazza Dante and the more recent Sip and Corte Lambruschini skyscrapers (P. Gambacciani & Ass.). The North Tower was designed by Som (1981) and stands between Via di Francia and Via A. Cantore, differing from the surrounding new and old environment both in aspect and materials employed. The plan is octagonal, with a spire roof in copper. The tower has 25 storeys and is 90 metres high to the eaves and is intended to suggest a balance between history and modernity. Traditional materials employed using unusual techniques have not led to a particularly satisfying effect. For example, the external facing of regularly alternating stone and glass strips create a sense of lightness which diminishes the perceived "weight" of the granite. The shape is based on the steeple of the church of San Donato and is intended from a regional point of view to give a sense of "Genoeseness" to the building, but with little success. The ordinary roads and flyovers and the port structures of San Benigno serve to separate the

North Tower from the group of skyscrapers by Piero Gambacciani & Ass., chief of which is the Wtc Tower (1981). The base is made up of a network of car parks and access ramps and cannot be said to constitute a proper urban front even along Via di Francia. In contrast to American skyscrapers, and even the North Tower, Gambacciani's buildings do not attempt to retain any sort of traditional relationship with pedestrians, so that the normal hallways, squares and pavements have been rejected in favour of an enclosed system. The Wtc Tower is a prism on a square base and is raised up by a network of pillars set back from the edge of the building. It differs markedly from the other two buildings in the complex. Its reflecting glass faces contrast with the aluminium panels on the corners and the dark surface has little to do with the new and old surrounding environment. The San Benigno complex in fact summarizes the principles of the town planning regulations: to recreate a metropolitan infrastructural centre in an underutilised area with a scattered residual urban environment, relying on service and communications technologies to determine the success of the venture, rather than on the architecture. [M. P. G.]

162
Church of Santa Maria della Cella (Sant'Agostino)
VICOLO APORTI 1
BUS 1, 2, 2/, 3, 7, 8, 18, 19, 20

Santa Maria della Cella is situated in the centre of medieval Sampierdarena and is built over an earlier chapel, which has been incorporated in the cloister, called *Sancti Petri de Arena*, where it was believed Saint Augustine's remains were temporarily kept on their journey to Pavia in 725, when it was placed under the authority of San Pietro in Ciel D'Oro. Bombing during the last war destroyed part of the cloister and brought to light the remains of the earlier church. The walls were crudely built and included a series of small arches and pilasters, while the semi-circular apse had five arches and two small splayed windows.

Santa Maria della Cella (1206-13) was built for Jacopo di Borgo and Battistella Doria and was taken over by the Augustinians in 1442, when the cloister was built. The choir was then rebuilt and family tombs introduced in the late sixteenth century, thus turning it into a family church. The Dorias were also responsible for building the dome (1639) and for adding the Baroque decorations.

The Augustinians surrendered the church in 1797 and it became the parish church of the ancient parish of San Martino. The most drastic rebuilding took place in the nineteenth century, with the arrangement of the façade by Angelo Scaniglia and the introduction of decorations inside the church by Nicolò Barabino. [M. M.]

163
Villa Imperiale Scassi (la "Bellezza")
VIA NICOLÒ D'ASTE 3
BUS 1, 2, 2/, 3, 7, 8, 18, 19, 20, 59

This is the most famous of all the villas in Sampierdarena and is traditionally known as "La Bellezza". It was built for Vincenzo Imperiale between 1560 and 1563 by Domenico and Giovanni Ponzello. It is slightly set back from the road with a large open space in front and in a close relationship with the nearby Villa Grimaldi and Villa Sauli. The model was Alessi's Villa Giustiniani Cambiaso but here the effect is heavier and the building is stretched out, with double the number of bays in the wings and less imaginative decoration than in the tri-partite cube of the villa in Albaro.
The ground plan is centred on the internal entrance hall and loggia and the drawing room and loggia on the main floor. The decoration inside the house was carried out by Bernardo Castello, Giovanni Carlone and Marcello Sparzo. The house was acquired by Onofrio Scassi at the beginning of the 19th century and restored by C. Barabino, with stuccos on the main floor by Michele Canzio. At present it is owned by the city council and has been converted into a school. In origin the villa relied for its full effect on the accompanying large terraced garden behind it, with pools, fountains and statues. In the 1930s, Via Cantore was driven through the garden to the north, thus destroying the intimate relationship between the house and its setting and emphasizing the rear façade in a complete overturning of the normal hierarchy of the fronts. The park is at present a public open space with facilities. [I. F.]

164
Villa Grimaldi (la "Fortezza")
via Palazzo della Fortezza 14
bus 1, 2, 2/, 3, 7, 8, 18, 19, 20

The house was built for Battista Grimaldi between 1559 and 1569 and designed by Bernardo Spazio and completed by Giovanni Ponzello. Recorded by Rubens during a visit in 1607, this building is considered a variation of Villa Giustiniani Cambiaso in Albaro and is one of the most important to come from Alessi's circle. The imposing and spare aspect of this square structure, with its pointed roof, has led it inevitably to be nicknamed "The Fortress", an image further enhanced by its raised position with respect to the road and the absence of any external decoration. The façade is divided into three sections, with a central loggia with three arches on the ground floor corresponding to windows and mezzanines in the storeys above, while the side walls each have an order of slightly projecting windows. Inside, the ground floor is arranged on an east-west axis and the piano nobile is set at right angles to it. The drawing room is of particular interest, as it is the largest ever built for the Genoese aristocracy.

The stucco decorations in the loggia on the piano nobile are by Andrea and Battista Carona based on designs by Luca Cambiaso, while the frescos of some of the rooms are attributed to Battista Perolli. The house was put to industrial use in the 19th century and was later taken over by Genoa city council and has now been converted into a school. [I. F.]

165
Palazzo dei Pagliacci
CORSO MARTINETTI 55
BUS 59, 66

Palazzo dei Pagliacci was built by an unknown architect before 1904 and is a good example of Art Nouveau architecture typical of bourgeois taste at the beginning of the 20th century.
The façade includes forms and decorations derived from the Viennese Secession, and the strong vertical and curving lines combine with the graffito decorations and horizontal cornices to provide a strong play of light and shade. It has been completely restored as part of the building's general conversion, as have the forged iron features and the details carved into the entrance steps. The overall effect is one of a perfect blending of structure and decoration.
Apart from a few outstanding figures, such as G. Coppedè, V. Borzani, G. Tallero and C. Fuselli, who are key figures in the development of Art Nouveau in Genoa, most of the architects and decorators working at the beginning of the century have sunk into anonymity. Perhaps many of these were unknown artists and craftsmen working for private clients who were aware of the aesthetic demands of the new century. [M. P. G.]

166
Ex-Excelsior Cinema Varietà
PIAZZA VITTORIO VENETO
BUS 18, 19, 20

In the building's present state (designed by Venceslao Borzani and built in 1921) very little can be seen of its original, intricate Art Nouveau decoration, particularly the masked panels at the base of the pilasters and the seated female figures below the two central pilasters with their arms raised to hold garlands, since vanished. The basically geometric decoration suggests a style lying between Jugendstil and the Secession. Inside, the decorations and furnishings have almost entirely disappeared, except for some traces which are still visible in a small adjacent building.

The comparison between the design and the original appearance of the building shows that all the arts dear to the Modernist movement were employed. Indeed, Borzani was one of the principal figures in Liguria in the first two decades of the 20th century and revealed a close attachment to both the style of Modernism and its overall view of architecture. [M. P. G.]

167
Villa Centurione del Monastero
PIAZZA DEL MONASTERO 6
BUS 1, 2, 2, 19, 20

The house was built by Barnaba Centurione in 1587 on the ruins of a monastery. Documents of the period indicate that the large cloister which still exists was built in the 14th century. In fact the new building was built against the south wall of the Gothic cloister, which was walled in, and an arcaded courtyard was built about three metres above the remaining sides of the cloister on the entrance floor.

The patron's intention to glorify himself is evident in the decorative cycle within the building. This was executed by Bernardo Castello and is particularly imaginative and effective; especially the deep drawing room on the main floor, with its tent vault and three tall windows.

The house remained in the Centurione family until 1882 and was acquired by the municipality of Sampierdarena in 1885, with the abortive idea of converting it into the town hall.

The cloister was brought to light during rebuilding in 1912. It was strengthened with reinforced concrete and connected to the ground floor, thus recreating the original appearance, with a high rusticated stucco base and intricate neo-Renaissance architectural decoration. The house is at present a secondary school and the cloister is now a gym. [I. F.]

168
"Gustavo Modena" Theatre
PIAZZA G. MODENA
BUS 18, 19, 20

Designed by Nicolò Bruno and built between 1856 and 1857, this is the only 19th-century Genoese hall to have come down to us basically intact; the quite substantial conversion carried out in 1920-22 by the architect's grandson, the engineer Raffaele Bruno, not being enough to make a fundamental impact.
The design is the work of a specialist (Teatro Civico in Chiavari, 1868; Teatro Sociale in Camogli, 1876; rebuilding of various theatres between 1868 and 1895) and is in the typical tradition of 19th-century theatres. The central body, incorporating the entrance, foyer and cloakrooms, is divided into three emphasised on the façade by the emphatically Neoclassical central section. The auditorium is horseshoe-shaped and is modelled on Barabino's Carlo Felice (1828), and contained four rows of boxes and a gallery above (removed in 1922, together with the last row of boxes, and replaced by a larger gallery) with a staircase at the entrance to the auditorium.
This is a common design among theatres in the smaller towns in Liguria, while in more important towns the staircase is an altogether grander affair and is given its proper place in the general scheme. After remaining in disrepair for a long time, the building has now been finally restored to its role of social aggregation. [N. D. M.]

169
Villa Durazzo Bombrini
VIA L. A. MURATORI 4
BUS 1, 2, 62, 63

Begun in 1752 for Giacomo Filippo II Durazzo, this palace is an interesting example of the application of the principles of 18th-century French residential architecture. It was designed by the military engineer Pierre P. de Cotte, involved from 1747 with Jacques de Sicre in building the defensive system on the hills, and who used ideas and furnishing schemes taken from Blondel's treatise (1737-38). Work continued until 1773 but the building was already lived in by 1757. In the 1770s and 1780s, E. Andrea Tagliafichi added the portico on the façade, the decorations in some of the rooms and, on the eastern edge of the huge Italian garden, the interesting "coffee house", which no longer exists but was painted by P. Gauthier (1818-32). The house passed into the hands of Filippo Ala Ponzoni and in 1865 it was acquired by the royal house of Savoy as the residence of Prince Odone. It was a hospital from 1892 to 1895 and was taken over by the Bombrini at the end of the century and the Ansaldo company in 1948, while today it belongs to Ilva. It is built around a large *cour d'honneur* and passing through the entrance, the hall and the drawing room one reaches the garden at the back with a view of the sea. The rest of the building is organized around independent "apartments". A particularly interesting architectural detail to the right of the entrance hall is the first cantilevered staircase built in Genoa, attributed to Tagliafichi as it is similar to the one installed by him in the palazzo in Via Balbi 1. [N. D. M.]

170
Villas of Cornigliano
VIA N. CERVETTO
BUS 1, 2, ~~2~~, 3, ~~8~~

The shore of Cornigliano, from the mouth of the Polcevera to the east and the promontory of Sant'Andrea to the west, formed a natural site for the extension of villas or country houses to the west of the city. They are mostly lined along the old "Roman road" on the flat section and on the slopes of the first hills. In spite of the great changes and intense urban development, it is still possible to see a large number of buildings dating from the 16th to the 18th century. The present Via Cevetto (previously Via alla Chiesa), an important internal thoroughfare, exemplifies this.

Villa Serra-Richini (no. 2) was built for the Serra family at the close of the 18th century and was later acquired by the Richini. It was then divided into flats. The late Neoclassical façade has a rusticated, projecting, central section. The park, with its series of fountains and pools, which used to connect the house to the road, has completely gone.

Villa Gianello-Carbone (no. 14) lies set back from the road surrounded by agricultural land. It has a broad front with seven sets of windows and a triple corner loggia on the piano nobile. A pebbled 18th-century pool can still be seen in the garden at the rear. It is at present in a state of total neglect.

Villa di Paolo-Spinola (nos. 23-25) was built by G. Ponzello in 1559-63. In spite of the substantial alterations to convert it into a series of flats, the influence of Alessi on the design is still apparent in the square body of the building divided into three sections and the loggia with a balcony and triple lights at the rear. The staircase is unusual in being originally designed with two flights with loggias and separated from the main building. Attached to the house is the tower of the same period with a corbelled projecting superstructure.

Villa Musso-Istituto Missionarie del "Sacro Cuore" (no. 30) is set up the hill from the road and is a sturdy building with a tent roof and flanked by a 16th-century tower. It has been converted into a school.

Villa Gentile-Bikley (no. 35) dates from the late 16th century and has a corbelled tower typical of the period. In 1885, it underwent restoration which altered its internal layout. The building is built on two floors with a mezzanine.

Villa Invrea-Padri Scolopi (no. 40), mentioned since 1757, still has its original structures and cross-vaulted staircase. It is now used as a library and social centre.

Villa Spinola-Doria-De Ferrari (no. 40) belongs, like the previous house, to the Scolopi Fathers and houses the Istituto Calasanzio. It was built on 16th-century remains by B. Bianco (1621-24) for G. D. Spinola. It is raised up and has a terraced roof and includes a large hallway from which two symmetrical flights of stairs lead with great effect to the upper floors. [G. S.]

171
Oratory of the Assunta
PIAZZA DEL SANTUARIO DI CORONATA
BUS 62

The building stands next to the church of Coronata, in a position dominating the valley of the Polcevera and the western hills. The oratory already existed in 1582 and is the only religious building of the Assunta complex to escape the bombing which irreparably damaged the church and convent.
The exterior is not particularly noteworthy and includes portals decorated with stuccowork and a marble Madonna. The interior provides one of the best examples of Genoese late Baroque. It has been called a "hall for a religious play", "worth visiting as the most beautiful of the Polcevera", and has extremely ornate decoration executed in the early 18th century. The statues, stuccos, gildings and frescos are skilfully blended with paintings by Gio Raffaele Badaracco, including his cycle of the Passion and an altarpiece depicting the "Assumption of the Madonna".
The vault bears frescos by Giuseppe Palmieri and the theatricality of the figures betrays a certain popular taste, revealing the patron's predilections. The furnishings and stuccos are all in the same rocaille manner: the high backs to the stalls produce an undulating effect on the walls which the stuccos continue and underline in a sort of echo. [I. F.]

172
Abbey of Sant'Andrea
VIA DELL'ACCIAIO 139
BUS 1, 2, 3, 22, 121

The abbey stands on the site of a Cistercian building of the 12th century above the *scoglio di Sant'Andrea* (St Andrew's rock), a promontory between Sestri and Cornigliano, where there was a small Benedictine monastery. In 1569 the Badia (abbey) was entrusted by Pius V to the Dominicans as the seat of the *Padre Inquisitore* of Genoa. In 1797, it was requisitioned and put up for sale by the Republic of Liguria. In the 19th century, it was by turns the property of Duke Vivaldi Pasqua, the shipbuilder Ludovico Peirano and, finally, Edilio Raggio, becoming a country mansion. After changing hands several more times it has now become offices and a conference centre.

In 18th-century plans, the complex seemed to be arranged around two large square cloisters with a church to one side set in extensive grounds reaching down to the sea. The present building is set back from the main coast road, whose traffic has been intensified by the building of the airport, and it has lost most of its park to the steelworks. It is now L-shaped and is the result of several rebuildings and was designed by Rovelli as Duke Vivaldi Pasqua's residence. It is strongly neo-Gothic in flavour, with a plethora of crenellations and pointed arches. [I. F.]

173
Christopher Columbus Airport
SESTRI PONENTE
BUS 121

The airport is set between the steelworks of the 1930s and the area of residential development of the 1950s and 1960s, in other words within the city itself – an extremely unusual position for a city airport. It was built on reclaimed land adjacent to the promontory of Sant'Andrea agli Erzelli and is in a strategic position, blocking the continuation of the port of Genoa, which had developed towards the west in various stages, and the port of Voltri.
The airport, regarded as provisional for a long time, was finally rebuilt in 1986 after a competition-contract of the Consorzio Autonomo del Porto and the Ministry of Transport (1971, Ingrani). It is on three levels in a roughly triangular shape with loadbridges stretching towards the runways. The open-plan interior provides easy access to all the various services. Although the materials used tend to date this sober and functional building, it remains an elegant attempt to combine good design with efficiency. [M. P. G.]

174
Church of Nostra Signora Assunta
Via Sestri
Bus 1, 2, 2', 3, 58, 61, 170

The church of Nostra Signora Assunta in Via Sestri dates from 1620 and is attributed to Rocco Pellone, who also built the high altar and the tabernacle. The richly decorated interior has a single nave and contains some fine paintings and frescos, including "Jesus in a boat woken by St Peter", by Domenico Fiasella, and "Moses and Daniel", a fresco by Nicolò Barabino.

The façade originally bore frescos by Gio Andrea Ansaldo but was altered in 1934 using a design by Piero Barbieri (1927): it is in three sections, with three arches framing the doors, and a big projecting cornice producing a strong shadow on the smooth, featureless wall. The pediment has a bronze relief of the "Assumption of the Virgin" by Luigi Venzano, while to the sides the statues of St. Joseph and St. John the Baptist emerge from the background, in a modern interpretation of the classicism of the Roman School. Barbieri was, in fact, a pupil of Piacentini and Giovannoni and, apart from a few commissions of lesser importance (Pontedecimo hospital, 1926; the church of Misericordia e Santa Fede; development of Villa Gruber, 1927; Hotel Columbia, 1929; public buildings of Santo Stefano D'Aveto, 1938), he was concerned mainly with town planning, drawing up schemes of an academic nature, such as the *Studio di Piano Regolatore e di Diradamento della Genova Medioevale* (1936), *Le piazze urbanistiche di Genova* (1937) and *Forma Genuae* (1938), the first history of the city's urban development. [M. P. G.]

175
Villa dei Gesuiti, Parodi
VIA VADO 39
BUS 1, 2, 2̸, 3, 3̸

In 1733, Stefano Spinola di Francavilla gave to the Jesuit Fathers a villa of his on the hills of Sestri, between Villa Lomellini Rostan to the east and Villa Pallavicini and Villa Spinola to the west, as a "holiday home" for the College. However, the building was evidently not entirely suitable for their needs and the Jesuits decided to make some alterations. The work, supervised by Brother Cesare Ferreri, must have been carried out quickly if the house was once again in use by 1735. The large sum spent and above all the final ground plan suggest the building was completely rebuilt. It stands on the highest point of the garden, with a long, low central body and two taller wings forming a shallow courtyard. The sides were designed to be used for the cells, with long corridors connecting them, and the main body was used for official purposes. An imposing hallway lined with columns was extended by a gallery leading to the garden at the rear. From the hall, two separate staircases led up to the piano nobile and the great drawing room.

Of particular interest is the monochromatic rocaille fresco decoration outlining the architectural details and providing *trompe l'œil* views of courtyards and gardens on the walls. The house passed into the hands of the Durazzo and Casanova families and was finally sold to the city council in 1905 by the banker Parodi. It is at present a school. [G. S.]

176
Workers' Houses
VIA C. ROSSI
BUS 22, 169

Completed in 1910, these are an important example of council housing built by building cooperatives *a proprietà divisa* (that is, the council residents could eventually become owners after several down payments and then eventual extraction), which became common in Genoa after 1860. In Sestri in particular the town planning scheme of 1910 led to intense development in the area between Via Menotti and Via Puccini, as well as the uncontrolled industrial development which saw factories and houses put up cheek by jowl. These houses are laid out at right angles to the main road, with the symmetrical block buildings lined up facing each other along a connecting road. They are four storeys high and contain two flats on each floor with narrow alleys between the buildings. The façades on Via Rossi were originally painted with a rusticated base, pilasters and lunettes, as well as windows painted in to match real ones on the opposite side. Very little remains of these details and the colouring has almost completely disappeared, except where it is protected by the cornices. The poise and style of this type of housing was in fact more suited to a bourgeois and petty bourgeois lifestyle rather than that of the working class, in spite of its siting in a densely-populated industrial area. It often turned out that the property redemption system forced those allocated a flat to give it up to someone better-off. [M. P. G.]

177
Ansaldo Cast Iron Foundries
VIA MULTEDO
BUS 1, 2, 2', 3, 3', 51

Designed in 1916, at present these foundries are unused and in a serious state of disrepair, but they nevertheless stand as witnesses to industrial growth in the iron and steel sector and in mecchanics, for war production in particular, which was started in 1906 by San Giorgio and continued by Ansaldo, an industrial giant owned by the Perrone family.

With orders guaranteed from the government for war production, Ansaldo employed Adolfo Ravinetti in 1915 to design the Campi (Vittoria) works, among others. His concept was based on 19th-century eclecticism, in which different materials could be combined, while also making use of the classical Roman tradition and modern ideas of industrial design using reinforced concrete.

With the benefit of hindsight the tight relationship between client and architect recalls the similar situation from 1909 to 1911 in Germany between Aeg and Peter Behrens, leaving aside the quality of Ravinetti's work and taking into account the different economic and market conditions in which the two industries found themselves. [M. P. G.]

178
Villa Pallavicini and Park
VIA I. PALLAVICINI
BUS 71, 93

Inspired by Tagliafichi's 18th-century garden and Villa Lomellini-Rostan, which has since been pulled down, the architect and set designer Michele Canzio drew up a design in 1837 for rebuilding the villa and relandscaping the garden in a 19th-century, Romantic, theatrical taste at the request of Marquess Ignazio Pallavicini.

The entrance to the villa, flanked by lower, twin structures, stands at right angles to Via Pallavicini, facing the station square. A long straight avenue leads over the railway line, built in 1856, to the courtyard in front of the villa on the hill of San Martino. The building itself is a solid, square block in the classical style, connected by scenic terraces and staircases to the botanic garden below. In fact, the park is the object of greatest interest and was laid out in the style of an English, picturesque park and was clearly heavily influenced by its creator's set designing experience. A conspiracy made of unexpected views and surprises traces out a compulsory path through games of water and sheets of vegetation, leading one past classical edifices and exotic constructions; all designed in theatrical sequence. It was completed in 1846 at the time of the first transformation of Pegli into a tourist resort and the conversion of villa and garden can perhaps be seen as a prescient foretaste of the future role of this small seaside town, which was to remain a famous holiday resort right up until the Second World War. [M. P. G.]

179
Cep Housing Estate
VIA PRÀ
BUS 1, 2, 2

The Cep (Coordinamento edilizia popolare) estate is made of an original nucleus, in the lower part of the complex, which dates from the 1950s, and a densely-built surrounding area developed at different stages during the 1970s and 1980s. The most recent part, Palmaro Due, was put up by the Valle company using a design by I. Gardella and was completed in 1985.

The first block, which was built before Law No.167 (1962) providing land for council housing, was originally conceived as part of the Ina Casa schemes, which were planned in a neo-Realist style for sites throughout the country by architects such as Quaroni and Ridolfi, and by Daneri in Genoa (Forte Quezzi and Bernabò Brea estates).

In 1965, the Peep (low-cost housing plan), which was formulated after Law 167, set out the main lines of the expansion of housing in the hills, both eastern and western. These proposals were held up by the centre-left administration but were approved by the first administration wholly of the left, whose policy of expanding development into the hills, thus opening the road to the building speculation of the following years, was of questionable benefit. These decisions prevented any real effort being made to restore the centre of the town, which lost inhabitants to the new quarters on the outskirts, thus encouraging the gutting and conversion of entire blocks (Piccapietra, Madre di Dio) which had been part of town planning schemes of the 1930s. [M. P. G.]

Villa Brignole Sale (Duchess of Galliera)
VIA N. DA CORTE
BUS 1, 96, 97

The villa stands on a site popular since the 14th century, when a certain Spinola Castle was to be found there. The Brignole Sale family built their villa on the ruins of this building in the late 17th-century and enlarged it in the 18th. The villa became a luxurious residence, even containing a theatre. The house became famous again in the 19th century, when the park was enlarged to include the Santuario delle Grazie, with the monastery of the Capuchins, to prevent them being expropriated by the State as Church property. The Dukes of Galliera are buried in its grounds. The house passed into the hands of the town council in 1931 and the park was opened to the public, while the villa was converted into a school. The building is raised above the garden and seems larger than it is in reality - a typical theatrical feature of Genoese architecture. It consists of a main body of modest size, with a winter garden and a long and narrow rear wing. The two entrances are set into the sides and point out the asymmetry of the building, as does the main entrance staircase, which appears off-centre with respect to the façade but matches the internal layout.

The great park was improved in 1870 by Rovelli on the English model and is in juxtaposition to the Italian garden at the front of the house. In accordance with tastes in landscape architecture, the park combines large patches of trees and winding avenues with quaint features, such as a refreshment lodge, a triumphal arch with a stele and a rustic Swiss hut. [M. P. G.]

181
Voltri Port
BUS 1, 96, 97, 191

The quays were built following the common practice in Genoa of reclaiming land from the sea - a system also used in the construction of the airport and other industrial developments along the coast. The port was designed for container traffic and is located on the shore in front of Villa Doria-Podestà, between Palmaro and Voltri; an area which has gradually become crowded since the 1960s with motorways and low-cost housing developments.

Work was begun in 1970 but was immediately held up. In 1976, changes to the port development plan gave it a new role and the following year the main quay and the offshore breakwater were built. There was a fresh interruption owing to financial difficulties and private investment was sought, although it did not reach the required levels. Work finally proceeded in 1984 with the construction of the first section of the east quay and is now finished.

The project has been on the drawing board in one form or another since 1919 and discussions with the Ministry have been almost as long, but the final result is a quayside built in line with the very latest technology (prefabricated reinforced concrete blocks). The port is still waiting to receive a railway link which will enable it to break its dependence on a motorway which has to all intents and purposes become a city bypass. [C.B.]

VIII.
VAL POLCEVERA
GIORGIO PIGAFETTA

In an anonymous 17th-century print, the urban expansion of Sampierdarena is seen from the sea displaying all its mature elegance. On the right, in the print, below the Lanterna, stand the spare, massive buttresses of the town walls. A few words describe this area simply as "Part of Genoa". To the left a pretty landscape, dotted with villas immersed in the greenery, unfolds along a stream crossed by a 16th-century bridge with twelve arches, and gradually blurs into the distance beyond the Appennines, suggesting distant horizons to the north.

This was how the valley of the Polcevera looked then, and would continue to do so for another three centuries. Today it has been reduced to being a convenient route for a motorway and railway and is clogged with small and medium-sized industrial developments, while every nook and cranny has been packed with housing. The modern visitor cannot help being struck by the loss of any sense of decency in the exploitation of this strip of land. Even so, here and there he can still find timid throwbacks to the old gracefulness, in the form of villas, palaces, churches and other buildings tucked away along a road at the bottom of the valley running up to Via Postumia. The so-called "Tavola del Polcevera" (Polcevera table) - dating from 117 B.C. and concerning Roman arbitration in a dispute between the Genuati and the Langensi - reveals the importance of the road, which crossed the Appennines at the Colle della Bocchetta.

Along that extremely ancient road with mostly commercial traffic there gradually arose over the centuries early forms of industrial activity (mills, ironworks, textile manufacturing) mixed in with modest terraced cultivations, vineyards and churches (including the important complex of San Bartolomeo della Certosa). These were later joined by several villas and palaces - some of high architectural quality - marking the area's takeover by the Genoese nobility from the 16th to the 19th century.

The first along the road is Villa Imperiale Casanova, in the Campi area, which was built in the late 16th century. Further inland stand Villa Dellepiane "dell'Olmo", Villa Spinola, Villa Durazzo Pallavicini, Villa Cambiaso and, finally, the Villa Serra complex, a curious example of a blend of different styles among buildings set in an extensive park. In front of an earlier 18th-century building, next to a huge crenellated tower and facing a Romantic English garden, stands an unexpected triple-pointed neo-Gothic pavilion, which Carlo Cusani put up towards the end of the 19th century for the Serra family.

But if a place does have a destiny, and if this can be read in the stones of its constructions, at either end of the valley can be found a building which illustrates and comments on that destiny. At the top of Mount Figogna, at over eight hundred metres, stands the Sanctuary of the Madonna della Guardia, whose view sweeps from the hinterland, and the vital source of its ancient trade, all the way to the port of Superba, at the mouth of the Polcevera. On the right bank of that estuary stands Palazza Durazzo Bombrini, built in the mid 18th century by Pierre Paul de Cotte, which was in industrial times to turn into a strategic hub of the very steel and shipbuilding industry which has played such a crucial role in the valley's fate to date.

182
Viaduct of the Genoa-Savona Motorway
BUS 7, 8

Built by the Società Condotte d'Acqua which won a contract from Anas (1960), and adopting a design by Riccardo Morandi and C. Cherubini, the imposing structure, completed in 1964, suggests two separate levels of use and perception. The first is clearly the most important and functionally clear: a motorway viaduct to cut east-west across the lower part of Val Polcevera which is occupied by a railway shunting yard and industrial and residential buildings. For those travelling eastwards on the motorway, the viaduct appears as a sort of giant entrance to the residential and "urban" nucleus of the city. In the opposite direction, clearly, it appears as an exit to the residential areas, the Riviera and southern Piedmont.

However, it is when travelling along Val Polcevera that the slender architectural features and environmental impact of the viaduct are best appreciated. Three "grasshopper" pylons support long, slender reinforced concrete supports from which are suspended symmetrical cantilevers making a strong and masterly statement in space; namely the vocation of the bridge to cross the valley in enormous steps. At the same time, however, those same pylons which are embedded in "such a dense fabric of earlier buildings", as Morandi himself said, bear witness to the rapid urban growth which Genoa has encountered in the years of development after the last war. [S. C.]

183
Church and Cloisters of San Bartolomeo della Certosa
VIA SAN BARTOLOMEO DELLA CERTOSA 15
BUS 7, 8, 22

The monastery, which lost its characteristic cells during the last century, today gives its name to an area of Rivarolo. It was built on land which was then deserted and so given to Luchino Di Negro in 1297. Its growth bears witness to the original religious vocation of this part of the valley, and was assisted by the protection of powerful families from the city, such as the Doria and Spinola who in 1472-80 built two chapels there (later dismantled), whose refined gateways in Brunelleschian style may today be seen at the Victoria & Albert Museum in London. The little which remains of the monastery, smothered by building development of the 1950s, is separated from the main road of Via Canepari by the railway bridge. The architecture of the complex displays in a somewhat confused manner successive alterations in Gothic and Renaissance style. The situation is complicated by the 19th-century restoration which, particularly in the apse of the church, highlighted the "Gothic" aspect. The main cloister, perhaps of Tuscan derivation and with a fine two-toned cobbled pavement (1572), and the second order of the lesser cloister are intact and can be dated to the opening years of the 16th century. The church with its beautiful octagonal dome covering (*tiburio,* 1562) shows Lombard influence and is completely frescoed by Giovanni Carlone. The vaults and a large part of the dome were restructured in the 19th century, whilst the frescos in the chapel of San Bartolomeo are original. Other canvases by Bernardo Castello, Badaracco and Carlone are conserved in the church and sacristy. [S. C.]

184
Church and Cloisters of San Nicolò del Boschetto
VIA DEL BOSCHETTO 29
BUS 63

As mentioned on a small plaque within the church, the original building was a small chapel erected in 1311 by Magnano Grimaldi. In 1410, it was given to the Benedictines and a century later, a church and monastery were built which were soon to take on great importance thanks to the large donations from the grandest Genoese families. It was chosen as a place of burial by the Doria, Spinola, Grimaldi and Lercari families and interesting funerary monuments survive to show this, but it also saw the passage of important figures such as King Louis XII of France and Francesco Sforza, Duke of Milan, who held an unusual service there at the entrance to the city. Transformed and enriched in the 17th and 18th centuries, the monastery was sacked by Austrian troops in 1748 and expropriated in 1810 to be transformed into apartments, with the church itself being turned into a factory. It was only returned to the Benedictines in this century, to be passed in 1960 to the Opera di Don Orione. The bell tower is all that remains of the 14th-century building. The chapel of San Benedetto dates from the mid 15th century. However, the features which most characterize the place are the monastery cloisters. The lesser cloister, giving directly on to the church, is a rare, complete example of the work of the Antelami masters who worked in the middle of the 15th century. The church interior, refurbished at the end of the 16th century, contains coeval frescos in the Cappella della Madonna and tombs and epitaphs of the Doria and Grimaldi families set into the floor (15th, 16th and 17th centuries). [S. C.]

185
Casino Serra Foltzer
VIA JORI 60
BUS 8, 22

The house, once belonging to the Serra family and recorded in Porro's plans (1836-38) with a layout similar to the present one, was built in 1858 by G. B. Cavalieri, mayor of Rivarolo. After passing through the hands of the industrialist Foltzer, the park became increasingly shabby and was used for improper purposes.
The house has a circular layout with four, small, crenellated, radial wings surmounted by slender turrets on the corners. A massive round tower topped with a little loggia stands above these. The modest decoration, comprising crenellations, corbels and pointed and polylobate cornices once highlighted by chromatic contrasts which have since disappeared, clearly show the house follows the tradition of a simple, restrained neo-Gothic style.
The interior opens on to a large, double-height central salon with a dome. From what it is possible to deduce from old maps, the sizeable park was bordered to the north by the Royal road for Turin (on to which the house itself gave) and stretched as far as the Polcevera torrent. The plot once had other buildings (greenhouses, service buildings) which have since been demolished. It is presently being restored. [G. S.]

Grandi Artiglierie Ansaldo Factory
CAMPI
BUS 1, 2, 3, 51, 52

An increased arms production was the vital stimulus for this industrial colossus, built in the inner suburbs of Cornigliano-Campi; named the Stabilimento Elettrotecnico per le Grandi Artiglierie of the Ansaldo company, it was under the control of the Perrone family in those years. It later changed its name to Stabilimento della Vittoria. It was built between 1915 and 1917 using a plan by Adolfo Ravinetti, employed by Ansaldo in 1915 as designer. He was given the task of putting together a series of projects for new constructions to be used in the increasingly sizeable arms industry.
For this factory, Ravinetti proposed no less than 6 possibilities, some of which highly detailed both in terms of ground plan and details, and using different construction materials (reinforced concrete, iron, glass, brick).
The decoration is provided by the articulation of the structures and volumes themselves and by the succession of rhythms which appear as a result of this. There are no sculpted or ornamental features except for some metal balusters and the brackets of the lamps at the entrance, which are finely decorated with the simple motifs appearing on the gates.
The imposing, severe project has a Latin cross ground plan with four aisles and one of the two transepts planned, which is divided longitudinally in two by a concrete wall lightened by geometric openings and broad openings between the slender columns which are filled with square windows in iron and

glass. The exterior and interior are well-preserved, but the image of the majestic triumphal arch suggested (as contemporary photographs show) by the structures at the western and eastern entrances, is completely changed. Today, solid gates have been installed for security reasons and so block off these entrances, and the two imposing columns, surmounted by a very wide, depressed arch which frame both entrances, have been completely levelled and flattened.

The load-bearing structure of the factory is in exposed reinforced concrete, with particular care being taken in the rather complicated system of beams and centering supporting the vaults; the impression today is of a strong, almost luminous design, the result of a deep understanding between project quality and technical knowledge, and between aesthetics and efficiency, which perhaps contrasts with the evident monumentality of the exterior.

The addition of a small aisle on the western side of the building, which caused the loss of the external surface and closed off the projection of the transept, is obvious. [S. C.]

187
Cige (Peep) Housing Estate
BEGATO
BUS 271

This extensive urban area in Begato (a part of Rivarolo) was built from 1976-86 by a consortium of building contractors which in 1975 formed Cige (Consorzio imprenditori edili genovesi; "Consortium of Genoese building contractors"). These blocks and related infrastructure were put up as part of a programme of public housing.

It comprises three sectors: 1, 2 and 9; the first (1976-81) was built almost wholly by the consortium, except for a small plot contracted out to Italposte, and it stretches from Via alla Costa di Rivarolo to the north-west and the viaduct of the A7 Genoa-Milan motorway to the east. It includes about 700 apartments, plus a number of apartment-hotels for the Ministry of Post and some shops.

Sector 2, between Via P. N. Cambiaso and the A12 Genoa-Livorno motorway, includes a main road, public parking, some parkland and a school, all built by Cige (1980-83). The building here was on a lesser scale than in sector 1 which includes two sets of roads (a main road and a secondary set of link roads extending about 1 km), as well as a nursery school and crèche and a football pitch and green space.

Sector 9 (1981-85) includes infrastructural elements (junction of the roads serving the three sectors, public parking and secondary link roads), and a certain number of apartments financed by companies using the "Fonds de rétablissement du Conseil de l'Europe".

The City Council's housing is of considerable importance and includes a complex called the "Diga" (dam), a large bridge-like structure joining the two sides of the valley. Proposed by the architect, P. Gambacciani, as a "walkway" across the valley, in reality it cuts the two zones like a barrier into distinct areas. The initial project planned a connection with the motorway and a railway station on the Casella line. Neither have been realized to date, although the old road for Begato has been rebuilt. [S. C.]

Villa Cattaneo "dell'Olmo" (Ansaldo Historical Archives) Ansaldo Research Centre
CORSO F. M. PERRONE 25/118
BUS 53, 63

Villa Cattaneo stands next to the Benedictine monastery of San Nicolò del Boschetto (14th century). At the beginning of the 15th century, it belonged to the illustrious Grimaldi family and then passed through several hands before becoming the property of the Cattaneo family midway through the 17th century. It was at this time that the house was turned into a grander estate.

After it was acquired by the Società Ansaldo in 1978, the palazzo and gardens were completely restored and used to house the company's historical archives; an extraordinary example of the care that even managers of industry take in the re-use of Genoese architectural heritage.

The house has three floors and an attic and is based on the typical Genoese house comprising a basic cube shape with a slate roof and a layout which met the requirements of the oligarchy of Genoa, especially in this case in view of the larger rooms.

The palazzo is reached across a parterre decorated with trees as is the entrance to the chapel on the first floor to the rear of the house. Within, the division between public and private rooms is quite clear; the former includes the Salone delle Feste on the piano nobile.

In these rooms, the division of the rooms is rendered uniform by the decoration, executed mainly by Giacomo Boni (18th century) in two phases together with the decoration in the chapel. Of only slightly later date is the decoration in the ground-floor rooms around the great hall and 18th-century stairway in which the traditional floors in slate octagons and marble squares are perfectly preserved. The siting of the research centre in the original location of the Cmi (Costruzioni metalliche industriali - Industrial metal constructions), built by Coopsette Reggio Emilia with a design by the Renzo Piano/Building Workshop in a joint venture with Cesen (1985-86), gives a concrete example of the desire to link corporate image with the restoration of the adjacent Villa Cattaneo as headquarters of a prestigious company archive. Without dismissing the problems of an area dominated by the culture of early industrial age hangars, the existing buildings have integrated themselves with abstract references to the architecture of the *Neue Sachlichkeit* (external stairs, walkways of a trellis structure, green window frames and white plaster work). [S. C.]

189
Villa Pinelli Serra
COMAGO-MANESSENO
BUS 7

Situated on the banks of the Secca torrent and surrounded by a large park, the house was for a long time abandoned after it was occupied by the military in the last war. However, it remains one of the most important examples of Genoese neo-Gothic architecture. Marchese Orso Serra commissioned Carlo Cusani around 1840 to transform the existing building and design the park around it. In the various forms adopted (the main house, cowshed, barn, cottage), the whole complex reveals a deep knowledge of English pattern books. Indeed, although the main house was adapted to the earlier volumes, it displays all the features of a Tudor cottage (the cuspidate features on the façade, the bow windows on the ground floor, the four-light windows in the loggia, the slender chimneys) which were perfectly illustrated in Loudon's plates of the period. A stylistic coherence dominates the whole complex: from the smallest details in the decoration (the monochrome frescos in the chapel, the little cast-iron columns, the oak panelling on the walls) to the general layout (the rustic look hidden by a crenellated tower, the "gothicked" stables and cowsheds with two-tone colours and pointed windows), and the way Cusani succeeded in making use of the natural lie of the land to create a picturesque landscape. The park, criss-crossed by twisting avenues and enlivened by thick patches of vegetation, tall sequoias and plays of water (now lost), has recently been restored. [G. S.]

190
Railway Viaduct
PONTEDECIMO-CAMPOMORONE
BUS 63

The 19th century saw a rapid growth in communications which in virtually all of Liguria until then had comprised just a few, poor roads. In 1852, the arrival of the railway was preceded in Genoa by an earlier link with Turin by "electric telegraph". Only a year later was an actual railway line begun, designed by the engineer Henry Maus (1846, assisted by the engineers Ranco, Bancheri, Braccio and Brunel) and built by the Azienda Generale delle Strade Ferrate. The official inauguration took place on 20 February 1854 in the presence of the royal family. The Genoa-Turin line counted a large number of tunnels, viaducts, curved and straight bridges. The Pontedecimo-Busalla stretch in particular required close study and clever solutions because of the steep slope and inadequacy of the locomotives of the period (in the Riccò valley, the incline reaches 35 per thousand). It was almost all to be replaced by the "Succursale dei Giovi" opened in 1889 (maximum gradient 16 per thousand). The highest viaduct cuts across the Val Polcevera on 16 arches - of which 7 superimposed - with rusticated base and terracotta upper parts. It rises majestically above the landscape at the outskirts of the city, although in the actual crossing of the valley, more and more buildings are appearing nearby, with the consequent risk of blocking out the last vestiges of an ancient rural area. [S. C.]

BIBLIOGRAPHY

ALIZERI, F., *Guida artistica per la città di Genova*, Grondona, Genoa 1846-47.
ALIZERI, F., *Guida illustrata del cittadino e del forestiero per la città di Genova e sue adiacenze*, Sambolino, Genoa 1875.
Catalogo delle ville genovesi, Comune di Genova, Genoa 1967.
COLMUTO, G., *Chiese barocche liguri a colonne binate*, in *Quaderni dell'Istituto di elementi di architettura*, No. 3, Faculty of Architecture, Genoa 1970.
FORTI, C. L., *Le fortificazioni di Genova*, Stringa, Genoa 1971.
Galeazzo Alessi e l'architettura del Cinquecento, Sagep, Genoa 1975.
DE NEGRI, E. M., *Ottocento e rinnovamento urbano. Carlo Barabino*, Sagep, Genoa 1977.
GROSSI BIANCHI, L. AND POLEGGI, E., *Una città portuale del Medioevo. Genova nei secoli X-XVI*, Comune di Genova, Genoa 1979 (1), p. 350; Sagep, Genoa 1980 (2); Sagep, Genoa 1987 (3).
AMT, *Storia del trasporto pubblico a Genova*, Sagep, Genoa 1980.
POLEGGI, E. AND CEVINI, P., *Le città nella storia d'Italia. Genova*, Laterza, Bari-Rome 1981, 1989 (2nd ed.).
DI RAIMONDO, A. AND MULLER PROFUMO, L., *Bartolomeo Bianco e Genova. La controversa paternità dell'opera architettonica fra '500 e '600*, Genoa 1982.
PATRONE, P. D., *Daneri*, Sagep, Genoa 1982, with introduction by E. D. BONA.
TCI, *Liguria*, Milan 1982.
POLEGGI, E. AND CARACENI, F., *Genova e Strada Nuova*, in *Storia dell'arte italiana*, Einaudi, Turin 1983, Vol. XII, pp. 299-361.
BALLETTI, F. AND GIONTONI, B., *Genova. Cultura urbanistica e formazione della città contemporanea 1850-1920*, Fabbiani, Genoa n.d. (but 1984).
Le ville del Genovesato. Albaro, Valenti, Genoa 1984.
Medioevo restaurato. Genova 1860-1940, C. BOZZO DUFOUR (ed.) in *Genova*, a. 64, 1984, special issue.
CARACENI, F., *Genova. Guida Sagep*, Genoa 1985 (7th ed.).
La pittura a Genova e in Liguria. Dagli inizi al Cinquecento (Vol. I), *Dal Seicento al primo Novecento* (Vol. II), Sagep, Genoa 1987.
La scultura a Genova e in Liguria: Vol. I, *Dalle origini al Cinquecento*, Cassa di Risparmio di Genova e Imperia, Genoa 1987; Vol. II: *Dal Seicento al primo Novecento*, 1988; Vol. III, *Il Novecento*, Genoa 1989.
Nove opere del porto vecchio, la costruzione del porto di Genova tra Otto e Novecento, E. POLEGGI (ed.), Sagep, Genoa 1987.
BERTELLI, C. AND NICOLETTI, A. *"Una gentile città moderna". L'espansione urbana tra Otto e Novecento: il caso di Albaro a Genova*, Angeli, Milan 1988.
L'ospedale della duchessa. 1888-1988, E. POLEGGI (ed.), Sagep, Genoa 1988.
POLEGGI, E., *Formazione e caratteri del Centro Storico e del Porto Vecchio / The historical evolution of the Historic Centre and the Old Port*, in COMUNE DI GENOVA, *Genova verso il/towards 1992*, Genoa 1988, pp. 139-152.
CEVINI, P., *Genova anni '30. Da Labò a Daneri*, Sagep, Genoa 1989.
Medioevo demolito, Genova 1860-1940, C. BOZZO DUFOUR AND M. MARCENARO (eds.), Pirella, Genoa 1990.
Cronache di progetto, il porto di Genova 1992, in *GB progetti*, No. 7, May-June 1991; *Genova dal mare: le aree progettuali, cronache di progetto*, in *GB progetti*, supplement to No. 8/9, November 1991.

La città dipinta. Genova '92, A. ROCCA AND G. SAMBONET (eds.), in *Lotus*, quaderno 17, 1991.
CARACENI, F., *Una strada rinascimentale. Via Garibaldi a Genova*, Genoa 1992.
DI BIASE, C., *Strada Balbi a Genova. Residenza aristocratica e città*, Genoa 1993.
NICOLETTI, A. M., *Via XX Settembre a Genova. La costruzione dell città tra Otto e Novecento*, Genoa 1993.
POLEGGI, E. (ed.), *Ripa porta di Genova*, Genoa 1993.
NICOLETTI, A., *Da via Giulia a via XX Settembre*, (forthcoming publication).

INDEX OF PLACES

PLACES	ENTRY
Abbey, Sant'Andrea	172
Accademia Ligustica di Belle Arti	68
Airport, Christopher Colombus	173
Albaro, new Lido	143
Albaro, council swimming pool	142
Albergo dei Poveri	108
Ansaldo, cast iron foundries	177
Ansaldo, Grandi Artiglierie factory	186
Ansaldo, research centre	188
Archbishop's Palace	22
Arco dei Caduti	124
Block of flats, Via O. De Gaspari 42	141
Block of flats, Via Montevideo 2	149
Boccadasse village	157
Bridge, monumental	74
Business centre, Madre di Dio	86
Business centre, San Benigno (North Tower and Wtc Tower)	161
Casa del Mutilato	122
Casa Ollandini	138
Casino Serra Foltzer	185
Castelletto Türcke	156
Castello De Albertis	95
Castello Mackenzie	102
Cathedral, San Lorenzo	12
Cemetery (Cimitero monumentale)	132
Church, Nostra Signora Assunta	174
Church, Nostra Signora del Carmine	4
Church, Sacra Famiglia	130
Church, San Bartolomeo della Certosa and cloister	183
Church, San Carlo	62
Church, San Donato	14
Church, San Filippo Neri and oratory	56
Church, San Giacomo di Carignano (Sacro Cuore)	82
Church, San Giorgio	20
Church, San Giovanni di Prè and hospice	2
Church, San Luca	53
Church, San Marcellino	113
Church, San Matteo	9
Church, San Nicolò del Boschetto and cloister	184
Church, San Pietro in Banchi	29
Church, San Siro di Struppa	134
Church, San Siro	52
Church, San Torpete	20
Church, Sant'Agostino	16
Church, Sant'Anna	104
Church, Sant'Ignazio and novitiate (state archives)	27
Church, Santa Croce e San Camillo	65
Church, Santa Maria Assunta in Carignano	26
Church, Santa Maria del Prato	152
Church, Santa Maria della Cella (Sant'Agostino)	162
Church, Santa Maria delle Vigne	7
Church, Santa Maria di Castello and convent	15
Church, Santa Maria Immacolata	99
Church, Santa Maria Maddalena	51
Church, Santa Marta	35
Church, Santo Stefano	18
Church, SS. Ambrogio e Andrea (Il Gesù)	24
Church, SS. Annunziata del Vastato	57
Church, SS. Annunziata di Portoria (Santa Caterina)	36
Church, SS. Nome di Maria e Angeli Custodi (Scuole Pie)	31
Cinema, ex Excelsior	166
Corte Lambruschini	125

Faculty of Architecture	88
Fiera del Mare	120
Fort Diamante	116
Fort Ratti	135
Fort Richelieu	136
Fort Santa Tecla	136
Fort Sperone	117
Funicular railway, Zecca-Righi	94
Galleria Mazzini	66
Hospital, Acuti block	148
Hospital, pediatric, "Istituto Giannina Gaslini"	146
Hospital, Sant'Andrea (Galliera)	80
Houses, fishermen's	119
Houses, tramway employees'	131
Houses, workers'	176
Houses, Opera Pia De Ferrari Galliera	112
Housing estate, Bernabò-Brea	145
Housing estate, Cep	179
Housing estate, Cige (Peep)	187
Housing estate, Costa degli Ometti	147
Housing estate, Forte Quezzi	133
Lanterna lighthouse	1
Loggia dei Mercanti	28
Macello Nuovo (new slaughterhouse)	8
Mercato Orientale	78
Museo del Tesoro di San Lorenz	90
Museum of Oriental Art, "E. Chiossone"	64
Museum, Sant'Agostino	87
"Nicola Bonservizi" ex-Fascist meeting house	144
Offices, new council	93
Offices, ex municipal technical (Fassolo)	110
Oratory, Assunta	171
Palazzata della Ripa	5
Palazzetto Criminale (state archives)	21
Palazzina Eridania	75

Palazzo Balbi-Cattaneo Adorno	58
Palazzo Balbi-Senarega	59
Palazzo Brignole (Bianco)	47
Palazzo Brignole (Rosso)	48
Palazzo Cattaneo Adorno	45
Palazzo degli uffici giudiziari	71
Palazzo dei Maruffi	13
Palazzo dei Giganti	76
Palazzo dei Pagliacci	165
Palazzo dell'Ateneo (ex Jesuit college)	61
Palazzo Andrea Doria (ex Lazzaro Doria)	10
Palazzo Doria Pamphili	63
Palazzo Doria Spinola	43
Palazzo Doria Spinola (Prefecture)	34
Palazzo Ducale	23
Palazzo Fieschi Ravaschieri, De Ferrari	32
Palazzo Grimaldi della Meridiana	49
Palazzo Grimaldi Doria-Tursi (town hall)	46
Palazzo Ilva	84
Palazzo Imperiale	30
Palazzo Lamba Doria	10
Palazzo Lercari Parodi	40
Palazzo Lomellini Patrone (regional military headquarters)	55
Palazzo Lomellini Podestà	44
Palazzo Pallavicino Carrega (Chamber of Commerce)	41
Palazzo Pallavicino-Cambiaso (Banca Pop. Brescia)	38
Palazzo Reale (ex Balbi, Durazzo)	60
Palazzo San Giorgio	6
Palazzo Spinola (Deutsche Bank)	42
Palazzo Spinola (national gallery)	50
Palazzo Spinola dei Marmi	11
Palazzo Spinola Gambaro (Banco di Chiavari e della Riviera Ligure)	39
Palazzo Spinola Pessagno	33
Palazzo Zuccarino	77
Piazza Colombo	79
Piazza Dante, tower blocks	85
Piazza della Vittoria	123

Piazza Raffaele De Ferrari	67
Ponte Caffaro	105
Ponte di Carignano	25
Port, old, projects for reusing the infrastructures	98
Port, industrial	159
Port, Voltri	181
Porta del Molo	19
Porta della Pila	126
Porta di Sant'Andrea (Soprana)	3
Porta di Santa Fede (dei Vacca)	3
Portello/Castelletto lift	91
Residential complex	137
Restaurant, San Pietro	121
Sampierdarena, town hall	160
Sanctuary, Nostra Signora di Loreto	107
Sanctuary, Madonna del Monte	128
Sanctuary, Madonnetta (Santa Maria Assunta)	106
Sanctuary, San Francesco da Paola (sailors' shrine)	114
School, Gioventù del Littorio (Faculty of Arts)	101
Seafront, eastern	139
Seminary, old	73
Silos, grain	97
Stadium, Luigi Ferraris	129
Station, maritime, Andrea Doria	109
Station, railway, Porta Principe	96
Stock Exchange	70
Strada Nuova	37
Teatro Comunale dell'Opera	69
Theatre, "Gustavo Modena"	168
Tower dei Maruffi	13
Tower, Embriaci	17
Towers, San Bernardino and Quezzi	118

Tunnels, "G. Garibaldi" and "N. Bixio" at Portello/Zecca	92
Urban park (Expo '92)	89
Via Cairoli	54
Via XX Settembre	72
Viaduct, Genoa/Savona motorway	182
Viaduct, railway	190
Villa Airolo Franzone	154
Villa Brignole Sale (Duchessa di Galliera)	180
Villa Canali Gaslini	140
Villa Cattaneo "dell'Olmo" (Ansaldo historical archives)	188
Villa Centurione del Monastero	167
Villa De Franchi/Raggio	155
Villa De Mari Gruber (American Museum)	103
Villa dei Gesuiti, Parodi	175
Villa Di Negro Rosazza (lo "Scoglietto")	111
Villa Durazzo Bombrini	169
Villa Pallavicini and park	178
Villa Giustiniani/Cambiaso	153
Villa Grimaldi (la "Fortezza")	164
Villa Imperiale di Terralba	127
Villa Imperiale Scassi (la "Bellezza")	163
Villa Mylius	83
Villa Pallavicino delle Peschiere	100
Villa Pinelli Serra	189
Villa Raggi	151
Villa Saluzzo/Bombrini (il "Paradiso")	150
Villa Serra/Gropallo	158
Villa Tomati	115
Villas of Cornigliano	170
Villetta di Negro	64
Yacht Club	81

INDEX OF NAMES

NAMES	ENTRY
Aalto, Alvar	121
Airolo (family)	154
Ala Ponzoni, Filippo	169
Albini, Franco	16, 22, 47, 48, 86, 87, 90, 93
Albini, Marco	87
Aldovrandini, U.	60
Alessi, Galeazzo	12, 19, 24, 25, 26, 37, 38, 40, 42, 62, 63, 151, 153, 163, 164
Alizeri, Federigo	16
Allegro	95
Andrea da Goano	9
Andreani, Aldo	133
Ansaldo, Andrea	29, 30, 111
Ansaldo, G. A.	96, 128, 150, 174
Antonio da Pordenone	63
Antonio da Sangallo the Younger	41
Armanino, Alfredo	98
Bacemo Lanfranco	17
Badano Tomaso	92
Badaracco, Gio Raffaele	171, 183
Bagnasco, Adriano	148
Balbi, Francesco M.	59
Balbi, Giacomo	59
Balbi, Gian Tomaso	54
Balbi, Gio Agostino	58
Balbi, Pantaleo	59
Balbi, Stefano	60, 61
Bancheri	190
Barabino, Antonio	16
Barabino, Carlo	21, 52, 67, 68, 69, 79, 80, 86, 132, 163, 168
Barabino, Nicolò	162, 174
Barberini, G. B.	108
Barbieri, Piero	82, 174
Baroni, Eugenio	122
Bartolozzi, Gian Paolo	98
Beccafumi, Domenico	63
Behrens, Karl	177
Bellati, Beniamino	123
Bensa, P. Emilio	55
Bertrand	116
Bianco, Bartolomeo	7, 46, 48, 53, 58, 59, 61, 62, 126, 170
Bianco, Giovanni Battista	7
Bifoli, Enrico	77, 149
Bisagno, Carlo	78
Bissoni (family)	11
Blondel, Jacques-François	169
Boccanegra, Guglielmo	6
Boito, Camillo	12, 74, 131
Bombrini (family)	150, 169
Bona, Enrico D.	108
Boni, Giacomo Antonio	60, 188
Borromini	56
Borzani, Venceslao	16, 165, 166
Bossio, Francesco (Mons.)	134
Braccialini, Mario	92, 119, 120
Braccio	190
Bramante	24
Brignole, Emanuele	73, 108
Brignole Sale (family)	48, 155, 180
Brignole Sale de Ferrari, Maria	80
Brignole Sale, Gio Francesco	48
Brignole Sale, Ridolfo	48
Brunel, Isambard Kingdom	190
Bruno, Nicolò	168
Bruno, Raffaele	168
Brusco, Giacomo	49, 54
Caccia Dominioni, Luigi	143
Calvi (family)	40
Calvi, Aurelio	34
Calvi, Felice	34
Calvi, Lazzaro	34
Calvi, Pantaleo	34
Cambiaso (family)	54, 153
Cambiaso, Giovanni	34
Cambiaso, Luca	9, 22, 34, 40, 43, 49, 100, 127, 153, 164
Campora, Giuseppe	95
Canali (family)	140
Canali di Althans	132
Caniggia, G. Franco	147
Cantone, Bernardino	26, 29, 34, 37, 38, 43, 44

Cantoni, Francesco 60
Cantoni, Gaetano 21
Cantoni, Simone 23
Canzio, Michele 14, 60, 100, 163, 178
Carbone, Dario 70, 76, 139, 143
Carissimo, A. 97
Carlo, Felice 168
Carlo, Giacinto
 di Santa Maria (father) 106
Carlone (brothers) 23, 69
Carlone, Andrea 48
Carlone, Bernardo 63
Carlone, G. B. 35, 108
Carlone, Giovanni 163, 183
Carlone, Luca 114
Carlone, Taddeo 28, 29, 63
Carona, Andrea 164
Carona, Battista 164
Carrega (family) 41
Casanova (family) 175
Casella, Daniele 7, 28, 29
Castello, Bernardo 42, 150, 163, 167, 183
Castello, Giovan Battista
 called Il Bergamasco 9, 30, 33, 34, 38, 41, 43, 44, 46, 49, 100, 127, 153
Castello, Lorenzo 101
Castello, Valerio 35, 59
Cattaneo (family) 20, 104, 188
Cattaneo, Lorenzo 127
Cavalieri, G. B. 185
Cebà, Ansaldo 55
Centurione, Barnaba 167
Ceppi, Carlo 96
Ceresola, Andrea called
 Il Vannone 23, 28, 29, 51, 52
Cervetto, Domenico 99
Cervetto, G. B. 54
Cervetto, Luigi A. 12
Ceschi, Carlo 18
Cibo, Innocenzo (archbishop) 22
Charles V 63
Cherubini, C. 182
Chessa, Luigi 69
Chiari, C. 120
Chini, Galileo 82
Cibo, Innocenzo (archbishop) 22
Ciruzzi, Aristo 98
Codeviola, Michele 118, 126
Coen Cagli, E. 159
Colombus, Christopher 18

Contri, Paride 142
Coppedè, Adolfo 70, 132
Coppedè, Gino 49, 77, 102, 140, 156, 165
Cordoni, Ludovico 78
Corradi, Pietro Antonio 48, 56, 59, 108, 114
Cosini, Silvio 63
Cremona, Ippolito 7
Crippa, Angelo 146, 149
Crosa di Vergagni,
 Giuseppe 81, 84
Crotta, M. Aurelio 6, 11, 12, 95
Crotti, G. 97
Cusani, Carlo 83, 189
Cybo (family) 53, 152

D'Andrade, Alfredo 3, 6, 11, 12, 14, 16, 18, 95, 152
Daneri, Luigi Carlo 113, 120, 121, 133, 137, 144, 145, 148, 179
Da Novi, Benedetto 63
Da Novi, Matteo 63
Da Rosio, Martino 1
Dasso, Marco 86
Dazzi, Arturo 124
De Albertis, Edoardo 124
De Albertis, Enrico 95
De Andreis (colonel) 118, 135
De Carlo, Giancarlo 130
De Castro (family) 15
De Cotte, Pierre P. 116, 118, 169
De Cristoforis, G. B. 97
De Ferrari, Gregorio 48, 59
De Ferrari, Lorenzo 35, 50, 60
De Fornari (family) 152
De Franchi (family) 155
De Langlade, Gerard 25
De Lellis, Camillo 65
Delmoro, Luigi 74
De Marchi, Angelo 152
De Mari, Ansaldo 126
De Mari, Stefano 103
De Sicre, Jacques 116, 118, 136, 169
Del Curto, Pier Antonio 63
Della Corte, Gaspare 7
Della Porta,
 Giovanni Giacomo 12
Della Porta (general) 19
Di Borgo, Jacopo 162

Di Gandria, Giovanni	12	Galliera, (dukes of)	112, 180
Di Negro (family)	111	Gamba, Cesare	72, 74
Di Negro, Luchino	183	Gambacciani, Piero	73, 98,
Di Negro, Orazio	111		125, 161, 187
Dodero (family)	157	Gambaro (family)	39
Dodero, Pietro	82	Gambaro, Pietro	99
Doggio, Angelo	26	Gandolfi, Francesco	90
Doria (family)	43, 50, 183, 184	Gandolfo, Gerolamo	73, 108
Doria, Andrea	9, 10, 37, 63	Gardella, Ignazio	23, 69, 73,
Doria, Antonio	34		88, 179
Doria, Battistella	162	Gardella, Jacopo	88
Doria, Gio Andrea	46, 63	Garibaldi, R.	98
Doria, Lamba	10	Garnier, Tony	155
Doria, Lazzaro	10	Garré, G. B.	79
Doria, Martino	9	Gaslini, Gerolamo	146
Doria, Nicolò (father)	104	Gauthier, Martin Pierre	154, 169
Dufour, Maurizio	15, 99	Gelasio II (pope)	12
Duplessis de Richelieu, Armand	136	Gentile, Leonardo	44
		Ghiso, Giovanni Battista	108, 128
Durazzo (family)	175	Ginatta, Cristoforo	123
Durazzo Brignole, Maria	47	Giovannoni, Gustavo	174
Durazzo, Eugenio	60	Giustiniani, Luca	153
Durazzo, Giacomo	62	Grassi, Orazio	24
Durazzo, Giacomo Filippo	116	Graziani, M.	95
Durazzo, Giacomo Filippo II	169	Gregotti, Vittorio	129
Durazzo, Gio Luca	111	Grimaldi (family)	53, 184, 188
Durazzo, Stefano	73	Grimaldi, Battista	36, 49, 164
		Grimaldi, Francesco	50
Embriaci (family)	15, 17	Grimaldi, Gerolamo	47, 49
Embriaco, G.	89	Grimaldi, Luca	44, 46, 47
Eugenio IV	15, 128	Grimaldi, Magnano	184
		Grimaldi, Nicolò	37, 46
Ferralasco, Marco	97, 98	Grossi Bianchi, Luciano	64,
Ferreri, Cesare	175		88, 145
Fiasella, Domenico	55, 174	Grosso, Orlando	3, 10, 16
Fieschi (family)	17, 23, 32	Gruber, Adolfo	103
Fieschi, Sinibaldo	32	Guarini	56
Filarete	108	Guidobono, Bartolomeo	106
Filippini, S.	98		
Flobert, Frederic	116	Haupt, Riccardo	74, 75, 155
Foltzer, Emilio	185	Helg, Franca	16, 86, 87
Fontana, Carlo	60		
Fontana, Luigi	98	Imperiale di Sant'Angelo (family)	127
Foscolo, Ugo	116		
Fragonard, Jean-Honoré	58	Imperiale, Gio Vicenzo	30, 163
Franzone (family)	154	Inglese, Ignazio	159
Fuselli, Carlo	76, 133, 165	Ingrani	173
Fuselli, Eugenio	122, 133, 148	Innocent II	22
		Innocent VIII	53
Gabrielli, Bruno	98, 139	Invernizzi, Angelo	85
Gaggini, Giovanni	12	Isola, Giuseppe	32
Galeotti, Sebastiano	32, 50		
Galletti, Guido	85	Labò, Mario	10, 37, 64, 121

256

Lagomaggiore, Giacomo 20, 49
Landolfo (bishop) 134
Lantana, G. B. 24
Larini, S. 88
Le Corbusier,
  (Ch./E. Jeanneret) 133, 144
Lercari (family) 184
Lercari, Franco 40, 51
Lomellini (family) 57
Lomellini, Giacomo 55
Lomellini, Stefano 45
Lomellini, Baldassarre 37
Lomellini, Nicolosio 30, 44, 30
Loudon 189
Louis XII 1, 127
Lurago, Giovanni 153

Mackenzie, Evans 49, 102
Malaponti, Angela 88
Mangiarotti, Angelo 120
Marcenaro, Caterina 47, 48, 90
Marchesi, Domenico
  da Caranca 22
Massardo (eng.) 73
Massone, Bartolomeo 32
Maus, Henry 190
Mazzuchetti, Alessandro 96
Melzi d'Eril (family) 155
Merano, G. B. 16
Michelucci, Giovanni 141
Mignacco, L. 94
Moncino, Michele 60
Montaldo, G. B. 56
Montorsoli, G. Angelo 9, 12, 63
Mor, Andrea 94, 130
Morandi, Riccardo 182
Morozzo della Rocca,
  Robaldo 110, 133, 138
Muttone, Carlo 53, 65
Mylius, Federico 83

Nardi, G. 88
Nardi Greco, Camillo 101
Negrone, Giulio 24
Negrone, Giovan Battista 128
Negrone, Luca 33
Nervi, Pier Luigi 113, 120

Olcese, Giorgio 64
Oliverio (friar) 6
Orazzini, Alessandro 98
Orsolino, Andrea 71
Orsolino, Gio Batta 73, 79, 128

Orsolino, Giovanni 128
Orsolino, Giovanni Pietro 39
Orsolino, Tomaso 153

Pallavicini, Ignazio A. 178
Pallavicino (family) 50
Pallavicino, Agostino 38
Pallavicino, Camillo 56
Pallavicino, Cipriano
  (archbishop) 22, 73
Pallavicino di San Pancrazio
  (family) 56
Pallavicino, Marcello (father) 24
Pallavicino, Tobia 30, 33, 38,
    41, 46, 100
Pallavicino-Grimaldi
  (family) 155
Palmieri, Giuseppe 171
Parodi (family) 175
Parodi, Cesare 80, 112
Parodi, Domenico 35, 60, 61
Parodi, Francesco M. 35, 95
Pateri (eng.) 133
Peirano, Ludovico 172
Pellone, Rocco 174
Perin del Vaga 63
Perolli, Battista 164
Perrone (family) 186
Perrone, F. M. 103
Peruzzi, Baldassarre 100
Pesce, Benvenuto 99
Pesce Maineri, Bartolomeo 131
Petondi, Gregorio 1, 54
Pfaltz, C. 94
Philip II 63
Piacentini, Marcello 85, 123,
    124, 161, 174
Piano, Renzo 89, 188
Picasso, Renzo 85
Pino, A. 98
Piola, Domenico 32, 35, 39, 48, 59
Piola, Paolo Gerolamo 29, 35, 48
Pisano, Nicolo 12
Piva, Alberto 16, 87
Pogliaghi, Ludovico 6
Polastri, Guglielmo 97, 98
Ponzello, Domenico 26, 46, 163
Ponzello, Giovanni 20, 26, 28, 29,
    42, 46, 51, 63,
    103, 163, 164, 170
Porcheddu
  (company) 70, 72, 76, 97
Porro, Ignazio 185

257

Portman	98	Scassi, Onofrio	163
Predasso	77, 140, 156	Schiaffino, Francesco M.	104, 108, 114
Puget, Pierre	26, 108		
Pulitzer	133	Selingeri (eng.)	91
		Semino, Andrea	27, 42, 43
Quaroni, Ludovico	130, 179	Semino, Antonio	6
		Semino, Mario	98
Raphael	33, 41	Semino, Ottavio	40
Raggio (family)	152	Serra (family)	158, 185
Raggio, Armando	155	Serra, Orso (marquis)	189
Raggio, Carlo	140	Sertorio (eng.)	91
Raggio, Edilio	172	Sforza, Francesco	184
Ranco, Luigi	190	Sibilla, Angelo	27, 69, 94, 98, 99, 130, 133
Ravaschieri, Manfredo	32		
Ravinetti, Adolfo	177, 186	Siro (bishop)	134
Reinhardt, Richard	69	Siro II (archbishop)	22
Repetto (company)	76	Sistus IV	36
Resasco, G. B.	28, 57, 79, 96, 132	Spalla, Giovanni	98
Ricca, Antonio Maria	31, 43, 106	Sparzo, Marcello	29, 63, 163
Ricca, Gio Antonio	31	Spazio, Bernardo	26, 39, 164
Ricca, Gio Antonio Jr.	20, 31	Spinola (family)	50, 53, 184
Ricca, Gio Giacomo	31	Spinola, Andrea	43
Riccio, Andrea	52	Spinola, Angelo Giovanni	42
Riccomanni, Leonardo	11	Spinola di San Pietro (family)	34
Ridolfi, Mario	179	Spinola, G. B.	43, 51, 62
Rizzo, Aldo Luigi	98	Spinola, G. Domenico	170
Roderio, Antonio	19, 63	Spinola, Giacomo	11, 45
Rolla Rosazza (family)	111	Spinola, Giulio	42
Romano, Giovanni	71	Spinola, Lazzaro	45
Ronco, Nino	74	Spinola, Luca	37
Rossi, Aldo	69	Spinola, Oberto	53
Rosso, Giuseppe	85	Spinola, Pantaleo	39
Rovelli, Luigi	82, 132, 172, 180	Spinola, Stefano di Francavilla	175
Rovelli, Antonio	82		
Rubatto, Carlo	12	Spinola, Tomaso	33, 38
Rubens, Peter Paul	24, 34, 41, 45, 50, 52, 58, 59, 164	Spinola, Veronica	114
		Storace, Bartolomeo	106
Saccorotti, G.	149	Tagliafichi, E. Andrea	58, 111, 169, 178
Saluzzo, Giacomo	128		
Saluzzo (marquis)	150	Tallero, Giuseppe	123, 155, 165
Salvago (family)	127	Tallone, Gaetano	25
Sanguineti, Gio Batta	20	Tassi, Agostino	111
Sansebastiano, Michele	76	Tavarone, Lazzaro	6, 12, 42, 150
Sauli (family)	26	Teodolfo II (bishop)	18
Sauli, Domenico	25, 31	Tibaldi, Pellegrini	24
Sauli, Stefano	25	Timosci, Luigi	89
Savoia, Odone	169	Tomasinelli, Francesco	97, 98
Savoy, Carlo Alberto	60	Torriglia, G. B.	108
Scamozzi, Vincenzo	32	Traverso, Mattia	82
Scaniglia, Angelo	160, 162	Türcke, Giovanni	156
Scaniglia, S.	108		
Scarpa, Carlo	69	Valeriani, Giuseppe	24

Vannone, Andrea	150	Viscardi, Giovanni Antonio	20
Vasari, Giorgio	37	Vitale, Daniele	88
Venzano, Luigi	174	Vivaldi (family)	45, 172
Veroggio, Benedetto	78	Viviano, Niccolò	48
Viano, Giacomo	47		
Vietti, Luigi	109, 119	Zappa, Giulio	145
Vinzoni, Matteo	25, 118	Zuccarino, Giuseppe	77

PROPRIETÀ LETTERARIA RISERVATA
© 1992 UMBERTO ALLEMANDI & C. SRL
© 1998 ENGLISH EDITION UMBERTO ALLEMANDI & C. SRL

FINITO DI STAMPARE PRESSO LE ARTI GRAFICHE GIACONE,
CHIERI (TORINO), NEL MESE DI SETTEMBRE 1998, PRINTED IN ITALY

FOTOLITO FOTOMEC, TORINO

DISTRIBUTORE ESCLUSIVO ALLE LIBRERIE
MESSAGGERIE LIBRI SPA

DISTRIBUTORE ESCLUSIVO ALLE EDICOLE
MESSAGGERIE PERIODICI SPA